Brian Fleming Research & Learning Library
Ministry of Education
Ministry of Training, Colleges & Universities
900 Bay St. 13th Floor, Mowat Block
Toronto, ON M7A 1L2

TALIS

Supporting Teacher Professionalism

INSIGHTS FROM TALIS 2013

This work is published on the responsibility of the Secretary-General of the OECD. The opinions expressed and arguments employed herein do not necessarily reflect the official views of the OECD member countries.

This document and any map included herein are without prejudice to the status of or sovereignty over any territory, to the delimitation of international frontiers and boundaries and to the name of any territory, city or area.

Please cite this publication as:
OECD (2016), *Supporting Teacher Professionalism: Insights from TALIS 2013*, TALIS, OECD Publishing, Paris. http://dx.doi.org/10.1787/9789264248601-en

ISBN 978-92-64-24859-5 (print)
ISBN 978-92-64-24860-1 (PDF)

TALIS
ISSN: 2312-9638 (online)
ISSN: 2312-962X (print)

The statistical data for Israel are supplied by and under the responsibility of the relevant Israeli authorities. The use of such data by the OECD is without prejudice to the status of the Golan Heights, East Jerusalem and Israeli settlements in the West Bank under the terms of international law.

Photo credits:
© Andersen Ross/Inmagine LTD
© Digital Vision/Getty Images
© Feng Yu/Stocklib
© Hero Images/Corbis
© Michael Brown/Stocklib
© Monkey Busines/Fotolia
© Pressmaster/Shutterstock
© Vetta Collection/iStock
© Tyler Olson/Shutterstock

Corrigenda to OECD publications may be found on line at: *www.oecd.org/publishing/corrigenda*.
© OECD 2016

You can copy, download or print OECD content for your own use, and you can include excerpts from OECD publications, databases and multimedia products in your own documents, presentations, blogs, websites and teaching materials, provided that suitable acknowledgement of OECD as source and copyright owner is given. All requests for public or commercial use and translation rights should be submitted to *rights@oecd.org*. Requests for permission to photocopy portions of this material for public or commercial use shall be addressed directly to the Copyright Clearance Center (CCC) at *info@copyright.com* or the Centre français d'exploitation du droit de copie (CFC) at *contact@cfcopies.com*.

Foreword

Teachers around the world are increasingly being asked to teach more diverse student populations, including disadvantaged and immigrant students, and students who may not be proficient in the country's principal language. Investing in teachers' professionalism is one way that education systems can help teachers face these challenges and, by doing so, ensure that all students receive the high-quality teaching they need to succeed.

This report shows how countries can do that most effectively by focusing on teacher professionalism.

Examining the nature of teacher professionalism around the world, this report focuses on teachers' knowledge, autonomy in decision making, and engagement in peer networks as hallmarks of teacher professionalism. The findings highlight the value of teacher collaboration, mentoring and pre-service formal education programmes.

The report is based on results from the OECD Teaching and Learning International Survey (TALIS) 2013. TALIS, the largest international survey of teachers, collects teachers' and principals' views about the teaching and learning environments in their schools and their working conditions.

Andreas Schleicher
Director, Directorate for Education and Skills

Acknowledgements

The OECD Teaching and Learning International Survey (TALIS) 2013 is the outcome of collaboration among the TALIS participating countries and economies, the OECD Secretariat, the European Commission and an international consortium led by the International Association for the Evaluation of Educational Achievement (IEA). This report was prepared by the FHI 360 Education Policy and Data Center, under the technical supervision of Carina Omoeva. Elizabeth Buckner was the lead author, with Charles Gale and Christine Van Keuren (Educational Policy Institute). Chapter 4 was developed and written by William C. Smith (RESULTS Educational Fund). The report was completed under the technical oversight of the OECD TALIS Team: Katarzyna Kubacka, Karine Tremblay, Jia He, and Noémie Le Donné, with help from Montserrat Gomedio. The report was edited by John Pierce. Communications assistance was provided by Jennifer Cannon and Cassandra Davis. Administrative and editorial assistance was provided by Emily Groves. The report benefited from the review and comments on earlier drafts by members of the TALIS Board of Participating Countries.

Table of contents

ABBREVIATIONS AND ACRONYMS	19
EXECUTIVE SUMMARY	21
CHAPTER 1 CONCEPTUALISING TEACHER PROFESSIONALISM	25
Introduction	26
Background	28
Conceptual framework: Domains of teacher professionalism	32
Outline of the report	39
CHAPTER 2 THE NATURE AND EXTENT OF TEACHER PROFESSIONALISM	45
Introduction	46
Teacher professionalism	46
System differences in teacher professionalism	48
Teacher professionalism, by domain	50
Models of teacher professionalism	57
Teacher professionalism and system-level factors	63
Discussion	67
CHAPTER 3 TEACHER PROFESSIONALISM AND POLICY-RELEVANT OUTCOMES	69
Introduction	70
Teacher perceptions of status, satisfaction and self-efficacy	71
Overall teacher professionalism	72
Teacher professionalism, by domain	74
Variation across education systems	78
The role of system-level factors	83
Differences by school level	85

TABLE OF CONTENTS

Discussion 86

CHAPTER 4 **EQUITY AND TEACHER PROFESSIONALISM** 91

Introduction 92

Identifying high-needs schools 93

Teacher professionalism domains, by high-needs categories 96

Teacher professionalism support gap 97

Within-system equity patterns.. 99

Cross-system differences in socio-economically disadvantaged schools............. 106

Predicting teacher satisfaction with their current work environment 109

Exploring differences in teacher professionalism effects 114

Discussion 116

CHAPTER 5 **POLICY RECOMMENDATIONS TO SUPPORT TEACHER PROFESSIONALISM** 119

Policy recommendations 120

Conclusion 122

ANNEX A **TECHNICAL ANNEX** 125

ANNEX B **SYSTEM-SPECIFIC PROFILES OF TEACHER PROFESSIONALISM** 137

ANNEX C **TEACHER PROFESSIONALISM SUPPORT GAPS BETWEEN HIGH AND LOW SECOND-LANGUAGE SCHOOLS** 177

ANNEX D **TEACHER PROFESSIONALISM SUPPORT GAPS BETWEEN HIGH AND LOW SPECIAL-NEEDS SCHOOLS** 179

ANNEX E **TEACHER PROFESSIONALISM SUPPORT GAPS BETWEEN HIGH AND LOW SOCIO-ECONOMICALLY DISADVANTAGED SCHOOLS** 181

ANNEX F **SYSTEM EQUITY PROFILES** 183

BOXES

Box 1.1 The importance of peer networks in teacher professionalism 34

Box 1.2 Technical notes on scale construction 37

Box 1.3 Technical notes on regression analysis 40

Box 2.1 Teacher professionalism scales 47

Box 3.1 Teacher professionalism indices 70

Box 3.2 Technical notes on regression analysis 72

Box 3.3 Technical notes on domain specific analyses 75

Box 3.4 Analysis of system variation 79

Box 3.5 Technical notes on system-level analysis 83

Box 4.1 Defining high-needs student groups 94

Box 4.2 Calculating the teacher professionalism support gap 98

Box 4.3 Focus on socio-economically disadvantaged schools 106

Box 4.4 Predicting teacher satisfaction with the current work environment 109

Box 4.5 Calculating effect differentials 114

FIGURES

Figure 2.1 Average values on the domains of teacher professionalism indices, by domain (ISCED 2). 48

Figure 2.2 Total professionalism index, by country (ISCED 2) 49

Figure 2.3 National averages on the knowledge base scale (ISCED 2) 51

Figure 2.4 Breakdown of knowledge base, by sub-scale 52

Figure 2.5 Mean values on knowledge base domain, by ISCED level 52

Figure 2.6 System averages on the autonomy scale (ISCED 2) 54

Figure 2.7 Average values on autonomy scale, by school level 55

Figure 2.8 System averages on peer networks scale (ISCED 2) 56

Figure 2.9 Average values on peer networks scale, by school level 57

Figure 2.10 Malaysia triangle graph (ISCED 2) 58

TABLE OF CONTENTS

Figure 2.11	East Asian systems particularly emphasise peer networks (ISCED 2)	59
Figure 2.12	Italy triangle graph (ISCED 2)	59
Figure 2.13	Northern and Central Europe emphasise autonomy (ISCED 2)	60
Figure 2.14	France triangle graph (ISCED 2)	60
Figure 2.15	Knowledge emphasis countries (ISCED 2)	61
Figure 2.16	Poland: Balanced high professionalism (ISCED 2)	61
Figure 2.17	Systems with a model of balanced high professionalism (ISCED 2)	62
Figure 2.18	Portugal triangle graph (ISCED 2)	62
Figure 2.19	Teacher professionalism profiles in Brazil and Mexico (ISCED 2)	63
Figure 2.20	Education expenditure (per pupil) and overall teacher professionalism (ISCED 2)	64
Figure 2.21	Overall teacher professionalism and teacher salary (ISCED 2)	65
Figure 2.22	Overall teacher professionalism and average class size (ISCED 2)	66
Figure 2.23	PISA scores and overall teacher professionalism (ISCED 2)	67
Figure 3.1	The relationship between overall teacher professionalism and teacher outcomes (ISCED 2)	74
Figure 3.2	The role of the knowledge base on teachers' perceptions and satisfaction (ISCED 2)	76
Figure 3.3	The role of autonomy on teachers' perceptions and satisfaction (ISCED 2)	77
Figure 3.4	The role of peer networks on outcomes (ISCED 2)	78
Figure 3.5	Patterns of relationships between professionalism and outcomes in select countries and economies (ISCED 2)	80
Figure 3.6	Country/economy-specific regression coefficients – overall professionalism index (ISCED 2)	81
Figure 3.7	Country/economy-specific regression coefficients for autonomy scale (ISCED 2)	82
Figure 3.8	Teacher professionalism and outcomes by educational level	86
Figure 4.1	Percentage of teachers, by second-language student concentration	94
Figure 4.2	Percentage of teachers, by concentration of students with special needs	95
Figure 4.3	Percentage of teachers, by socio-economically disadvantaged student concentration	96
Figure 4.4	Domain means, by second-language and special-needs concentration	97
Figure 4.5	Domain means, by socio-economically disadvantaged concentration	97
Figure 4.6	Latvia – more equitable second-language pattern	100

TABLE OF CONTENTS

Figure 4.7	Estonia – less equitable second-language pattern	100
Figure 4.8	Finland – replacement second-language pattern	101
Figure 4.9	Alberta (Canada) – more equitable special-needs pattern	102
Figure 4.10	The Netherlands – less equitable special-needs pattern	102
Figure 4.11	France – replacement special-needs pattern	103
Figure 4.12	Georgia – more equitable socio-economically disadvantaged pattern	103
Figure 4.13	Israel – less equitable socio-economically disadvantaged pattern	104
Figure 4.14	Singapore – socio-economically disadvantaged pattern	105
Figure 4.15	Teacher professionalism support gap, by percentage of teachers in high socio-economically disadvantaged schools	107
Figure 4.16	Mean PISA standard deviation and teacher professionalism support gap	108
Figure 4.17	Mean PISA standard deviation and autonomy support gap	108
Figure 4.18	The association between the autonomy scale and teacher satisfaction with their current work environment	111
Figure 4.19	The association between the knowledge scale and teacher satisfaction with their current work environment	112
Figure 4.20	The association between the peer networks scale and teacher satisfaction with current work environment	113
Figure 4.21	Knowledge support gap, by knowledge effect differential	115
Figure 4.22	Peer networks support gap, by peer networks differential	115
Figure 4.23	Effect differentials, by percentage of teachers in high socio-economically disadvantaged schools	116
Figure A.1	Distribution of knowledge base scale	131
Figure A.2	Distribution of autonomy scale	132
Figure A.3	Distribution of peer networks scale	132
Figure B.1	Profile of Abu Dhabi (United Arab Emirates)	138
Figure B.2	Profile of Alberta (Canada)	139
Figure B.3	Profile of Australia	140
Figure B.4	Profile of Brazil	141
Figure B.5	Profile of Bulgaria	142
Figure B.6	Profile of Chile	143

TABLE OF CONTENTS

Figure B.7   Profile of Croatia 144
Figure B.8   Profile of Cyprus 145
Figure B.9   Profile of the Czech Republic 146
Figure B.10 Profile of Denmark 147
Figure B.11 Profile of England (United Kingdom) 148
Figure B.12 Profile of Estonia 149
Figure B.13 Profile of Finland 150
Figure B.14 Profile of Flanders (Belgium) 151
Figure B.15 Profile of France 152
Figure B.16 Profile of Georgia 153
Figure B.17 Profile of Iceland 154
Figure B.18 Profile of Israel 155
Figure B.19 Profile of Italy 156
Figure B.20 Profile of Japan 157
Figure B.21 Profile of Korea 158
Figure B.22 Profile of Latvia 159
Figure B.23 Profile of Malaysia 160
Figure B.24 Profile of Mexico 161
Figure B.25 Profile of the Netherlands 162
Figure B.26 Profile of New Zealand 163
Figure B.27 Profile of Norway 164
Figure B.28 Profile of Poland 165
Figure B.29 Profile of Portugal 166
Figure B.30 Profile of Romania 167
Figure B.31 Profile of the Russian Federation 168
Figure B.32 Profile of Serbia 169
Figure B.33 Profile of Shanghai (China) 170
Figure B.34 Profile of Singapore 171
Figure B.35 Profile of the Slovak Republic 172
Figure B.36 Profile of Spain 173

Figure B.37	Profile of Sweden	174
Figure B.38	Profile of the United States	175

Figure F.1	Equity profile of Abu Dhabi (United Arab Emirates)	184
Figure F.2	Equity profile of Alberta (Canada)	185
Figure F.3	Equity profile of Australia	186
Figure F.4	Equity profile of Brazil	187
Figure F.5	Equity profile of Bulgaria	188
Figure F.6	Equity profile of Chile	189
Figure F.7	Equity profile of Croatia	190
Figure F.8	Equity profile of Cyprus	191
Figure F.9	Equity profile of the Czech Republic	192
Figure F.10	Equity profile of Denmark	193
Figure F.11	Equity profile of England (United Kingdom)	194
Figure F.12	Equity profile of Estonia	195
Figure F.13	Equity profile of Finland	196
Figure F.14	Equity profile of Flanders (Belgium)	197
Figure F.15	Equity profile of France	198
Figure F.16	Equity profile of Georgia	199
Figure F.17	Equity profile of Iceland	200
Figure F.18	Equity profile of Israel	201
Figure F.19	Equity profile of Italy	202
Figure F.20	Equity profile of Japan	203
Figure F.21	Equity profile of Korea	204
Figure F.22	Equity profile of Latvia	205
Figure F.23	Equity profile of Malaysia	206
Figure F.24	Equity profile of Mexico	207
Figure F.25	Equity profile of the Netherlands	208
Figure F.26	Equity profile of New Zealand	209
Figure F.27	Equity profile of Norway	210

Figure F.28 Equity profile of Poland 211

Figure F.29 Equity profile of Portugal 212

Figure F.30 Equity profile of Romania 213

Figure F.31 Equity profile of the Russian Federation 214

Figure F.32 Equity profile of Serbia 215

Figure F.33 Equity profile of Shanghai (China) 216

Figure F.34 Equity profile of Singapore 217

Figure F.35 Equity profile of the Slovak Republic 218

Figure F.36 Equity profile of Spain 219

Figure F.37 Equity profile of Sweden 220

Figure F.38 Equity profile of the United States 221

TABLES

Table 1.1	Variation in teacher professionalism reform strategies (a few examples)	29
Table 2.1	System means on teacher professionalism domains (ISCED 2)	50
Table 2.2	Components of knowledge base scale, by ISCED level	53
Table 2.3	Components of autonomy scale, by ISCED level	55
Table 2.4	Components of peer networks scale, by ISCED level	57
Table 3.1	Overview of the TALIS questions used in the teacher perceptions of status, satisfaction and self-efficacy	71
Table 3.2	Relationship between teacher professionalism and teacher outcomes (ISCED 2)	73
Table 3.3	Table of coefficients on teacher professionalism indices (ISCED 2)	76
Table 3.4	The relationship between outcomes and alternate educational policies	85
Table 4.1	Identifying high-needs schools	93
Table 4.2	Most equitable, mixed equity and least equitable countries/economies for teacher professionalism support	105

Table 4.3	Association between teacher professionalism domains and teacher's satisfaction with current work environment by socio-economically disadvantaged concentration – complete sample	110
Table A.1	Knowledge domain variables	127
Table A.2	Cronbach's alpha of knowledge domain items, by ISCED level	127
Table A.3	SEM goodness of fit indicators of knowledge scales	127
Table A.4	Goodness of fit indicators for a two-factor latent knowledge variable	128
Table A.5	Correlations between knowledge domain scales and indices	128
Table A.6	Autonomy domain variables	129
Table A.7	Cronbach's alpha and inter-item correlation for autonomy	129
Table A.8	Goodness of fit indicators for autonomy scale, by ISCED level	129
Table A.9	Correlations between autonomy domain scales and indices	129
Table A.10	Variables in peer networks domain	130
Table A.11	Cronbach's alpha for peer networks domain by ISCED level	130
Table A.12	Goodness of fit indicators for the peer networks scale	130
Table A.13	Correlations between peer networks domain scales and indices	131
Table A.14	Distribution of knowledge base scale	131
Table A.15	Distribution of autonomy domain scale	132
Table A.16	Distribution of peer networks domain scale	132
Table A.17	Teacher professionalism outcome variables	133
Table A.18	Covariates in regression models	135
Table A.19	Regression models	135
Table A.20	Additional controls	136
Table B.1	Profile of Abu Dhabi (United Arab Emirates)	138
Table B.2	Profile of Alberta (Canada)	139
Table B.3	Profile of Australia	140
Table B.4	Profile of Brazil	141
Table B.5	Profile of Bulgaria	142
Table B.6	Profile of Chile	143
Table B.7	Profile of Croatia	144

TABLE OF CONTENTS

Table B.8	Profile of Cyprus	145
Table B.9	Profile of the Czech Republic	146
Table B.10	Profile of Denmark	147
Table B.11	Profile of England (United Kingdom)	148
Table B.12	Profile of Estonia	149
Table B.13	Profile of Finland	150
Table B.14	Profile of Flanders (Belgium)	151
Table B.15	Profile of France	152
Table B.16	Profile of Georgia	153
Table B.17	Profile of Iceland	154
Table B.18	Profile of Israel	155
Table B.19	Profile of Italy	156
Table B.20	Profile of Japan	157
Table B.21	Profile of Korea	158
Table B.22	Profile of Latvia	159
Table B.23	Profile of Malaysia	160
Table B.24	Profile of Mexico	161
Table B.25	Profile of the Netherlands	162
Table B.26	Profile of New Zealand	163
Table B.27	Profile of Norway	164
Table B.28	Profile of Poland	165
Table B.29	Profile of Portugal	166
Table B.30	Profile of Romania	167
Table B.31	Profile of the Russian Federation	168
Table B.32	Profile of Serbia	169
Table B.33	Profile of Shanghai (China)	170
Table B.34	Profile of Singapore	171
Table B.35	Profile of the Slovak Republic	172
Table B.36	Profile of Spain	173
Table B.37	Profile of Sweden	174

TABLE OF CONTENTS

Table B.38 Profile of the United States 175

Table C.1   Gaps in teacher professionalism between high and low second-language schools 178

Table D.1   Gaps in teacher professionalism between high and low special-needs schools 180

Table E.1   Gaps in teacher professionalism between high and low socio-economically
            disadvantaged schools.. 182

Abbreviations and acronyms

AAD	Abu Dhabi, United Arab Emirates
AUS	Australia
BFL	Flanders, Belgium
BGR	Bulgaria
BRA	Brazil
CAB	Alberta, Canada
CHL	Chile
CSH	Shanghai, China
CZE	Czech Republic
DNK	Denmark
EFA	Education for All
ENG	England, United Kingdom
ESP	Spain
EST	Estonia
FIN	Finland
FRA	France
GEO	Georgia
HLM	Hierarchical linear modeling
HRV	Croatia
ISCED	International Standard Classification of Education
ISL	Iceland
ISR	Israel
ITA	Italy
JPN	Japan
KOR	Korea

ABBREVIATIONS AND ACRONYMS

LVA	Latvia
MEX	Mexico
MYS	Malaysia
NLD	Netherlands
NOR	Norway
NZL	New Zealand
OECD	Organisation for Economic Co-operation and Development
PISA	Programme for International Student Assessment
PLC	Professional learning communities
POL	Poland
PRT	Portugal
ROU	Romania
RUS	Russian Federation
SGP	Singapore
SRB	Serbia
SVK	Slovak Republic
SWE	Sweden
TALIS	Teaching and Learning International Survey
UNESCO	United Nations Educational, Scientific and Cultural Organization
USA	United States

Executive summary

This report examines the nature and extent of support for teacher professionalism using the Teaching and Learning International Survey (TALIS) 2013, a survey of teachers and principals in 34 countries and economies around the world, with data collected from an additional 4 systems after the original data collection, making a total of 38. Teacher professionalism is conceptualised here as a composite of three domains: 1) a knowledge base, which includes necessary knowledge for teaching (including pre-service and in-service training); 2) autonomy, which is defined as teachers' decision making over aspects related to their work; and 3) peer networks, which provide opportunities for information exchange and support needed to maintain high standards of teaching. It then measures the extent of teacher professionalism in an education system by calculating the average number of best practices that teachers benefit from across TALIS countries and economies.

DOMAINS OF TEACHER PROFESSIONALISM

Despite substantial system-level variation, there are clear areas of emphasis across the three domains of teacher professionalism. For example, the report finds that teachers have more support for pre-service education than in-service professional development. They are least likely to receive financial support for in-service professional development outside working hours.

Across all TALIS countries and economies, school-based autonomy is the domain with the least support overall. Since items related to teacher autonomy were asked only in the principal questionnaire, they represent practices as they apply to the entire school as reported by principals rather than individual teachers. According to these reported practices, teachers exercise decision making over only two areas of a possible five, on average. With respect to support for peer networks, teachers are most likely to have received feedback from peers and supervisors based on direct observations, and are less likely to participate in a network of teachers devoted to professional development or a formal induction programme.

While most of the analysis is focused on lower secondary teachers (ISCED 2), the report finds important differences across school levels. Both primary and lower secondary teachers are much more likely than upper secondary teachers to have gone through a pre-service education programme. In contrast, at the upper secondary level, teachers are likely to have higher levels of autonomy compared to primary and lower secondary.

EXECUTIVE SUMMARY

In addition, there are important differences in how TALIS countries and economies approach teacher professionalism. Although most countries and economies have similar support systems for their teachers' knowledge base, there are larger differences across educational systems in terms of their support for peer networks, and substantial differences in terms of the amount of school-based decision making (i.e. autonomy) that teachers enjoy. In some systems teachers exercise very little autonomy as measured by TALIS 2013, whereas in others they participate in an average of four areas of decision making out of the possible five captured by this survey. As a way of identifying patterns across systems, the report proposes five models of teacher professionalism depending on the domain that is most emphasised (Chapter 2).

TEACHER SATISFACTION, STATUS, AND SELF-EFFICACY

In examining the relationship between teacher professionalism and policy-relevant teacher outcomes: perceived status, satisfaction with profession and school environment, and perceived self-efficacy, the report finds that overall levels of teacher professionalism are positively associated with all four outcomes. Both the knowledge base and peer networks scales are statistically significantly predictive of perceptions of higher status and satisfaction across all countries and economies, while the autonomy scale is generally not (with some exceptions).

The report also looks at country-specific relationships between teacher professionalism and teachers' satisfaction and perceptions of status and self-efficacy, and finds that the role of teacher professionalism matters more in some countries/economies than others. This suggests that country-specific policy environments and teaching cultures mediate the relationship between teacher professionalism and outcomes.

EQUITY CONCERNS IN TEACHER PROFESSIONALISM

The report also examines professionalism support gaps, which are defined as differences in support for teacher professionalism in schools with high levels of disadvantage as compared to those with low-levels of disadvantage. High-needs schools are those schools which have a large percentage of their student body identified in one of three high-needs categories: second-language learners, students with special needs, or students that are socio-economically disadvantaged. In exploring the differences in teacher support present at high-needs and low-needs schools, the report found that the greatest variation in teacher support is often found in the autonomy domain. Although this must be interpreted with some caution, given that autonomy measures were surveyed in the principal questionnaire and therefore applied to all teachers in a school, it does suggest that, between high-needs and low-needs schools, the autonomy available to teachers, in general, differs. Across high-needs categories, the largest disparity in teacher support within countries occurs in schools at different levels of socio-economic disadvantage.

As can be expected, TALIS 2013 indicates that the way and degree to which teachers are supported can influence their satisfaction with their present employment. Important for equity concerns, the association between teacher professionalism support and teacher satisfaction is greater for teachers in high-needs schools, suggesting that one of the best investments such schools can make in increasing teacher satisfaction is providing practices that support teacher professionalism.

POLICY IMPLICATIONS

The report shows that overall higher levels of teacher professionalism are beneficial for teachers – however, it recognises the complexity of supporting teacher professionalism in different contexts. An important issue to consider is whether one model for teacher professionalism is preferable, or if a higher value on teacher professionalism is necessary and desirable in all educational systems.

This report does not make any assumptions about what policies will work best in any one education system, but does offer policy recommendations about how to support teacher professionalism. Specifically, this report suggests policies should consider:

- requiring teachers to participate in pre-service formal teacher education programmes that expose teachers to pedagogy and provide opportunities for practice teaching;
- expanding induction and mentoring programmes;
- supporting teachers in conducting classroom-based individual or collaborative research;
- encouraging teachers' participation in networks of other teachers for information exchange.

These policy interventions may be particularly beneficial in schools with high proportions of students who suffer from socio-economic disadvantage, and in secondary schools.

Conceptualising teacher professionalism

This chapter outlines the background of the Teaching and Learning International Survey (TALIS). It then introduces the goals of this thematic report on teacher professionalism, which has been based on the TALIS 2013 data. It discusses the different forms and aspects of teacher professionalism and the existing literature on the topic. The chapter also introduces the research questions and the methods underlying the current report.

CONCEPTUALISING TEACHER PROFESSIONALISM

INTRODUCTION

In recent decades, countries and organisations around the world, including the OECD, have grappled with how to best address new challenges in their education systems, such as their diversifying student bodies and their students' need to develop new skills for the global economy. While there are many competing ideas about how education systems can best respond to changing needs, scholars have increasingly advocated investing in teacher quality as a reform approach (Darling-Hammond, 2013). Investing in teachers makes sense – after all, high-quality teaching is considered perhaps the single most important factor in student learning (Rhoton and Stiles, 2002).

How can governments train, recruit and retain these high-quality teachers? Research suggests that the status of the teaching profession is a critical factor in attracting more and better teachers (Barber and Mourshed, 2007). Meanwhile, retaining good teachers depends on factors such as job satisfaction and professional growth (Brunetti, 2001). As such, teachers' beliefs about their perceived status, self-efficacy and job satisfaction must be viewed as important and policy-relevant mediators of the overall supply of high-quality teacher labour.

This report draws on data from the Teaching and Learning International Survey (TALIS) 2013 to investigate teacher professionalism and its relationship to teachers' perceptions and satisfaction. TALIS 2013 is an international survey focused on understanding the working conditions of teachers and principals in schools. It is implemented as a collaborative effort by OECD members and partners. Its primary objective is to help countries review and develop policies that foster the conditions for effective schooling. TALIS focuses on lower secondary education (ISCED Level 2), although participating countries and economies also have the option to survey teachers in primary and upper secondary schools. This thematic report is based on the second cycle of TALIS, which was implemented in 2012-13, the goal of which was to fill gaps in the evidence base on effective teaching and learning practices. TALIS 2013 builds on the first cycle of TALIS, implemented in 2007-08. The following 34 countries and economies participated in TALIS 2013: The following 34 countries and economies participated in TALIS 2013: Abu Dhabi, United Arab Emirates; Alberta, Canada; Australia; Flanders, Belgium; Brazil; Bulgaria; Chile; Croatia; Cyprus;[1] the Czech Republic; Denmark; England, United Kingdom; Estonia; Finland; France; Iceland; Israel; Italy; Japan; Korea; Latvia; Malaysia; Mexico; the Netherlands; Norway; Poland; Portugal; Romania; Serbia; Singapore; the Slovak Republic; Spain; Sweden and the United States;[2] with 4 additional economies participating at a later stage (Shanghai, China; Georgia; New Zealand; and the Russian Federation).

The potential of professionalism as a reform approach is that it is viewed as a way of both improving teacher quality while also enhancing teachers' perceptions of their status, job satisfaction and efficacy. Professionalism "…seeks to invest in knowledgeable practitioners who can make sound decisions about how to shape education for the specific clients they serve." (Darling-Hammond, 2013: 124). Although there is no consensus in the definition of a "high-quality teacher", it is well documented that teachers who participate in strong mentoring (Borman and Dowling, 2008) or induction programmes (Feiman-Nemser, 2003), have autonomy in curriculum and teaching activities (Watkins, 2005), collaborate with their peers (Borman and Dowling, 2008; Darling-Hammond, 2006) and take on leadership roles (Berry, Smylie and Fuller, 2008) are more likely to positively impact student achievement. These practices, associated with teacher professionalism, are also linked to teacher longevity.

Professionalism takes various forms cross-nationally – many nations have initiated policy changes "…to upgrade the status, training, and working conditions of teachers." (Pearson and Moomaw, 2005: 40). For

CONCEPTUALISING TEACHER PROFESSIONALISM

example, governments such as the United States and United Kingdom have attempted to professionalise teaching by raising minimum credentials for entry and clarifying the professional standards (i.e. required attributes, skills and knowledge) required by all teachers. In the United States, the No Child Left Behind Act required all schools to have a "highly qualified teacher" in order to set a minimum standard of professional knowledge required by teachers. Other countries, such as Ireland, created teaching councils as a national professional body in charge of self-regulation, while some have supported teacher professional learning through the creation of professional learning committees (PLCs). For example, in Singapore, the Ministry of Education led large-scale implementation of PLCs at the school level, with school administrators given substantial autonomy to implement the PLCs (Lee and Lee, 2013).

However, more than two decades into the move to professionalise teaching, a thorough understanding is still lacking of what teacher professionalism looks like in different contexts, and how teacher professionalism is related to outcomes of interest, including the recruitment and retention of high-quality teachers. Evans (2008) explains that, in many countries, external accountability for professionalism has created a "prescribed" professionalism dictated by national policies and standards, which differs from the "enacted" professionalism that exists in teachers' practices. To link teacher professionalism to teacher-level outcomes, there is a need to understand what enacted professionalism looks like – in other words, the policies and practices, often implemented at the school level, that are designed to support teachers' growth as professionals, and how this affects their perceptions and attitudes towards teaching.

Drawing on data from TALIS 2013, which includes teachers' and principals' reports of their individual and school-wide practices, this study moves the conversation beyond prescribed professionalism as it is embedded in national policies to examine enacted professionalism as practiced in schools. It draws on an extensive review of the literature on the school-based practices and national policies that promote teacher professionalism to conceptualise teacher professionalism, describe the nature of professionalism in different countries and economies and, finally, investigate how professionalism is related to teachers' perceptions and satisfaction.

Research questions

Drawing on the literature on teacher professionalism, this study anticipates that teachers' perceptions of their status and self-efficacy, and their satisfaction with their jobs and the teaching profession, will all be higher in contexts where teachers are accorded greater professional autonomy, responsibility, and opportunities for professional development.

To build the knowledge base on teacher professionalism, this study explores three related topics: 1) the extent and nature of teacher professionalism cross-nationally; 2) how teacher professionalism is related to important policy-relevant outcomes, including teachers' perceived status, self-efficacy and job satisfaction; and 3) whether teacher professionalism is equally distributed across schools. Concretely, the study is centred on three related research questions:

1. What does teacher professionalism look like cross-nationally?

2. How does the nature and extent of teacher professionalism affect teachers' perceptions of the status of teaching, their job satisfaction, their commitment to teaching and their self-efficacy?

3. Does teacher professionalism differ by school composition (school socio-economic status [SES], percentage of second-language learners, percentage of students with a disability), indicating inequitable access to teacher professionalism? Does the importance of teacher professionalism for a teacher's sense of satisfaction with the profession differ by school composition?

CONCEPTUALISING TEACHER PROFESSIONALISM

BACKGROUND

Teacher professionalism in historical perspective

Historically, the conceptualisation of the professional and of professionalism referred to the level of autonomy and internal regulation exercised by members of an occupation in providing services to society (Evans, 2008). Early researchers evaluated whether changes in a particular livelihood were a result of external forces exerting pressure and influence inward on an occupation, or were due to the internal motivation and efforts of the members of the profession itself. In 18th and 19th century Europe, the distinction between occupations and professions lay in the level of institutionalisation of the members of a given trade and the level to which a profession carried a requirement for special knowledge, a formalised code of conduct and a mandate to carry out particular services given out by the state, which served as "…the guarantor of legal order [and] the promoter of culture…" (Siegrist 2015: 97). Through deliberate institutionalisation, the state fostered the intellectual development of members of the professions and cultivated the growth of professions that were of fundamental importance to the development of the state. Over time, the classic definition of the professions was expanded, and university professors and upper secondary teachers were recognised as the experts for education, aesthetics and morality (Siegrist, 2015).

In the 20th century, the professionalisation of teaching was faced with a counterforce: the growing standardisation of curricula and standards and, with them, the emergence of externally imposed accountability. The expansion of educational opportunity around the world over the course of the century led to the expansion of the ranks of teachers and scripted lesson plans became increasingly common in many education systems. Popkewitz (1994) argues that, as more women joined the profession, the level of autonomy and latitude over instructional content saw a downward trend, while external regulation went on the rise.

At the turn of the 21st century, however, there was renewed focus on teacher professionalism as an approach to educational reform – as improving teacher quality became viewed as the key to student achievement, teacher professionalism gained greater prominence. In 2000, the international community met in Dakar, Senegal, to reconfirm their commitment to the World Declaration on Education for All, during which they committed to promoting teacher professionalisation by ensuring that all teachers had adequate pay, access to professional development and the opportunity to participate in decision making concerning matters that affect the profession (see also Harris-Van Keuren and Silova, 2015).[3]

Nonetheless, the meaning of teacher professionalism, and the nature and extent of professionalism practices, varies significantly across countries. Varied approaches to professionalism may reflect cultural and historical differences, or differences in national and local policy priorities.

Between 2008 and 2014, most OECD countries introduced reforms in the area of teacher policy (OECD, 2015). Table 1.1 highlights the diversity of reforms adopted. As the table shows, policies include those that regulate entry into the profession, improve teacher education programmes, regulate teacher compensation and establish mechanisms for external accountability and community oversight. Some countries focused on regulating entry and pay: for example, Denmark is allowing colleges more autonomy in programmatic development of teacher education, the Netherlands is mandating teacher registration and Portugal is raising the bar on entrance into pre-service pedagogical university admissions, while Estonia established policies affecting teacher compensation and contract type. Other

countries have increased the importance of teacher voice. Iceland, for example, adopted a teacher policy that specifically listed a more significant role of the teachers union in the central government's educational decision-making processes. Policies designed to regulate teacher quality similarly run the gamut from the more stringent national evaluation systems, such as in Korea, to providing greater authority for schools and the local community to "…design appraisal policies that suit their own circumstances…", as in the United Kingdom (OECD, 2015: 7). External control is high in Ireland, which provided local stakeholders the authority to discipline and discharge teachers from service.

In short, while the interest in teacher quality and the improvement of learning outcomes is a shared concern across OECD countries, the areas of emphasis for policy reform vary substantially. In other words, there is no single way for countries to promote teacher professionalism – rather, there are different approaches and models that make sense in different contexts. In general, however, countries seek to establish a system for producing and maintaining teacher knowledge base – i.e. training and professional development, as well as their internal and external evaluation and accountability. These elements, along with compensation and recruitment and retention practices, ultimately affect the role and extent of professionalisation among teachers.

Table 1.1   **Variation in teacher professionalism reform strategies (a few examples)**

Country	Policy	Description
Denmark	Reform of teacher education in Denmark	The university colleges will be granted more autonomy in setting programme structures and determining the content of modules for development of teacher profiles.
Estonia	Increasing teacher salaries	Increase teacher salaries, changing the calculation base from contractual hours to full-time employment pay.
Iceland	Council for Teachers' Education and Professional Development	Increased representatives from the teachers' union, teacher training institutions and Ministry of Education.
Ireland	Procedures for Induction and Procedures and Criteria for Probation	Local control to formally discipline and eventually dismiss primary and secondary school teachers.
Korea	National Teacher Professional Development and Evaluation System (NTPDES)	New evaluation system to improve teacher effectiveness.
Netherlands	Registration for teachers	Registration for teachers to monitor their formal qualifications and their professional development, which was voluntary, will become compulsory.
Portugal	Entrance exam for all new teachers	Pre-service entrance exam for all new teachers in compulsory education.
United Kingdom	New arrangements for managing teacher performance	Aim to give schools and local authorities more freedom to design appraisal policies that suit their own circumstances.

Source: OECD (2015), *Education Policy Outlook 2015: Making Reforms Happen*, http://dx.doi.org/10.1787/9789264225442-en.

Teacher professionalism in high-performing education systems

While teacher professionalism reforms vary significantly across OECD countries, it may be instructive to turn to a few high-performing education systems for potential lessons regarding the role and space of the teacher. Interestingly, there is almost just as much variation in approaches to teacher professionalism among high performers as in the rest of the world. Hong Kong, China, for example, has introduced higher levels of teacher autonomy than its neighbours in East Asia. As the OECD notes in its recent *Lessons from PISA* publication (2014), school administrators and teachers in Hong Kong, China are given the freedom to customise the curriculum, materials and methods. This breadth and depth of autonomy has fostered high teacher professional self-esteem and the internal motivation for continuous professional development. Even with low-performing schools, the government does not intervene in school management, relying instead on the decision-making power of the school administration and teachers (OECD, 2014). By contrast, Shanghai, China embraces a more top-down approach, where the municipal government designs the policies, manages the schools and improves instruction (OECD, 2014). Teachers in Shanghai, China are comprehensively and rigorously trained in pre-service programmes and subsequent regular professional development (OECD, 2014: 110). They are expected to implement the standards and curricular approaches defined by the government and generally have less authority and autonomy in the delivery of instructional content and a narrower space for interpretation of curricular objectives (Lai and Lo, 2007).

High-quality teachers and school leaders have formed the cornerstone of the Singapore education system and are a major reason for its high performance. Singapore has developed a comprehensive system for selecting, training, compensating and developing teachers and principals, thereby creating tremendous capacity at the point of education delivery (OECD, 2014). In Singapore, professional development is defined by apprenticeship, mentoring, and collaborative learning environments (National Institute of Education, 2009). Much professional development is school-based, led by staff developers who identify teaching-based problems or introduce new practices. This accords the teaching profession greater autonomy over professional development and facilitates a teacher-led culture of professional excellence (OECD, 2014). Finally, Korea – another East Asian PISA high performer – places a high value on the teacher candidate selection process and pre-service teacher training and has a national evaluation process, strengthened through recent reforms as noted above, all of which serve to ensure only the best and the brightest join the ranks of teachers (OECD, 2014).

In Europe and North America, the usual above-average PISA performers – Australia, Canada, Finland and the Netherlands – have traditionally been commended for their strong teacher professionalisation practices and the latitude provided for teachers to customise learning (OECD, 2013b). Most notably, researchers argued that Finland's early success on PISA was explained by the fact that it "…publicly recognises the value of its teachers and trusts their professional judgments in schools…" (Sahlberg, 2010: 1). Similarly, Webb et al. (2004) document how Finnish teachers tend to emphasise autonomous decision making in their own conceptions of their professionalism. However, as the places traditionally occupied by Finland and the rest of the early top scorers began to shift, the linkages between a particular set of policies surrounding teachers and the results on PISA became less clear. A model that was highly successful in one context may not be as successful in another, as it is layered over the traditional and cultural frameworks that govern the relationship between the teacher, the state and the society at large.

In addition to understanding the variation in the conceptualisation of teacher professionalism across countries and economies, it is important to acknowledge that teacher quality and, consequently, levels of teacher professionalisation are not equally distributed within countries. Countries and economies may include multiple education systems and different policies governing different parts of the system. Furthermore, the extent of teacher professionalism also varies vertically within systems, with schools at different levels of the socio-economic ladder functioning with different levels of teacher professionalism. The next section discusses these considerations.

Teacher professionalism within countries

Within countries, equity concerns around teachers' access to structures that support their professional growth is highlighted by the unequal distribution of high-quality teachers in high-needs schools (i.e. schools with a student body with a high proportion of socio-economically disadvantaged students, second-language learners or students with special needs). This includes tendencies for more-experienced teachers, certified teachers, or teachers working in their subject area speciality to disproportionately work in high-income and low-minority schools in OECD countries (Imazeki and Goe, 2009; Jacob, Vidyarthi and Carroll, 2012; Peske and Haycock, 2006; OECD, 2005), schools with fewer Roma students in Eastern Europe (Kertesi and Kézdi, 2011; Sorbe, 2014), and urban schools in much of the global south (Mulkeen, 2006).

In this report, the unequal distribution of quality teaching is identified as a "professionalism gap", and defined as the differences in teacher support activities between high-needs and low-needs schools. This professionalism gap often runs parallel to student achievement gaps. In their analysis of the gap in support services across three states in the United States, Johnson et al. (2004) found that 91% of teachers in high-income schools had a mentor compared to just 65% of teachers in low-income schools. When mentor relationships were established in low-income schools, the participants were less likely to have meaningful conversations around curriculum and lesson planning, instructional practices and classroom management. Teachers in low-income schools also had less flexibility in curriculum and were more likely to be required to explicitly prepare for standardised tests, which led the authors to conclude that "…low-income schools fail to support new teachers as well as high-income schools." (Johnson et al., 2004-15). Additional research in the United States and internationally reinforces the presence of a professionalism gap, suggesting that high-needs schools are less likely to have induction or mentor programmes (Darling-Hammond et al., 2009), have fewer resources and lower quality curriculum (Darling-Hammond, 2006) and provide for an array of essential work conditions that address the sociological, psychological and physical demands of teaching (Johnson, 2006).

The teacher professionalism gap compounds problems in high-needs schools by increasing teacher turnover and decreasing teacher satisfaction. In a meta-analysis of 34 studies on the factors associated with teacher retention, Borman and Dowling (2008) found that teachers working in high-poverty schools or schools with large minority populations were more likely to leave their current place of employment. These compositional factors, when combined with findings around collaborative teacher practices and mentoring, led the authors to conclude that "…the characteristics of teachers' work conditions are more salient for predicting attrition than previously noted in the literature." (Borman and Dowling, 2008: 398).

Multiple factors accelerate teacher turnover in high-needs schools. First, high-poverty schools are more likely to employ less-experienced and less-educated teachers (Imazeki and Goe, 2009). Second, many of the activities that guard against teachers exiting the school are absent or severely underdeveloped in many high-needs schools. These include high levels of autonomy (Guarino, Sanibañez and Daley, 2006); comprehensive induction programmes that include mentors, time for collaboration, a reduced teaching load and a focus on networking (Smith and Ingersoll, 2004); and adequate administrative support (Ingersoll, 2001). Finally, teacher attrition is more common in schools that consist of a disproportionate number of unqualified teachers, suggesting that "…having more effective colleagues is a working condition in and of itself." (Berry, Smylie and Fuller, 2008: 37). All three of these characteristics correlate with the traits of high-needs schools, compounding the difficulties faced by these schools.

CONCEPTUALISING TEACHER PROFESSIONALISM

CONCEPTUAL FRAMEWORK: DOMAINS OF TEACHER PROFESSIONALISM

This section outlines the conceptual framework used to guide the remainder of the analysis. It includes information on how teacher professionalism is measured and an overview of hypotheses about the relationship between teacher professionalism and teacher perceptions and satisfaction. The conceptual framework is based on theories of teacher professionalism, which conceptualise teacher professionalism as having three major domains, namely: 1) knowledge base; 2) autonomy; and 3) peer networks.

In order to measure how well education systems support teachers' professionalism in each of these domains, the report identifies best practices for supporting teacher professionalism from the literature. The extent of teacher professionalism in an education system is measured by calculating the average number of best practices implemented in that system. Each of the domains of teacher professionalism is scaled from 0 to 5, with 5 representing a theoretical maximum where all practices within the domain are observed. The overall index of teacher professionalism adds up values on the three domains, with values ranging from a theoretical minimum of 0 to a possible maximum of 15. In reality, most teachers find themselves in environments where these practices are partially observed.

The conceptual framework then discusses how teacher professionalism is thought to be related to teachers' perceptions and satisfaction.

Conceptualising teacher professionalism

This section details the evidence supporting the inclusion of each best practice in the teacher professionalism index. As Servage observes, "…no shortage of literature puzzles over whether teaching is a profession, a semi-profession, a vocation or 'work that anyone can do'." (2009: 150). In the conception of teacher professionalism, this study follows Sexton (2007) in that teacher professionalism need not map onto the classic profession directly – instead, what matters is teachers' "practitioner professionalism", which includes the skills, attitudes and practices that are required for teachers to be effective educators (Sexton, 2007). As such, the domains of professionalism conceptualised and used in this study have been modified in line with the literature specific to teaching.

This report draws on theories of classic professionalism and its application to teaching to conceptualise teacher professionalism as consisting of three major domains: 1) professional knowledge; 2) teachers' autonomy in decision making; and 3) high peer networks. This classification is based on that of Wang, Lai and Lo (2014), who explain that "…professional knowledge is a set of knowledge the professional uses in teaching and learning that is acknowledged through qualifications and memberships. Teacher autonomy means that teachers have the ability to make some decisions in their work." (Wang, Lai and Lo, 2014: 434). High peer networks "…implies that teachers are responsible for students' development and for their own professional work." (Wang, Lai and Lo, 2014: 434). The remainder of this section discusses the literature on how each of these domains supports the improvement of teacher practice.

Professional knowledge base

Mastery of a complex body of professional knowledge is a core element of the classic professions, and most scholars have "…subscribed to the existence of, and indeed, fundamental importance of, a knowledge base in teaching." (Sexton, 2007: 83). Professional knowledge is defined as the set of knowledge the professional uses in teaching and learning that is acknowledged through qualifications and memberships. Teachers' professional knowledge base requires advanced or graduate-level education and specialised knowledge of subject matter, pedagogy and classroom management,

typically acquired through participation in initial teacher training programmes and continuous in-service professional development.

Formal teacher education

In a review of the research on teacher education, Linda Darling-Hammond (2000) finds that:

> …substantial evidence indicates that teachers who have had more preparation for teaching are more confident and successful with students than those who have had little or none. Recent evidence also indicates that reforms of teacher education creating more tightly integrated programmes with extended clinical preparation interwoven with coursework on learning and teaching produce teachers who are both more effective and more likely to enter and stay in teaching. (Darling-Hammond, 2000: 166)

Research also suggests that both subject-specific content knowledge and pedagogical knowledge are important for teachers' performance (Darling-Hammond, 2000). Additionally, studies have found that teachers who have some graduate-level training are both better prepared and more effective than those who enter the profession with the equivalent of an ISCED 5 (BA degree) (Wang et al., 2003).

Professional development opportunities

At the same time, ongoing learning through professional development is increasingly recognised as a core component of teachers' overall professional learning (Darling-Hammond, 2006). Research suggests that high-quality professional development can improve teacher practices and develop teachers' professional knowledge base (Desimone, et al., 2002; Mukeredzi, 2013). It is also expected that school and policy environments that support teachers' professional development are those where they participate more fully. Support for teacher professional development can take various forms, including providing designated time for professional development opportunities and offering financial or other incentives for participation. Inadequate support for professional development is seen as undermining professionalism (see Lynch, Hennessy and Gleeson, 2013: 498).

Practitioner research

Additionally, a number of scholars, including Sexton (2007), argue for an urgent consideration of how to tie more closely the theoretical knowledge base learned in teacher education programmes to teachers' classroom practices. Sexton suggests that "action-research" initiatives be used to deepen teachers' knowledge (2007: 96). Lynch, Hennessy and Gleason (2013) and Gonzalez, Moll and Amanti (2013) also argue for more opportunities for practitioner research as a way of deepening the knowledge base of teaching. For this reason, teachers' participation in individual or collective research is included as a component of the knowledge base.

Autonomous decision-making

Autonomy

Autonomy, or freedom to make decisions over one's work, is a second core component of the classic professions. For teachers, autonomy has been defined as autonomy over curricular choices, instructional planning and classroom standards of conduct (Pearson and Moomaw, 2005). Autonomy is closely related to both decision making and empowerment because it recognises teachers' capacity for sound professional judgment. Dondero (1997) links teacher autonomy closely to teachers' participation in school-based decision making and argues that both are necessary for professional growth. In empirical research, Pearson and Moomaw conceptualise empowerment, autonomy and professionalism as separate concepts, but find that all three are correlated, stating that "…teachers who felt empowered perceived a higher degree of professionalism." (2005: 46). Empowerment is more strongly correlated to professionalism

CONCEPTUALISING TEACHER PROFESSIONALISM

than is general or curricular autonomy. Examining research on the effect of autonomy, Dondero explains why this might be, stating that "…autonomy leads to a sense of ownership and empowerment where workers aim to grow within their profession and to seek increased responsibility." (1997: 1).

School-based decision making

School-based decision making is one area where teachers exert and develop their professionalism. Autonomy as decision making does not mean teachers are necessarily involved in school-based management; rather, it points to teachers' ability to make decisions over key aspects related to their work – curriculum, assessment, student discipline, etc. This definition of teacher autonomy aligns to the literature, which states that "…teachers and principals must have the authority to make key decisions about the services they render, and any top-down imposition of change is counter to the development of professionalism." (Firestone and Bader, 1992; Pearson and Moomaw, 2005: 41).

In the school setting, autonomy means that teachers are able to make key decisions about their work, including decisions over curricular content, pedagogical practices and assessment techniques. Pearson and Moomaw (2005) explain that collaborative autonomy takes place when teachers have the opportunity to work with administrators in making decisions related to curriculum, instruction and scheduling. For the purposes of this study, autonomy refers to collaborative autonomy, in which teachers are involved in a collective decision-making process. This study conceptualises higher levels of autonomy as existing when teachers are part of decision making in more domains of school life.

Peer networks

Peer regulation is a core component of classic professionalism; peers are responsible for setting high standards and ensuring that members are accountable to those standards (see also Box 1.1). In the literature on teacher professionalism, the development of professional networks and, with them, of high standards for performance across the profession through the professional peer networks, can be considered a form of internal accountability, which exists independently of externally imposed accountability (Sexton, 2007).

> **Box 1.1 The importance of peer networks in teacher professionalism**
>
> Supporting high professional standards requires a shift from viewing teaching as a solitary activity, owned by each teacher, to a view of teaching as a professional activity open to collective observations, study and improvement. Education systems can promote high standards by establishing peer networks of knowledge sharing, collaboration and support.

Maintaining high professional practices takes various forms, most of which emphasise peer collaboration and networks of information exchange, knowledge sharing and collective standard setting. In practice, responsibility for maintaining high professional standards means active engagement in other teachers' development through participation in school learning communities, engaging in peer feedback, and participation in mentoring and induction programmes at the school level.

Mentoring

Mentoring, which is defined in the literature as an intentional relationship, promotes teachers' professional growth by both expanding their knowledge base and supporting them emotionally

CONCEPTUALISING TEACHER PROFESSIONALISM

(Troman, 1999). Lai argues that "...mentoring plays an important role in enhancing novice teachers' opportunities to learn within the contexts of teaching." (2005: 12). Although effects of mentoring vary based on the nature of the mentorship, research has found that mentoring programmes can be mutually beneficial for both mentors and mentees (Banji and Ayankunle, 2013; Hall et al., 2008; Heirdsfield et al., 2008). Mentoring supports high standards for teachers by facilitating knowledge sharing and developing new teachers' skills (Fox and Wilson, 2015: 94). Important to this analysis is the role that mentors play in supporting the development of performance standards, which takes many forms, including by providing specific instructions about how to improve teaching, providing learning materials and resources, engaging in mutual evaluation, sharing professional knowledge and skills, and providing feedback (Bullough et al., 2003; Maynard, 2000; Bray and Nettleton, 2006; Le Maistre, Boudreau and Pare, 2006; Killcullen, 2007). As Mertz explains "...a good advisor, like a good supervisor, would quietly assess the competence and effectiveness of the new colleague and be willing to help the teacher assess and improve her or his performance so that it meets or exceeds the career expectations for the position." (2004: 552).

Induction

Induction programmes are formal programmes that provide support, guidance and orientation to new teachers in the transition to their first teaching position. These programmes help introduce new teachers to professional networks that help set standards and expectations of their work and ease their transition to the profession. Mentoring is often an important component of induction programmes, but not the same (Smith and Ingersoll, 2004; Portner, 2005). Examining the effects of mentoring and induction programmes, Smith and Ingersoll (2004) find that induction programmes are most effective when they include a set of complementary measures, such as a general induction programme, a seminar with other new teachers, a supportive mentor in the same field, common planning time, regularly scheduled collaboration with other teachers, regular supportive conversations with administrators, as well as participation in an external network of teachers. Teachers participating in such comprehensive programmes were found to be much less likely to leave the profession after one year than those who received none of these supports (Smith and Ingersoll, 2004).

Professional development plans

The professional development plan is a practice that requires teachers to determine their professional needs and set goals for themselves for developing their teaching practice. It is considered part of the peer networks domain because it is established in consultation with supervisors and mentors to promote professional development and high standards. As Jaquith et al. explain, it is a practice that aims to monitor and promote teachers' accountability and professional development by providing a "...mechanism to evaluate the quality of the continuing education to prevent it from becoming merely an exercise in accumulating credits and hours." (2010: 6). A 2010 report on four states in the United States examined the policy frameworks supporting high standards for teacher professionalism and found that, along with induction and mentoring, professional development plans are considered a best practice and are required in three of the four states (Jaquith et al., 2010).

Peer feedback

Peer feedback on teacher practice is one way that teachers and schools can ensure effective teaching. Sheeler, Ruhl and McAfee explain that "...teachers who attempt to try new teaching methods must receive regular feedback about the impact of new practices on student learning." (2004: 394). Empirical studies show that feedback has the largest impact on teachers' practices when it is immediate (Sheeler,

Ruhl and McAfee, 2004). Empirical research suggests that teachers' practices respond to feedback from both peers and supervisors (Sheeler, Ruhl and McAfee, 2004: 61) and that the feedback be given from a source the teacher deems to be credible (Pultorak, 2014).

Professional learning communities

The professional learning community (PLC) is one model by which schools create opportunities for professional learning and socialisation. Lee and Lee explain that "…with the realisation that teachers cannot do it alone in the isolation of their classrooms, the PLC school movement represents the aspirations for teacher collaborative networks to tackle the challenges of the new order." (2013: 436). Similarly, scholars have argued that the PLC can be a "…tool to surface good practices and combat teacher individualism." (Lee and Lee, 2013: 439). On her part, Servage (2009) emphasises the role that PLCs play in creating shared norms and expectations among teachers through socialisation. She argues that "…a professional learning community has considerable potential to produce both individually and collectively held norms and beliefs about the knowledge and practices that make a teacher a professional." (Servage, 2009: 152). This is because "…teachers experience greater professionalism through their engagement with one another in collaborative work." (Servage, 2009: 153). PLCs have also been recognised as a cornerstone of innovative learning environments (OECD, 2013a). Empirically, Jaquith et al. find that the states in their study of effective professional development have all "…embraced the use of school-based professional learning communities – collaborative teams which focus on professional development and key school improvement initiatives." (2010: 7).

Measures of teacher professionalism

Constructing a measure of teacher professionalism

For the analysis, a separate scale is developed for each domain of teacher professionalism – knowledge base, autonomy and peer networks – to study the nature and extent of teacher professionalism cross-nationally. To capture the nature and extent of teacher professionalism in different countries, this study draws on the academic literature on best practices – outlined earlier in this chapter – to create three separate scales of teacher professionalism, with each aligning to a specific domain. This approach draws on both the theory on classical professionalism, as well as empirical research on institutional practices that are shown to improve teacher performance. Using three distinct scales of professionalism allows the analysis to account for the fact that while each of the individual components of an index (i.e. knowledge base, belonging to peer networks, etc.) are supported by the literature, they are not necessarily highly correlated with one another empirically, meaning that the presence of one element does not always mean the presence of the other two in the same environment.

The scale created through the composite additive approach has the advantage of being both easily interpretable and comparable across countries and domains: a country with a higher score on a specific domain (such as a knowledge base, for example) adopts more policies and practices to promote teacher professionalism through that domain than one with a lower score.

Box 1.2 shows the items used in constructing the three scales. More information on scale construction can be found in the Technical Annex, Annex A. Each scale is naturally weighted by the number of indicators to give each a possible range of zero to five. Chapter 2 examines the nature of teacher professionalism in each country or economy and provides a visual representation of its professionalism.

CONCEPTUALISING TEACHER PROFESSIONALISM

Box 1.2 **Technical notes on scale construction**

Constructing an additive scale

In constructing the three scales of professionalism, three composite, additive scales are created. These scales weigh each factor equally and create an additive scale that ranges from 0-5. The composite additive approach, which is based on tangible, observed practices, is more appropriate for the measurement of teacher professionalism applied in this study than other approaches, such as confirmatory factor analysis or structural equation modelling, which rely on inter-item correlations to capture a latent construct (such as, for example, job satisfaction). The additive approach to scale construction is driven by the theory, and recognises that, in practice, not all elements of a common construct may be simultaneously observed. Many schools face situations of limited financial and human resources – when faced with an array of best practices, they make choices and trade-offs about which practices and policies to implement in support of professionalism. An additive scale that weighs all elements important to professionalism equally allows us to identify these trade-offs and assign higher scores to those systems where all practices recommended by research on professionalism are implemented.

Teacher professionalism sub-indices

1. Knowledge base best practices – drawn from TALIS 2013 teacher questionnaire
   - pre-service formal education
   - participation in formal teacher education programme
   - breadth of content covered in teacher education programme
   - support for in-service professional learning
   - types of support provided for ongoing professional development during and outside working hours (time, monetary, non-monetary)
   - participation in long-term professional development
   - support for practitioner research
   - participation in practitioner or action-research

2. Autonomy – drawn from TALIS 2013 principal questionnaire
   - decision-making over curriculum choices
   - decision-making over learning materials
   - decision-making over course content
   - decision-making over assessment policies
   - decision-making over discipline policies

3. Peer networks – drawn from TALIS 2013 teacher questionnaire
   - participation in a formal induction programme
   - participation in formal mentoring programme
   - received peer feedback on teaching based on direct observation
   - development of a professional development plan
   - participation in network supporting teacher professional development

CONCEPTUALISING TEACHER PROFESSIONALISM

The link between teacher professionalism and recruitment and retention

Teachers' professionalism is associated with a variety of policy-relevant outcomes of interest, specifically teachers' perceptions and their satisfaction. Chapter 3 investigates how teacher professionalism on each domain affects the following outcomes using multi-level regression analysis. The report investigates the relationship between teacher professionalism and four specific outcomes:

1. *Perceived status:* The study hypothesises that perceptions of status will be positively associated with levels of professional autonomy and higher knowledge-base requirements. The status of certain occupations also varies cross-nationally – in some countries teaching may be a higher-status profession than in other countries due to historical, cultural or economic factors.

2. *Satisfaction with teaching as a profession*: Research suggests that teachers with greater levels of autonomy will have higher levels of satisfaction with the profession, and hence will be more committed to teaching as a career.

3. *Satisfaction with the work environment*: It is expected that teachers who have more autonomy and more community responsibility over their professions will have higher levels of job satisfaction.

4. *Perceived self-efficacy*: Teachers with higher levels of professionalism are expected to have higher levels of self-efficacy.

Each of the variables measuring teachers' perceptions and satisfaction is drawn directly from the TALIS 2013 teacher questionnaire.

Individual and school and system-level factors

A number of individual, school- and system-wide factors are associated with teachers' perceived status, self-efficacy and job satisfaction. At the individual level, teachers' perceptions will vary based on individual characteristics and experiences in the labour market. This study builds on the hypothesis that individual teachers' perceptions of status will vary based on their attributes, including their gender, teaching experience and subject-matter expertise.

Additionally, the context in which they teach may affect their perceptions of status and self-efficacy. Factors associated with their schools, including school resources, the student body composition, administrator practices of shared decision-making and professional development opportunities may all affect teachers' perceptions of status. For example, the OECD publication *New Insights from TALIS 2013* (OECD, 2014a) shows that participating in an induction programme helps to predict future participation in professional development activities, which in turn may be associated with higher levels of satisfaction and retention. Further, the level of schooling is also an important factor in predicting outcomes. The TALIS report states that teachers in upper secondary experience "…higher levels of self-efficacy but lower levels of job satisfaction…" (OECD, 2014b) – this suggests the need to examine each outcome separately by school level.

This study accounts for these factors while investigating whether countries and school contexts with higher levels of teacher professionalisation report higher perceptions and satisfaction. Importantly, it is anticipated that opportunities for professional development and higher levels of autonomy and responsibility will be associated with higher levels of job satisfaction and commitment to the profession and self-efficacy. However, it is possible that not all three are equally important. In particular, one might

predict that a higher knowledge base, associated with more specialised knowledge, has a stronger association with status and self-efficacy, while autonomy and peer networks, associated with teachers' work environments, are more associated with job satisfaction, as well as satisfaction with teaching as a profession. Therefore, each domain is examined separately.

Analysis of teacher professionalism from an equity perspective

To understand how teachers' access to support for teacher professionalism varies within countries by school type, the report examines differences in the level of support provided to teachers in different environments. Focusing on equity, the report defines a high-needs school as one where over 30% of the student population are classified as either second language learners, students with special needs, or students that are socio-economically disadvantaged. As a basis of comparison, it defines a second group of lower-needs schools – where less than 11% of students are classified into one of the three high-needs groups. The teacher professionalism support gap is then measured as the difference in the support available for teachers in the two environments – calculated as the difference on each of the teacher professionalism scales in the two environments.

OUTLINE OF THE REPORT

This section outlines the remainder of the final report. Chapter 2 provides a closer look at what teacher professionalism looks like in a cross-system perspective. It shows descriptive statistics of teacher professionalism and its component scales, including a profile of professionalism in each country, which graphically displays the nature and extent of professionalism by plotting each country's mean values on each scale in a triangle plot. The chapter also examines cross-system means for professionalism in each domain, and compares the descriptive statistics on each scale to the other two.

Chapter 3 provides the results of regression analyses (see Box 1.3) predicting each of the four outcomes of interest: status, job satisfaction, commitment and self-efficacy. The analysis accounts for the nested structure of the data within schools, which are embedded within national education systems. The regression models show the relationship of teacher professionalism, represented by each domain, on the key outcomes of interest, namely perceived status, job satisfaction, commitment and self-efficacy.

The combined model predicts each of the dependent variables as a function of individual, school- and system-level variables. In addition to the TALIS data, the chapter accounts for system-level factors drawn from the OECD's 2014 *Education at a Glance* publication. It presents results while controlling for other measures of teacher professionalism, including relative teacher salary measures and whether an education system has a test-based accountability system to evaluate teachers.

Chapter 4 explores within-system equity patterns, following the analytic approaches laid out in Chapters 2 and 3. To address differences in access to professional support activities by school composition, schools within each national sample are subdivided into high-, medium-, and low-needs schools based on the school's demographics. In addition to exploring the distribution of teacher professional support activities separately in each of these three categories, a composite "more challenging schools" category is used based on the definition in the 2013 TALIS main report (OECD, 2014b). The chapter explores whether the relationship between available teacher professional support practices and teacher satisfaction and commitment to teaching differs by the relative composition of the school with some dimensions of professionalism being of greater value to teachers in high-needs schools.

CONCEPTUALISING TEACHER PROFESSIONALISM

> Box 1.3 **Technical notes on regression analysis**
>
> **Policy relevant outcomes**
>
> 1. Status – Agree or strongly agree with the statement "I think that the teaching profession is valued in society" (TALIS variable: TT2G46H)
>
> 2. Satisfaction with Profession – Satisfaction with Profession (TALIS scale: TJSPROS)
>
> 3. Satisfaction with Current Work Environment – Teacher Job Satisfaction (TALIS scale: TJOBSATS)
>
> 4. Self-efficacy – Teacher Self-Efficacy (TALIS scale: TSELFEFFS)
>
> **Regression analyses**
>
> In this study, the analysis controls for important individual and school-level factors while focusing on the relationship between teacher professionalism and perceived status, self-efficacy, job satisfaction and commitment to the profession. It is expected that these system-level factors will influence the extent of teacher professionalism – in systems where educational standards are higher and teacher-training credentials closely regulated, we anticipate higher levels of professionalism. Because both levels shape professionalism, we will account for both system-wide context factors and school-level practices in the indices of teacher professionalism. This conceptual framework outlines what teacher professionalism is, how it might be measured and compared cross-nationally, and how it affects the supply of high-quality teachers.

By examining teacher professionalism along three separate domains, this study sheds light on how knowledge, autonomy and peer networks are associated with each of the outcomes of interest. This insight can be used to address the major issues of teacher recruitment and retention in specific system contexts. In Chapter 5, the report discusses the policy implications of the study and generates policy-relevant recommendations for enhancing teacher professionalism and equity in access to high-quality teaching.

Notes

1. Note by Turkey: The information in this document with reference to "Cyprus" relates to the southern part of the Island. There is no single authority representing both Turkish and Greek Cypriot people on the Island. Turkey recognises the Turkish Republic of Northern Cyprus (TRNC). Until a lasting and equitable solution is found within the context of the United Nations, Turkey shall preserve its position concerning the "Cyprus issue".

   Note by all the European Union Member States of the OECD and the European Union: The Republic of Cyprus is recognised by all members of the United Nations with the exception of Turkey. The information in this document relates to the area under the effective control of the Government of the Republic of Cyprus.

2. Data for the United States is not included in this report because they did not meet international participation rates. Country profiles for the United States are presented in Annexes B and F, for information purposes.

3. The Education for All Strategy 9 states, in part: "Teachers at all levels of the education system should be respected and adequately remunerated; have access to training and on-going professional development and support,

including through open and distance learning; and be able to participate, locally and nationally, in decisions affecting their professional lives and teaching environments." (UNESCO, 2000: 20).

A note regarding Israel
The statistical data for Israel are supplied by and under the responsibility of the relevant Israeli authorities. The use of such data by the OECD is without prejudice to the status of the Golan Heights, East Jerusalem and Israeli settlements in the West Bank under the terms of international law.

References

Banji, F.J. and S. Ayankunle (2013), "Open education resources and teacher professional development in Nigeria: Prospects and challenges", http://pcfpapers.colfinder.org/handle/5678/125.

Barber, M. and M. Mourshed (2007), "How the world's best-performing school systems come out on top", McKinsey & Company, http://mckinseyonsociety.com/downloads/reports/Education/Worlds_School_Systems_Final.pdf.

Berry, B., M. Smylie and E. Fuller (2008), "Understanding teacher work conditions: A review and look to the future", Center for Teaching Quality, November 2008, www.teachingquality.org/sites/default/files/Understanding%20Teacher%20Working%20Conditions-%20A%20Review%20and%20Look%20to%20the%20Future.pdf.

Borman, G.D. and N.M. Dowling (2008), "Teacher attrition and retention: A meta-analytic and narrative review of the research", *Review of Educational Research*, Vol. 78/3, pp. 367-409.

Bray, L. and P. Nettleton (2006), "Assessor or mentor? Role confusion in professional education", *Nurse Education Today*, Vol. 27, pp. 848-855.

Bullough Jr, R.V. et al. (2003), "Teaching with a peer: A comparison of two models of student teaching", *Teaching and Teacher Education*, Vol. 19, pp. 57-73.

Brunetti, G.J. (2001), "Why do they teach? A study of job satisfaction among long-term high school teachers", *Teacher Education Quarterly*, Vol. 28/3, pp. 49-74.

Darling-Hammond, L. et al. (2009), "Professional learning in the learning profession: A status report on teacher development in the United States and abroad", National Staff Development Council, http://learningforward.org/docs/pdf/nsdcstudy2009.pdf.

Darling-Hammond, L. (2006), "Securing the right to learn: Policy and practice for powerful teaching and learning", *Educational Researcher*, Vol. 35/7, pp. 13-24.

Darling-Hammond, L. (2000), "How teacher education matters", *Journal of Teacher Education*, Vol. 51(3), pp. 166-173.

Darling-Hammond, L. and A. Lieberman (eds.) (2013), *High Quality Teaching and Learning: Changing Policies and Practices*, Routledge, London.

Desimone, L.M. et al. (2002), "Effects of professional development on teachers' instruction: Results from a three-year longitudinal study", *Educational Evaluation and Policy Analysis*, Vol. 24/2, pp. 81-112.

Dondero, G.M. (1997), "Organizational climate and teacher autonomy: Implications for educational reform", *International Journal of Educational Management*, Vol. 11(5), pp. 218-221.

Evans, L. (2008), "Professionalism, professionality and the development of education professionals", *British Journal of Educational Studies*, Vol. 56/1, pp. 20-38.

Feiman-Nemser, S. (2003), "What new teachers need to learn", *Educational Leadership*, Vol. 60/8, pp. 25-29.

Firestone, W.A., and B.D. Bader (1992), *Redesigning teaching: Professionalism or bureaucracy?*, SUNY Press, Albany, N.Y.

Fox, A.R. and E.G. Wilson (2015), "Networking and the development of professionals: Beginning teachers building social capital", *Teaching and Teacher Education*, Vol. 47, pp. 93-107.

Gonzalez, N., L.C. Moll and C. Amanti (2013), *Funds of Knowledge: Theorizing Practices in Households, Communities, and Classrooms*, Routledge, New York.

Guarino, C.M., L. Santibañez and G.A. Daley (2006), "Teacher recruitment and retention: A review of the recent empirical literature", *Review of Educational Research*, Vol. 76/2, pp. 173-208.

Hall, K.M. et al. (2008), "More than a place to teach: Exploring the perceptions of the roles and responsibilities of mentor teachers", *Mentoring & Tutoring: Partnership in Learning*, Vol. 16(3), pp. 328-345.

Harris-Van Keuren, C. and I. Silova (2015), "Implementing EFA Strategy No. 9: The evolution of the status of the teaching profession (2000-2015) and the impact on the quality of education in developing countries: three case studies", Background Paper for the Global Monitoring Report 2015, ED/EFA/MRT/2015/PI/08, UNESCO, http://unesdoc.unesco.org/images/0023/002324/232402e.pdf.

Heirdsfield, A.M. et al. (2008), "Peer mentoring for first year teacher education students: The mentors' experience", *Mentoring & Tutoring: Partnership in Learning*, Vol. 16(2), pp. 109-124.

Imazeki, J. and L. Goe (2009), "The distribution of highly qualified, experienced teachers: Challenges and opportunities", *TQ Research and Quality Brief*, August 2009, National Comprehensive Center for Teacher Quality, www.gtlcenter.org/sites/default/files/docs/August2009Brief.pdf.

Ingersoll, R. (2001), "Teacher turnover and teacher shortages: An organizational analysis", *American Education Research Journal*, Vol. 38, pp. 499–534.

Jacob, A., E. Vidyarthi and K. Carroll (2012), "The irreplaceables: Understanding the real retention crisis in America's urban schools", TNTP, http://tntp.org/assets/documents/TNTP_Irreplaceables_2012.pdf.

Jaquith, A. et al. (2010), "Teacher professional learning in the United States: Case studies of state policies and strategies. Summary report", Learning Forward, Stanford Center for Opportunity Policy in Education, http://learningforward.org/docs/pdf/2010phase3report.pdf?sfvrsn=0.

Johnson, S.M. et al. (2004), "The support gap: New teachers' early experiences in high-income and low-income schools", *Education Policy Analysis Archives*, Vol. 12/61, 29 October 2004, pp. 1-25, http://dx.doi.org/10.14507/epaa.v12n61.2004.

Johnson, S.M. (2006), *The Workplace Matters: Teacher Quality, Retention, and Effectiveness*, National Education Association, Washington, DC.

Kertesi, G. and G. Kézdia (2011), "The Roma/non-Roma test score gap in Hungary", *The American Economic Review*, Vol. 101/3, pp. 519-525.

Kilcullen, N.M. (2007), "Said another way: The Impact of mentoring on clinical learning", *Nursing Forum*, Vol. 42(2), pp. 95-104.

Lai, E. (2005), "Mentoring for in-service teachers in a distance teacher education programme: views of mentors, mentees and university teachers", paper presented at the Australian Association for Research in Education International Education Research Conference, Parramatta.

Lai, M. H. and Lo, L. N. K. (2007) "Teacher professionalism in education reform: The experience of Hong Kong and Shanghai", *Compare: A Journal of Comparative Education*, Vol. 37(1), pp. 53-68.

Lee, D. and W.O. Lee (2013), "A professional learning community for the new teacher professionalism: The case of a state-led initiative in Singapore schools", *British Journal of Educational Studies*, Vol. 61(4), pp. 435-451.

Le Maistre, C., S. Boudreau, and A. Pare (2006), "Mentor or evaluator? Assisting and assessing newcomers to the professions", *The Journal of Workplace Learning*, Vol. 18(6), pp. 344-354.

Lynch, R., J. Hennessy and J. Gleeson (2013), "Acknowledging teacher professionalism in Ireland: the case for a Chartered Teacher initiative", *Irish Educational Studies*, Vol. 32/4, pp. 493-510.

Maynard, T. (2000), "Learning to teach or learning to manage mentors? Experiences of school-based teacher training", *Mentoring and Tutoring*, Vol. 8(1), pp. 17-30.

Mertz, N.T. (2004), "What's a mentor, anyway?", *Educational Administration Quarterly*, Vol. 40(4), pp. 541 560.

Mukeredzi, T.G. (2013, "Professional development through teacher roles: conceptions of professionally unqualified teachers in rural South Africa and Zimbabwe", *Journal of Research in Rural Education*, Vol. 28/11, pp. 1-16, http://sites.psu.edu/jrre/wp-content/uploads/sites/6347/2014/02/28-11.pdf.

Mulkeen, A. (2006), "Teachers for rural schools: A challenge for Africa", Association for the Development for Education in Africa.

National Institute of Education (2009), "A teacher education model for the 21st Century: A report by the National Institute of Education, Singapore", www.nie.edu.sg/files/spcs/Te21_online_ver.pdf.

OECD (2015), *Education Policy Outlook 2015: Making Reforms Happen*, OECD Publishing, Paris, http://dx.doi.org/10.1787/9789264225442-en.

OECD (2014a), *Lessons from PISA for Korea*, Strong Performers and Successful Reformers in Education, OECD Publishing, Paris, http://dx.doi.org/10.1787/9789264190672-en.

OECD (2014b), *TALIS 2013 Results: An International Perspective on Teaching and Learning*, TALIS, OECD Publishing, Paris, http://dx.doi.org/10.1787/9789264196261-en.

OECD (2013a), *Innovative Learning Environments*, Educational Research and Innovation, OECD Publishing, Paris, http://dx.doi.org/10.1787/9789264203488-en.

OECD (2013b), *PISA 2012 Results: What Makes Schools Successful (Volume IV): Resources, Policies and Practices*, PISA, OECD Publishing, Paris, http://dx.doi.org/10.1787/9789264201156-en.

OECD (2005), *Teachers Matter: Attracting, Developing and Retaining Effective Teachers*, Education and Training Policy, OECD Publishing, Paris, http://dx.doi.org/10.1787/9789264018044-en.

Pearson, L.C. and W. Moomaw (2005), "The relationship between teacher autonomy and stress, work satisfaction, empowerment, and professionalism", *Educational Research Quarterly*, Vol. 29/1, pp. 38-54.

Peske, H.G. and K. Haycock (2006), "Teaching inequality: How poor and minority students are shortchanged on teacher quality," a Report and Recommendations by the Education Trust, http://edtrust.org/wp-content/uploads/2013/10/TQReportJune2006.pdf.

Popkewitz, T. (1994), "Professionalization in teaching and teacher education: Some notes on its history, ideology, and potential", *Teaching & Teacher Education*, Vol. 10/1, pp. 1-14.

Portner, H. (2005), *Teacher Mentoring and Induction: The State of the Art and Beyond*, Corwin Press, Thousand Oaks, CA.

Pultorak, E.G. (2014), *Reflectivity and Cultivating Student Learning: Critical Elements for Enhancing a Global Community of Learners and Educators*, Rowman & Littlefield, Lanham, MD.

Rhoton, Jack and Katherine E. Stiles (2002), "Exploring the professional development design process: Bringing an abstract framework into practice", *Science Educator*, Vol. 11/1, pp. 1-8.

Sahlberg, P. (2010), "The secret to Finland's success: Educating teachers", *Stanford Center for Opportunity Policy in Education – Research Brief*, September 2010, https://edpolicy.stanford.edu/sites/default/files/publications/secret-finland%E2%80%99s-success-educating-teachers.pdf.

Scheeler, M.C., K.L. Ruhl and J.K. McAfee (2004), "Providing performance feedback to teachers: A review", *Teacher Education and Special Education: The Journal of the Teacher Education Division of the Council for Exceptional Children*, Vol. 27(4), pp. 396-407.

Servage, L. (2009), "Who is the 'professional' in a professional learning community? An exploration of teacher professionalism in collaborative professional development settings", *Canadian Journal of Education/Revue canadienne de l'éducation*, Vol. 32(1), pp. 149-171.

Sexton, Michael (2007), "Evaluating teaching as a profession – implications of a research study for the work of the teaching council", *Irish Educational Studies*, Vol. 26/1, pp. 79-105.

Siegrist, H. (2015), "Profession and Professionalization, History of", in J.D. Wright (ed.), *International Encyclopedia of Social and Behavioral Sciences*, 2nd Edition, Elsevier, Philadelphia, PA, pp. 95-100, http://dx.doi.org/10.1016/B978-0-08-097086-8.62020-2.

Smith, T.M. and R.M. Ingersoll (2004), "What are the effects of induction and mentoring on beginning teacher turnover?", *American Educational Research Journal*, Vol. 41/3, pp. 681-714.

Sorbe, S. (2014), "Tackling labour mismatches and promoting mobility in Hungary", *OECD Economics Department Working Papers*, No. 1122, OECD Publishing, Paris, http://dx.doi.org/10.1787/5jz2px6jtpmt-en.

Troman, G. (1999), "Researching primary teachers' work: examining theory, policy and practice through interactionist ethnography", in Hammersley, M. (ed.) *Researching School Experience: Ethnographic Studies of Teaching and Learning*, Falmer Press, London, pp. 33-50.

UNESCO (2000), "The Dakar Framework for Action: Education for all: Meeting our collective commitments", Adopted by the World Education Forum Dakar, Senegal, 26-28 April 2000, UNESCO Publishing, Paris, http://unesdoc.unesco.org/images/0012/001211/121147e.pdf.

Wang, A.H. et al. (2003), "Preparing teachers around the world", *Policy Information Report*, Policy Information Center, Educational Testing Service, Princeton, NJ, www.ets.org/Media/Education_Topics/pdf/prepteach.pdf.

Wang, L., M. Lai and L.N.K. Lo (2014, "Teacher professionalism under the recent reform of performance pay in Mainland China", *Prospects*, Vol. 44/3, pp. 429-443.

Watkins, P. (2005), "The principal's role in attracting, retaining, and developing new teachers: Three strategies for collaboration and support", *The Clearing House*, Vol. 79/2, pp. 83-87.

Webb, R., et al. (2004), "A comparative analysis of primary teacher professionalism in England and Finland", *Comparative education*, Vol. 40(1), pp. 83-107.

2

The nature and extent of teacher professionalism

This chapter examines the nature and extent of teacher professionalism in countries and economies participating in the Teaching and Learning International Survey (TALIS) 2013. The chapter provides an in-depth look at which domains of teacher professionalism tend to be emphasised across countries, what specific practices within each domain are most prevalent, and whether teacher professionalism differs by school level. Additionally, it examines how teacher professionalism differs across countries and economies, investigating which education systems have the highest levels of teacher professionalism overall, which domains systems emphasise, and the various models of professionalism that education systems follow.

2. THE NATURE AND EXTENT OF TEACHER PROFESSIONALISM

> **Highlights**
>
> - Findings of this chapter indicate that the nature of teacher professionalism in a system is related to the system's teaching culture or policy priorities.
> - The nature and extent of teacher professionalism differs across systems. Teacher autonomy is emphasised among several European systems, while peer networks tend to be emphasised among East Asian countries.
> - For the systems participating in the TALIS option at lower and upper secondary education levels, autonomy is higher for teachers of upper secondary grades, while emphasis on the development of knowledge base and building peer networks are relatively lower, in comparison to lower secondary and primary education.

INTRODUCTION

The chapter shows that the global averages on each of the teacher professionalism indices are between two and three out of five possible points, which suggests that schools and nations are implementing roughly half of all best practices consistently. Yet average values on each domain of teacher professionalism – knowledge, autonomy and peer networks – differ by school level. Teacher professionalism at the primary and lower secondary level emphasises the domains of knowledge and peer networks, with low levels of autonomy, while at the upper secondary level, teacher professionalism has higher values in the autonomy domain. Differences in the nature of teacher professionalism across school levels may reflect both differences in the nature of teaching, as well as dominant ideas about the role of the teacher: the greater content specificity at upper secondary level seems to imply more autonomy for teachers, less peer influence over peer networks and more emphasis on content knowledge accompanied by a reduced emphasis on pedagogical knowledge.

Countries are very similar in their support for the knowledge base domain, where the mean values for most participating countries and economies range narrowly between two and three. In contrast, systems exhibit much more diversity in terms of their support for autonomy and peer networks. This variation could indicate that these domains are more likely to reflect national priorities and differences in cultures of teaching. Additionally, the analysis of cross-country trends suggests that there are regional patterns for teacher professionalism.

TEACHER PROFESSIONALISM

As discussed in Chapter 1, this study conceptualises teacher professionalism as consisting of three domains: 1) knowledge, exemplified by the presence of teaching credentials and support for continued professional development; 2) autonomy, or the amount of decision-making power teachers have over aspects of their teaching, as reported by principals; and, 3) peer networks, conceptualised as the role that teachers play in regulating their own peer networks of practice and exemplified through school-based programmes that involve teachers in peer socialisation, guidance and feedback.

Each of the domains of teacher professionalism is scaled from 0 to 5.0, with 5.0 representing a theoretical maximum where all practices within the domain are observed for a given teacher. In reality, most teachers find themselves in environments where these practices are partially observed.

THE NATURE AND EXTENT OF TEACHER PROFESSIONALISM

Box 2.1 **Teacher professionalism scales**

Knowledge base scale

1. Participated in formal teacher education programme
2. Exposed to subject-specific content in teacher education programme
3. Exposed to pedagogy in teacher education programme
4. Exposed to practice in teacher education programme
5. Participates in individual or collaborative research
6. Receives financial support to pay for professional development
7. Receives time release for professional development during working hours
8. Receives salary supplement for professional development outside working hours
9. Receives non-monetary support for professional development outside working hours
10. Participates in extended professional development activities

Autonomy scale

1. Autonomy over content
2. Autonomy over course offerings
3. Autonomy over discipline practices
4. Autonomy over assessment
5. Autonomy over materials

Peer networks scale

1. Participates in formal induction
2. Mentoring programme at school
3. Participates in network of teachers
4. Receives feedback from direct observations
5. Receives personalised professional development plan

Figure 2.1 shows the TALIS averages of the three domains of teacher professionalism. The figure shows that the mean value across all surveyed lower secondary (ISCED 2) teachers is 2.68 out of 5.0 on the knowledge base scale, 2.21 on the autonomy scale and 2.99 on the peer networks index. These averages suggest that across TALIS countries and economies, averages on each domain of teacher professionalism range between 2 and 3; in other words, of the best practices identified in the literature, systems implement roughly half.

The figure shows that the knowledge and peer networks domains have higher averages across all TALIS countries and economies than the autonomy domain. This suggests that, overall, the practices related to teacher autonomy are implemented less often than those related to professional development and professional collaboration on teaching standards through peer networks.

THE NATURE AND EXTENT OF TEACHER PROFESSIONALISM

Because the scales are calculated by adding up the total number of best practices, implementation of a few best practices may affect mean values significantly. The differences in mean values on each of these indices may be affected by only a few education systems' practices, or could represent broad differences across all nations, suggesting the need for more detailed analysis of system-level variation. There are also a number of reasons to think that teacher professionalism may vary across school levels – both because of the nature of teaching and learning and because dominant ideas about the role of the teacher in students' development may differ at different school levels (OECD, 2014). As such, this report also examines how values on each domain vary across school levels. At the same time, a note of caution is advised when comparing across education levels, given that the TALIS option for primary schools was completed by 6 systems (Denmark; Flanders, Belgium; Finland; Mexico; Norway and Poland), and the option for upper secondary schools by 11 systems (Abu Dhabi, United Arab Emirates; Australia; Denmark; Finland; Georgia; Iceland; Italy; Mexico; Norway; Poland and Singapore). To explore these sources of variation, the remainder of this chapter examines how indices of professionalism vary across systems, school levels, and by specific practices.

▪ Figure 2.1 ▪
Average values on the domains of teacher professionalism indices, by domain (ISCED 2)

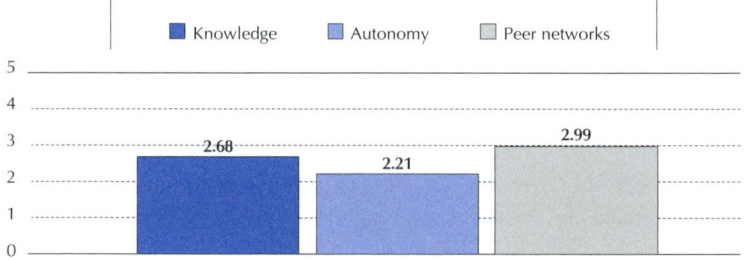

Source: OECD (2013), *Teaching and Learning International Survey (TALIS): 2013 complete database*, http://stats.oecd.org/index.aspx?datasetcode=talis_2013%20.

SYSTEM DIFFERENCES IN TEACHER PROFESSIONALISM

The nature of teacher professionalism varies both in terms of a system's overall level of teacher professionalism and the domain the country or economy emphasises. Figure 2.2 graphs education systems' overall level of teacher professionalism, broken down by their value on each domain. Overall values range from a maximum of 10.1 in the Russian Federation to a minimum of 5.8 in Portugal. This distribution suggests that, generally speaking, teachers in the Russian Federation will be exposed to two of every three best practices, while those in Portugal and in countries towards the bottom end of the spectrum will benefit from slightly more than one out of three.

Because teacher professionalism is a composite index, meaning an index created by summing the total number of implemented best practices, countries and economies with the highest overall values on teacher professionalism generally have high values on all three domains. As the figure shows, the education systems with the highest values on the composite index are the Estonia, New Zealand, the Russian Federation and Singapore. Seven of the ten education systems with the highest overall professionalism are located in Europe, while two (New Zealand and Singapore) are outside Europe. The

THE NATURE AND EXTENT OF TEACHER PROFESSIONALISM

three Latin American countries (Brazil, Chile and Mexico) score at the lower end of the overall index, while Portugal and Spain are the two countries with the lowest levels of teacher professionalism on the composite index in the surveyed TALIS systems.

■ Figure 2.2 ■
Total professionalism index, by country (ISCED 2)

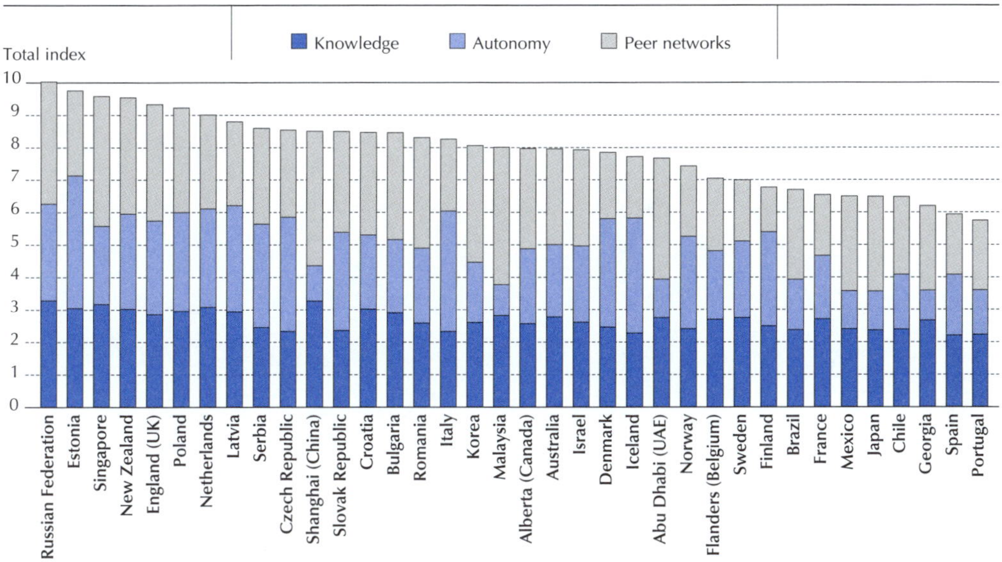

Source: OECD (2013), *Teaching and Learning International Survey (TALIS): 2013 complete database*, http://stats.oecd.org/index.aspx?datasetcode=talis_2013%20.

Table 2.1 lists each system's value on each domain and codes their values along a spectrum from zero to five (at the high end). One may note the geographic concentration of education systems with high values on autonomy, with all of these countries and economies located in Europe. In general, East Asian, Middle Eastern and Latin American systems have less autonomy afforded to teachers. This would suggest that the degree of decision making and control over school processes on the part of teachers may be in part influenced by cultural norms.

Meanwhile, only two of the education systems that emphasise peer networks are in Europe, namely England (United Kingdom) and Romania. Rather, high peer networks tend to be emphasised most among East Asian countries and economies, and the few Latin American and Middle Eastern systems represented in TALIS also score highest on the peer networks scale. This finding implies a cultural difference in the degree to which countries promote networking and peer feedback among teachers, with East Asian countries and economies such as Malaysia; Shanghai, China; and Singapore among the systems with the highest values on this measure.

2
THE NATURE AND EXTENT OF TEACHER PROFESSIONALISM

Table 2.1 System means on teacher professionalism domains (ISCED 2)

System	Knowledge	Autonomy	Networks
Abu Dhabi (United Arab Emirates)	2.8	1.2	3.7
Alberta (Canada)	2.6	2.3	3.1
Australia	2.8	2.2	3.0
Brazil	2.4	1.6	2.8
Bulgaria	2.9	2.3	3.3
Chile	2.4	1.7	2.4
Croatia	3.0	2.3	3.2
Czech Republic	2.3	3.5	2.7
Denmark	2.5	3.4	2.1
England (United Kingdom)	2.9	2.9	3.6
Estonia	3.1	4.1	2.6
Finland	2.5	2.9	1.4
Flanders (Belgium)	2.7	2.1	2.2
France	2.7	2.0	1.9
Georgia	2.7	0.9	2.6
Iceland	2.3	3.6	1.9
Israel	2.6	2.4	3.0
Italy	2.3	3.7	2.2
Japan	2.4	1.2	2.9
Korea	2.6	1.9	3.6
Latvia	2.9	3.3	2.6
Malaysia	2.8	1.0	4.3
Mexico	2.4	1.2	2.9
Netherlands	3.1	3.0	2.9
New Zealand	3.0	2.9	3.6
Norway	2.4	2.9	2.2
Poland	3.0	3.1	3.2
Portugal	2.2	1.4	2.1
Romania	2.6	2.3	3.4
Russian Federation	3.3	3.0	3.8
Serbia	2.5	3.2	3.0
Shanghai (China)	3.3	1.1	4.2
Singapore	3.2	2.4	4.0
Slovak Republic	2.4	3.0	3.1
Spain	2.2	1.9	1.9
Sweden	2.7	2.4	1.9

Source: OECD (2013), *Teaching and Learning International Survey (TALIS): 2013 complete database*, http://stats.oecd.org/index.aspx?datasetcode=talis_2013%20.

TEACHER PROFESSIONALISM, BY DOMAIN

The correlations between teachers' values on the three domains are quite low (see Annex A). This indicates that as a system adopts more of the identified best practices in one domain, they do not necessarily do so in the other two. This suggests there is no single underlying concept of teacher professionalism that drives education systems' values on all three domains; rather, teacher professionalism as practiced in schools should be considered a composite of three separate domains. Schools and systems may choose to emphasise one over the other two, or they may choose to focus on all three at the same time. Because implementation of best practices differs across domains, this section examines each domain individually, focusing on which practices are most common within each domain and how the domains vary across school levels.

THE NATURE AND EXTENT OF TEACHER PROFESSIONALISM

Knowledge base scale

As discussed in Chapter 1, items measuring teachers' knowledge base do not capture the extent of teachers' content knowledge in any given subject; rather, they assess the extent to which teachers have received training in areas recognised as important to the practice of teaching – subject-specific content and pedagogy, as well as practice teaching. They also include supports for in-service professional learning. Figure 2.3 shows national averages on the knowledge base scale, which range from 3.3 in the Russian Federation and Shanghai, China to a low of 2.2 in Portugal and Spain. As is clear, the range of national means is not large – at 1.1, the difference between education systems with the highest and lowest mean on the knowledge base scale is only two out of ten possible best practices, suggesting that countries/economies participating in TALIS implement similar policies to develop teachers' knowledge base.

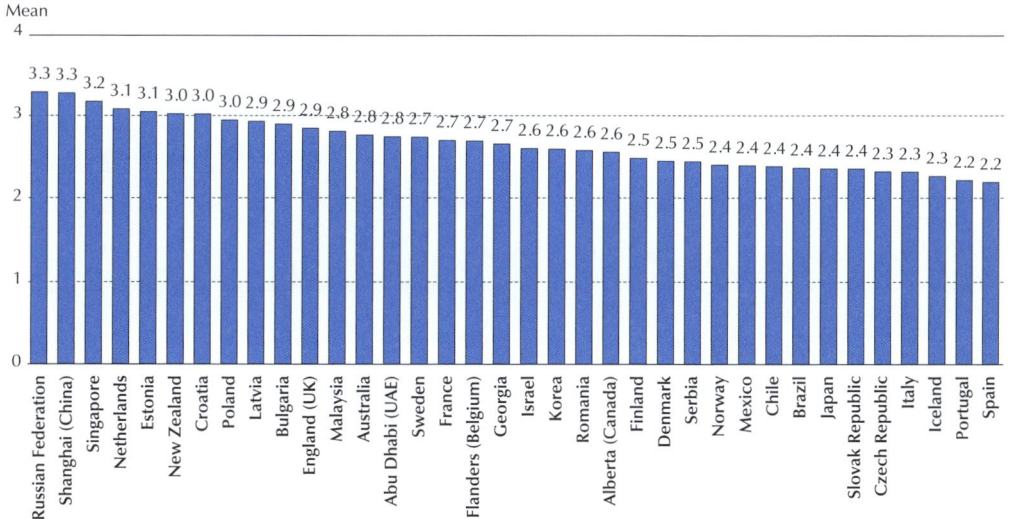

■ Figure 2.3 ■
National averages on the knowledge base scale (ISCED 2)

Source: OECD (2013), *Teaching and Learning International Survey (TALIS): 2013 complete database*, http://stats.oecd.org/index.aspx?datasetcode=talis_2013%20.

The items in the knowledge base scale can be classified into two categories: 1) the knowledge needed to enter the profession (i.e. pre-service formal education); and 2) supports for ongoing professional learning (i.e. in-service professional development).

Figure 2.4 presents a stacked bar plot, which breaks down the knowledge base scale into percentages – indicating the percentage of the total scale that is accounted for by implementation of pre-service practices compared to the percentage accounted for by in-service professional development practices. Were systems to support pre-service and in-service practices equally, each would contribute 50% of a country's total value on the knowledge base scale. As the figure shows, however, in almost all participating countries and economies, values on the pre-service training compose roughly 60-70% of their total values on the knowledge base scale – suggesting more emphasis on pre-service educational requirements, with fewer supports for in-service professional development. Among countries and economies participating in TALIS, it appears as though teachers may need more supports for in-service professional learning, though teachers' specific needs may vary and further research may be warranted into which types of supports are most effective.

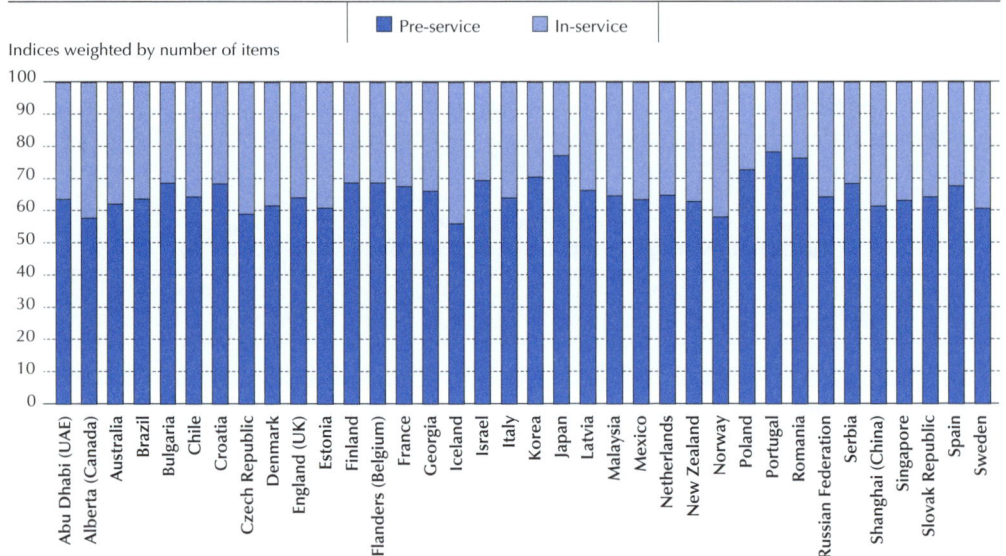

• Figure 2.4 •
Breakdown of knowledge base, by sub-scale

Source: OECD (2013), *Teaching and Learning International Survey (TALIS): 2013 complete database*, http://stats.oecd.org/index.aspx?datasetcode=talis_2013%20.

Knowledge base by ISCED level

Within education systems, average values on the knowledge base scale also vary across school levels. Figure 2.5 shows the average number of best practices in the knowledge base scale, out of a possible five, implemented by school level.[1] The figure shows that the mean number of practices at the primary and lower secondary level are nearly identical at 2.66 and 2.68, respectively. Meanwhile, the value at the upper secondary level is somewhat lower, at 2.43, and statistically significantly different (p<0.001), suggesting that the average number of practices in upper secondary schools is not the same as in primary and lower secondary schools.

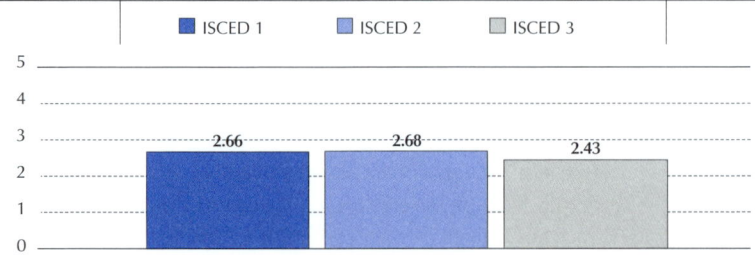

• Figure 2.5 •
Mean values on knowledge base domain, by ISCED level

Source: OECD (2013), *Teaching and Learning International Survey (TALIS): 2013 complete database*, http://stats.oecd.org/index.aspx?datasetcode=talis_2013%20.

THE NATURE AND EXTENT OF TEACHER PROFESSIONALISM

Support for teachers' knowledge base includes pre-service and in-service supports for professional development. As such, it may seem surprising that the mean value on the knowledge base scale is statistically the same at the primary and lower secondary levels, but is lower at the upper secondary level, where teachers can be expected to have the most content knowledge. To investigate the reasons for differences across school levels, responses to each item are examined.

Table 2.2 presents percentages of teachers who had received each form of knowledge in the knowledge base – an item-by-item analysis not only explains variation across school levels, but also sheds light onto the specific best practices in the knowledge base domain that are more common than others at different levels. The table shows that the majority of all teachers at all school levels are likely to enter the profession through participation in a formal education programme, which includes exposure to the content of the courses they teach, as well as exposure to pedagogy and practice.

Table 2.2 also sheds light on why teachers in upper secondary schools have lower values on the knowledge base scale – a lower percentage of teachers in secondary schools have participated in formal teacher education programmes, and a much lower percentage have been exposed to on-the-job practice in their education programmes. This is not surprising, as in many countries and economies, teachers in secondary schools are seen as content specialists and may not be required to participate in teacher education programmes (Akiba, LeTendre and Scriber, 2007; OECD, 2014). In short, it appears as though the additional content knowledge acquired by secondary teachers is possibly at the expense of their training in other relevant areas, including pedagogy and on-the-job practice.

Table 2.2 also shows that there are large differences in the types of support teachers receive for professional learning, with financial support (i.e. paid professional learning) the most common, followed by long-term training.[2] However, other types of supports are uncommon – the table shows that very few teachers received salary supplements or forms of non-monetary support for professional learning outside working hours. Indeed, systems that emphasise professional development activities during work hours may not offer support for such activities outside working hours at the school.

Table 2.2 **Components of knowledge base scale, by ISCED level**

Item in knowledge base scale	ISCED 1	ISCED 2	ISCED 3
Participated in teacher education programme	88.20%	87.30%	69.20%
Exposure to subject-specific content in teacher ed. programme	72.70%	74.20%	72.70%
Exposure to pedagogy in teacher ed. programme	71.30%	68.60%	65.80%
Exposure to practice in teacher ed. programme	69.70%	68.50%	53.90%
Participates in individual or collaborative research	40.20%	43.70%	42.90%
Receives financial support to pay for professional learning	68.20%	64.00%	63.10%
Receives time release for professional learning	45.50%	49.60%	42.40%
Receives salary supplement for professional learning	4.60%	12.20%	6.30%
Receives non-monetary support for professional learning	9.60%	14.70%	14.00%
Participates in extended-time professional learning activities	63.00%	52.90%	56.50%

Note: Not all countries and economies surveyed teachers at ISCED 1 or ISCED 3. Analyses on ISCED 1 include the following systems: Denmark; Finland; Flanders, Belgium; Mexico; Norway; and Poland. Analyses on ISCED 3 include Abu Dhabi, United Arab Emirates; Australia; Denmark; Finland; Georgia; Iceland; Italy; Mexico; Norway; Poland; and Singapore. The analyses were replicated using the subset of five countries that surveyed all three school levels and similar results were obtained.

Source: OECD (2013), *Teaching and Learning International Survey (TALIS): 2013 complete database*, http://stats.oecd.org/index.aspx?datasetcode=talis_2013%20.

Very few teachers both enter the profession with no knowledge and receive no supports for continued professional learning; however, at the same time, very few teachers receive all types of support for

2 THE NATURE AND EXTENT OF TEACHER PROFESSIONALISM

professional learning. This means that very few teachers receive all five supports for a knowledge base. As shown in Table 2.2, the limited number of teachers receiving full support is due largely to the very low percentage of teachers who receive salary support and other forms of non-monetary support for continued professional learning.

Autonomy scale

As defined in Chapter 1, autonomy refers to types of decision-making that teachers exercise in their schools. The autonomy scale has five measures, each a different area where teachers can make decisions, including decisions over materials, curriculum, course offerings, discipline procedures and assessment policies. As shown above, average values on the autonomy scale are lower than those on the knowledge base or peer networks scales in general.

Figure 2.6 plots each system's average on the autonomy scale, which represents the number of areas of school-based decision making teachers participate in on average. Averages range from a high of 4.1 in Estonia to a low of 0.9 in Georgia. As the figure indicates, the maximum score on the autonomy scale is much higher and the minimum much lower than the knowledge base scale; as a result, the range in means (i.e. 3.2) on the autonomy scale is three times as high as the range in means on the knowledge base scale (i.e. 1.1), indicating substantially more cross-national variation in scores on the autonomy scale than the knowledge base scale.

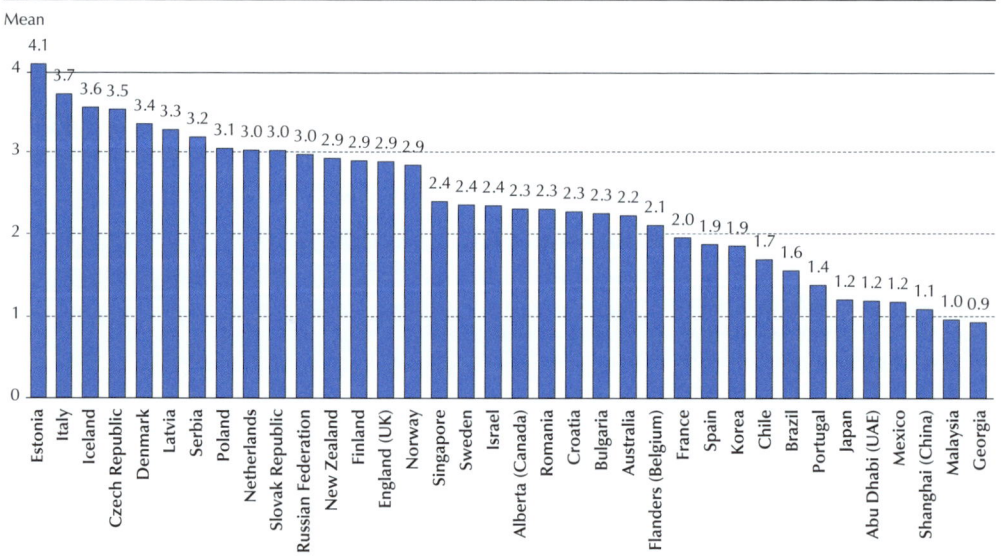

■ Figure 2.6 ■
System averages on the autonomy scale (ISCED 2)

Source: OECD (2013), *Teaching and Learning International Survey (TALIS): 2013 complete database*, http://stats.oecd.org/index.aspx?datasetcode=talis_2013%20.

Autonomy by school level

To examine differences in autonomy by school level, Figure 2.7 shows the average number of areas of decision-making for each school level – at the primary level, the average is 1.51; at the lower secondary level, it is 2.21; and at the upper secondary level the average is 2.56. This suggests that of five possible areas where teachers could exert decision-making authority, they are involved in decisions in only one or two of those areas at the primary level, while they are involved in two or three at the upper secondary level, across the systems participating in these options. These averages are statistically significantly different from both of the other levels, suggesting that there are real differences in the amount of decision-making teachers have at each level.

■ Figure 2.7 ■
Average values on autonomy scale, by school level

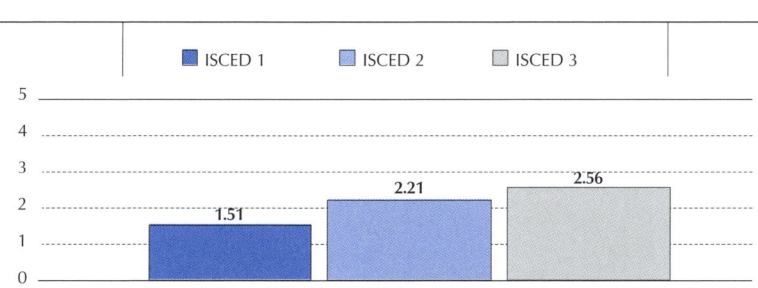

Source: OECD (2013), *Teaching and Learning International Survey (TALIS): 2013 complete database*, http://stats.oecd.org/index.aspx?datasetcode=talis_2013%20.

Table 2.3 provides the percentage of all surveyed teachers whose principals state that teachers in their school are involved in decision making over that area, indicating the types of decision-making areas that are most common across the TALIS systems and education levels. At all levels, principals report that teachers have the most say over what materials are used in their courses. Additionally, upper secondary teachers have more say in almost all aspects of decisions at the school than teachers at lower levels – they are much more likely to have a say in decisions over content and materials used in class, as well as assessment policies and course offerings. In contrast, teachers at the primary level in the participating systems have the lowest values on the autonomy scale, largely due to very low percentages of teachers who have a choice over course offerings or content.

It is interesting to note that, across the systems that survey teachers at the upper secondary level (ISCED 3), the mean value on the autonomy scale (2.56) is relatively high compared to mean values at the other two domains, suggesting that teacher professionalism in upper secondary schools is more closely related to levels of teacher autonomy, in contrast to other levels of teaching. The statistically significant differences in decision making at various school levels may reflect differences in the nature of teaching at different levels – where teachers at upper levels are trained in a specific subject and are treated more as subject-matter experts than at lower levels.

Table 2.3 **Components of autonomy scale, by ISCED level**

Item	ISCED 1	ISCED 2	ISCED 3
Autonomy over content	27.60%	42.70%	57.10%
Autonomy over course offerings	13.70%	35.10%	46.30%
Autonomy over discipline practices	30.70%	39.30%	34.00%
Autonomy over assessment	33.60%	39.20%	48.60%
Autonomy over materials	49.70%	66.50%	70.80%

Note: Not all countries and economies surveyed teachers at ISCED 1 or ISCED 3. Analyses on ISCED 1 include the following systems: Denmark; Finland; Flanders, Belgium; Mexico; Norway; and Poland. Analyses on ISCED 3 include Abu Dhabi, United Arab Emirates; Australia; Denmark; Finland; Georgia; Iceland; Italy; Mexico; Norway; Poland; and Singapore. The analyses were replicated using the subset of five countries that surveyed all three school levels and similar results were obtained.

Source: OECD (2013), *Teaching and Learning International Survey (TALIS): 2013 complete database*, http://stats.oecd.org/index.aspx?datasetcode=talis_2013%20.

2 THE NATURE AND EXTENT OF TEACHER PROFESSIONALISM

Peer networks scale

The peer networks scale is calculated based on the number of best practices related to information exchange and feedback among peers present at the school. The scale is based on the percentage of teachers who participate in formal induction and mentoring programmes, participate in a professional network of other teachers, receive feedback based on direct observations and whose school supports individual professional development plans.

■ Figure 2.8 ■
System averages on peer networks scale (ISCED 2)

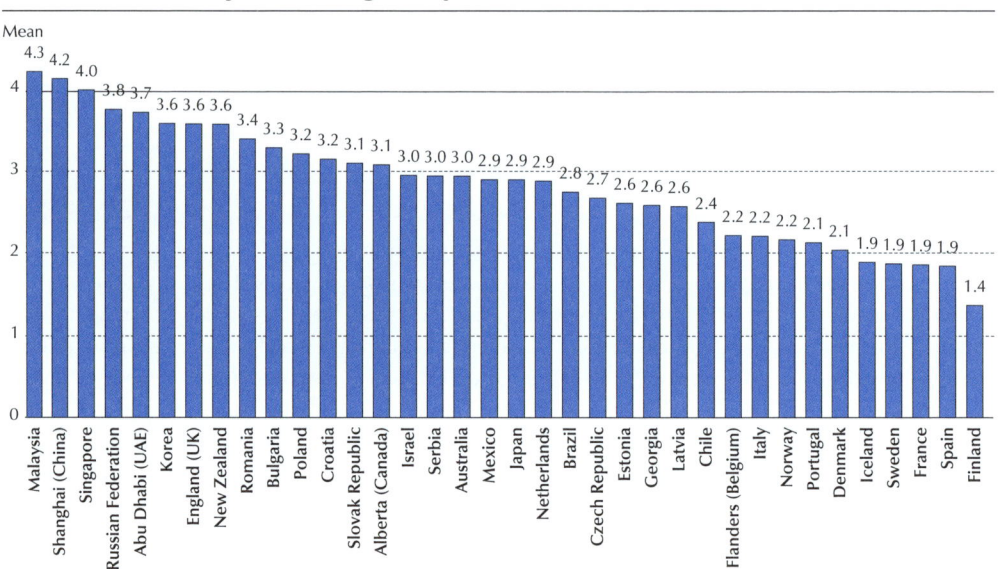

Source: OECD (2013), *Teaching and Learning International Survey (TALIS): 2013 complete database*, http://stats.oecd.org/index.aspx?datasetcode=talis_2013%20.

Figure 2.8 plots national means on the peer networks scale, which range from a maximum of 4.3 in Malaysia to a minimum of 1.4 in Finland. The range between systems at the top end of the spectrum of the peer networks domain and those at the low end is 2.9, indicating that those at the top end implement almost three more best practices on average than those at the bottom end. It is clear that the peer networks scale exhibits more cross-system variation than the knowledge base scale, but less than the autonomy scale.

Peer networks by school level

To examine differences in the peer networks scale by school level, Figure 2.9 graphs average values on the peer networks scale by school level. As is clear from the figure, scores are highest on this index among primary and lower secondary schools (3.01 and 2.99, respectively), with upper secondary schools having the lowest values (2.63). The patterns for the peer networks domain across school levels mirror those in the knowledge base scale. As with the knowledge base scale, the differences between primary and lower secondary schooling are statistically significantly different (p<0.001) than those at upper secondary schools, suggesting real differences in the number of practices implemented at each level rather than differences due to random error.

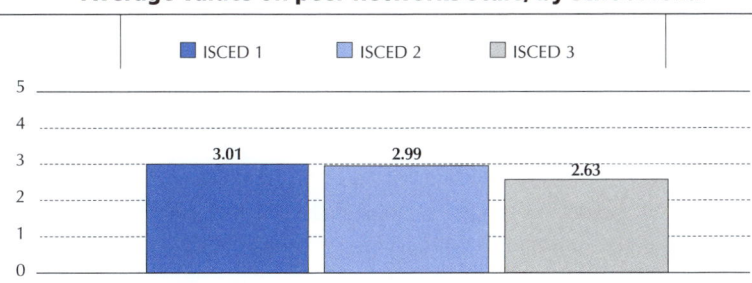

• Figure 2.9 •
Average values on peer networks scale, by school level

Source: OECD (2013), *Teaching and Learning International Survey (TALIS): 2013 complete database*, http://stats.oecd.org/index.aspx?datasetcode=talis_2013%20.

Table 2.4 shows the percentage of teachers stating that they benefit from each of the best practices identified in the peer networks domain. There is significant variation in terms of the best practices implemented in schools. The majority of teachers at all levels surveyed stated that either they personally participated in a mentoring programme at their school as a mentor or mentee, or their school supports an active mentoring programme,[3] that they received feedback based on direct observations of their teaching and that they have a personalised professional development plan. In contrast, roughly a third of teachers participate in a network of teachers designed specifically for their professional development, while approximately 50% of teachers stated that they participate in a formal induction programme.

It is important to note that, compared to the other two ISCED levels, teachers in systems participating at the upper secondary level are substantially less likely to participate in a mentoring programme (52.7% compared to 66.2% in lower secondary) or receive feedback on direct observations (63.2% compared to 75% in lower secondary). The nature of upper secondary school teachers as subject-matter experts may be a contributing factor in lower rates of peer regulation at this level – for example, it is possible that teachers at the upper secondary level are, in many cases, the only teacher of a certain subject in their school. As is clear in Table 2.4, across all levels, many teachers would likely benefit from participation in a formal induction programme and a formal network of teachers focused on professional learning.

Table 2.4 **Components of peer networks scale, by ISCED level**

Item	ISCED 1	ISCED 2	ISCED 3
Participates in formal induction	48.80%	52.50%	47.60%
Mentoring programme at school	60.50%	66.20%	52.70%
Participates in network of teachers	38.60%	37.40%	33.50%
Receives feedback from direct observations	81.10%	75.00%	63.20%
Receives personalised professional development plan	72.20%	67.50%	66.20%

Note: Not all countries surveyed teachers at ISCED 1 or ISCED 3. Analyses on ISCED 1 include the following systems: Denmark; Finland; Flanders, Belgium; Mexico; Norway; and Poland. Analyses on ISCED 3 include Abu Dhabi, United Arab Emirates; Australia; Denmark; Finland; Georgia; Iceland; Italy; Mexico; Norway; Poland; and Singapore. The analyses were replicated using the subset of five countries that surveyed all three school levels and similar results were obtained.

Source: OECD (2013), *Teaching and Learning International Survey (TALIS): 2013 complete database*, http://stats.oecd.org/index.aspx?datasetcode=talis_2013%20.

MODELS OF TEACHER PROFESSIONALISM

The cross-national variation in TALIS countries' and economies' emphasis suggests that there may be particular models of teacher professionalism. To further examine these models, the next section

presents country-specific means on all three domains. The following sets of triangle graphs show system mean values on the knowledge base, autonomy and peer networks scales on a two-dimensional plane. Values are plotted as a triangle, where the points represent the values of the three indices for each country. The shapes of the triangles provide a visual representation of where each education system's priorities lie, and whether the system emphasises one or two of the domains of professionalism over a third. The visual makes clear the cross-system variation in the degree to which countries and economies value different domains of teacher professionalism.

The analysis identifies five models of teacher professionalism: 1) high peer networks-low autonomy; 2) high autonomy; 3) knowledge emphasis; 4) balanced approach, high professionalism; 5) balanced approach, low professionalism. Interestingly, despite some exceptions, many countries and economies can be grouped into various models of professionalism based on geographic or cultural similarities. This section describes the identified models and highlights a few systems that exemplify each.[4]

Model 1: High peer networks – low autonomy

The first model for teacher professionalism is characterised by high values on the peer networks index, coupled with low levels of autonomy and moderate to high values on the knowledge base scale. Systems following this model have above a 3.0 on the peer networks domain and tend to have a value on the autonomy scale of less than 3, with many as low as 1. As shown in Figure 2.10, the high peer networks-low autonomy model is exemplified by Malaysia, which has a mean of roughly 4.3 on peer networks and a mean of only 1.0 on the autonomy scale. As a triangle plot shows, this model tends to take the shape of a low triangle with a wide base visibly skewed towards peer networks.

▪ Figure 2.10 ▪
Malaysia triangle graph (ISCED 2)

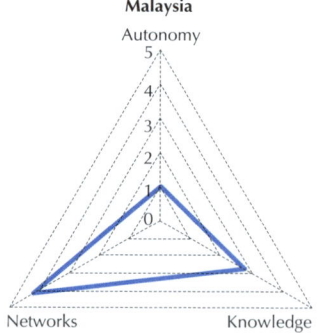

Source: OECD (2013), *Teaching and Learning International Survey (TALIS): 2013 complete database*, http://stats.oecd.org/index.aspx?datasetcode=talis_2013%20.

Model 1 is most common to East Asian economies, which emphasise peer networks and knowledge and have low levels of autonomy. With the exception of Singapore, East Asian systems fall relatively low on the autonomy scale, while emphasising the other two domains. This is shown clearly as the blue triangles are pulled further along the bottom edges (towards networks and knowledge) than towards the top (autonomy). Korea (3.6); Malaysia (4.3); and Shanghai, China (4.2) are other education systems where peer networks are given the greatest priority. Interestingly, Shanghai, China (3.3); and Singapore (3.2) also have high values on the knowledge base domain. Across all countries and

THE NATURE AND EXTENT OF TEACHER PROFESSIONALISM

economies in the global sample, Shanghai, China is among the highest ranked in knowledge and peer networks, at 3.3 and 4.2 respectively (see Figure 2.11).

■ Figure 2.11 ■
East Asian systems particularly emphasise peer networks (ISCED 2)

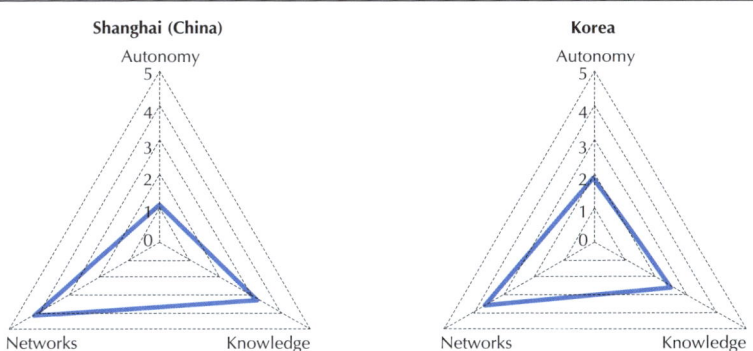

Source: OECD (2013), *Teaching and Learning International Survey (TALIS): 2013 complete database*, http://stats.oecd.org/index.aspx?datasetcode=talis_2013%20.

Model 2: High autonomy

Model 2 is characterised by having a high value on autonomy. Because many countries and economies have low values on autonomy, the countries that give teachers significant decision-making power stand out as a distinct model. Systems in Model 2 (high autonomy) will typically have scores above 3.0 on the autonomy scale, and autonomy will be the domain they emphasise the most. In certain systems, namely Denmark, Finland and Italy, the high value on the autonomy scale is accompanied by a relatively low value on the peer networks scale (<2.3). As shown in Figure 2.12, Model 2 is exemplified by Italy, which has the second highest value on the autonomy scale of any system, with a mean of 3.7. Italy also has low scores on the peer networks scale and moderate value on the knowledge base scale, giving it the shape of a tall isosceles triangle.

■ Figure 2.12 ■
Italy triangle graph (ISCED 2)

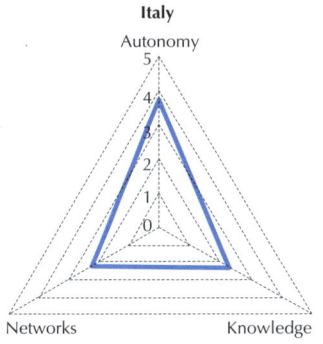

Source: OECD (2013), *Teaching and Learning International Survey (TALIS): 2013 complete database*, http://stats.oecd.org/index.aspx?datasetcode=talis_2013%20.

2 THE NATURE AND EXTENT OF TEACHER PROFESSIONALISM

As shown in Figure 2.13, the high autonomy model is found in Northern and Central Europe, where countries tend to score relatively higher on the autonomy variables. The Czech Republic (3.5) and Denmark (3.4) are the fourth and fifth highest autonomy-scale countries, while Finland, Iceland, Norway and the Slovak Republic also follow the high autonomy model. That said, many other nations have relatively high values on both the autonomy scale and the peer networks scale.

■ Figure 2.13 ■
Northern and Central Europe emphasise autonomy (ISCED 2)

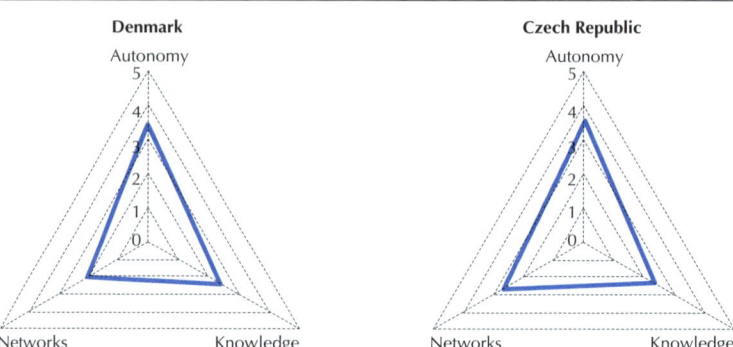

Source: OECD (2013), *Teaching and Learning International Survey (TALIS): 2013 complete database*, http://stats.oecd.org/index.aspx?datasetcode=talis_2013%20.

Model 3: Knowledge emphasis

Model 3 is characterised by an emphasis on knowledge. Countries and economies in this model have higher scores on the knowledge domain than any other domain, with a value generally above 2.7 on the knowledge base scale. This emphasis on knowledge is typically accompanied by low values on the peer networks scale and moderate values on the autonomy scale. Model 3 is not common among TALIS-surveyed countries and economies; although most have relatively high scores on knowledge, they tend to also have high scores on another domain as well. The knowledge emphasis model seems to be common to Francophone and Dutch-speaking economies, exemplified by France, (2.7) but also found in Flanders, Belgium (3.1) and the Netherlands (2.7).

■ Figure 2.14 ■
France triangle graph (ISCED 2)

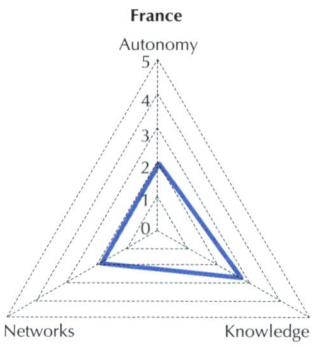

Source: OECD (2013), *Teaching and Learning International Survey (TALIS): 2013 complete database*, http://stats.oecd.org/index.aspx?datasetcode=talis_2013%20.

THE NATURE AND EXTENT OF TEACHER PROFESSIONALISM

As shown in Figure 2.14 and Figure 2.15, the knowledge emphasis model is exemplified by France and also found in other European economies, including Flanders, Belgium and the Netherlands, all of which have high values on the knowledge base domain, but relatively moderate or low values on the other two.

■ Figure 2.15 ■
Knowledge emphasis countries (ISCED 2)

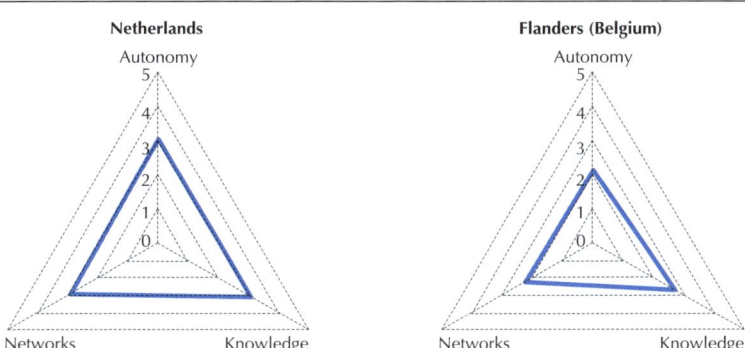

Source: OECD (2013), *Teaching and Learning International Survey (TALIS): 2013 complete database*, http://stats.oecd.org/index.aspx?datasetcode=talis_2013%20.

Model 4: Balanced domains, high overall professionalism

Model 4 is characterised by both equal and high values on all three domains. When plotted as a triangle plot, this model takes the shape of a large equilateral triangle – with values on each index at or above 3.0. As depicted in Figure 2.16, the balanced, high-professionalism model is exemplified by Poland, which has a mean of roughly 3.0 on all domains.

■ Figure 2.16 ■
Poland: Balanced high professionalism (ISCED 2)

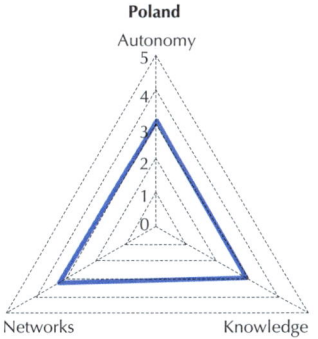

Source: OECD (2013), *Teaching and Learning International Survey (TALIS): 2013 complete database*, http://stats.oecd.org/index.aspx?datasetcode=talis_2013%20.

Countries and economies in Model 4 tend to have among the highest overall values on the teacher professionalism index because they have high values on all three domains (see Figure 2.17). These systems also represent a high degree of overall teacher professionalism according to proposed measures. England, United Kingdom; Estonia; New Zealand; Poland and the Russian Federation are all among the highest on the overall professionalism measure.

THE NATURE AND EXTENT OF TEACHER PROFESSIONALISM

■ Figure 2.17 ■
Systems with a model of balanced high professionalism (ISCED 2)

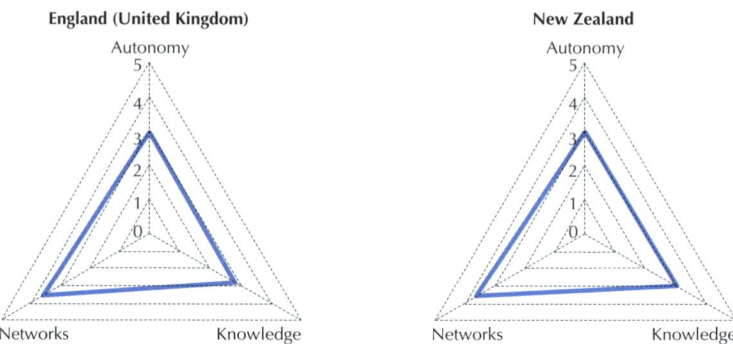

Source: OECD (2013), *Teaching and Learning International Survey (TALIS): 2013 complete database*, http://stats.oecd.org/index.aspx?datasetcode=talis_2013%20.

Model 5: Balanced domains, low professionalism

The fifth model of professionalism also takes a balanced approach, but this model has generally low levels of teacher professionalism on all three domains – which is conceptualised as a value of less than 3.0 on all three scales. As depicted in Figure 2.18, the balanced, low-professionalism model is exemplified by Portugal, which has values of 1.4-2.2 on all domains.

■ Figure 2.18 ■
Portugal triangle graph (ISCED 2)

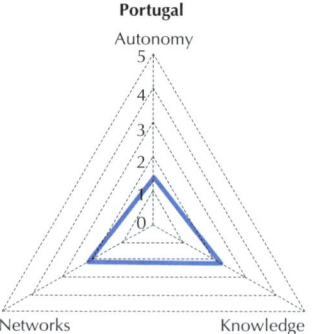

Source: OECD (2013), *Teaching and Learning International Survey (TALIS): 2013 complete database*, http://stats.oecd.org/index.aspx?datasetcode=talis_2013%20.

The balanced, low-professionalism model is common to the three countries from Central and Latin America, Chile, Brazil and Mexico. As shown in Figure 2.19, both Brazil and Mexico have small triangles pulled slightly in the direction of peer networks, demonstrating lower levels of the teacher professionalism index in all three domains.

THE NATURE AND EXTENT OF TEACHER PROFESSIONALISM

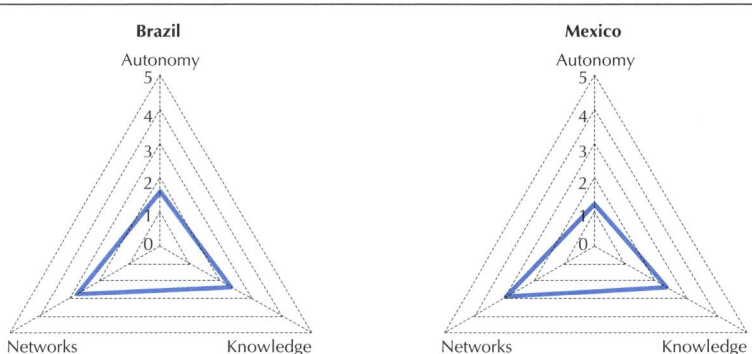

• Figure 2.19 •
Teacher professionalism profiles in Brazil and Mexico (ISCED 2)

Source: OECD (2013), *Teaching and Learning International Survey (TALIS): 2013 complete database*, http://stats.oecd.org/index.aspx?datasetcode=talis_2013%20.

The Latin American countries do not appear to emphasise any one domain, and they tend to have lower index values on all three domains of teacher professionalism. Chile is among low-scoring countries on the knowledge domain with 2.4, while Brazil and Mexico are medium to low among the peer networks group, with values of 2.8 and 2.9. Among all countries and economies, only a handful have lower values on the knowledge base scale than any of the three Latin American countries.

Although every education system is different, the five models identified here suggest overarching patterns of how countries can approach teacher professionalism and offer fruitful areas for comparison.

TEACHER PROFESSIONALISM AND SYSTEM-LEVEL FACTORS

While recognising that systems approach teacher professionalism differently, factors that promote professionalism and the role of professionalism in predicting other policy-relevant outcomes are ultimately interesting. In this section, the bivariate relationships between teacher professionalism and other system-level factors, including wealth, student-teacher ratios and PISA score outcomes are examined. Because investing in teacher professionalism requires some commitment of resources, one may wonder whether wealthier countries and economies are more likely to show higher values on teacher professionalism, as they are able to invest more in costly programmes or policies.

Figure 2.20 shows the combined teacher professionalism index plotted against government per-pupil education expenditure. Contrary to expectation, there appears to be no relationship between educational expenditure and the teacher professionalism index.

The emerging trend showing geographic differences suggests that analyses of the linkages of professionalism with teacher outcomes, such as job satisfaction, motivation, perception of status and self-efficacy must take into account the overall geographic and economic context. However, the differences in the direction of relationships mean that higher teacher professionalism is not a mere function of allocating more resources, and that a number of systemic or cultural factors may be at play – some of which are explored in Chapter 3.

THE NATURE AND EXTENT OF TEACHER PROFESSIONALISM

■ Figure 2.20 ■
Education expenditure (per pupil) and overall teacher professionalism (ISCED 2)

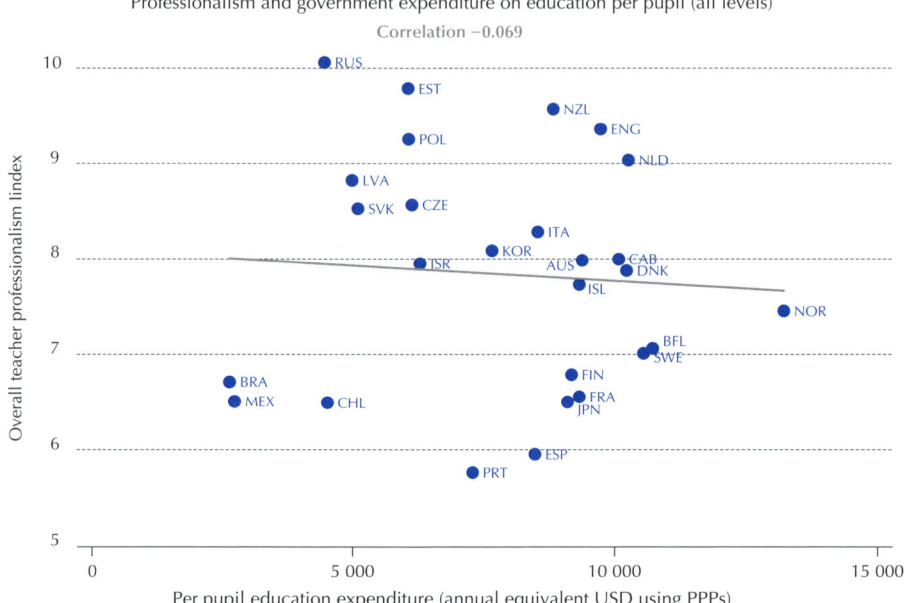

Source: OECD (2013), *Teaching and Learning International Survey (TALIS): 2013 complete database*, http://stats.oecd.org/index.aspx?datasetcode=talis_2013%20; World Bank (The) (2015), *World Development Indicators 2015*, http://data.worldbank.org/products/wdi.

Teacher pay and working conditions

Because the measured level of teacher professionalism reflects systems' policy concerning teachers, it is also possible that countries and economies that invest heavily in their teachers are those where teachers also command higher salaries or are better able to advocate for better working conditions. Figure 2.21 and Figure 2.22 examine how overall values of teacher professionalism are related to mediating factors, including teacher pay and working conditions. Figure 2.21 plots the relationship between overall professionalism and average teacher salaries relative to other tertiary educated employees in the labour market. It is reasonable to assume that countries and economies that invest in higher salaries may also be more likely to support policies related to teacher professionalism. However, there is no evidence that this is the case across systems. Figure 2.21 actually suggests a negative relationship between overall values of teacher professionalism and relative salary, indicating a potential trade-off between dedicating resources towards support for professionalism practices or teacher compensation. However, this relationship is highly sensitive to which systems are included: for example, Portugal and Spain have low levels of the teacher professionalism index, but relatively high salaries, which contributes to the appearance of a negative relationship. This suggests that teacher professionalism policies may be driven by policy decisions distinct from their relationship to those governing compensation.

THE NATURE AND EXTENT OF TEACHER PROFESSIONALISM

■ Figure 2.21 ■
Overall teacher professionalism and teacher salary (ISCED 2)

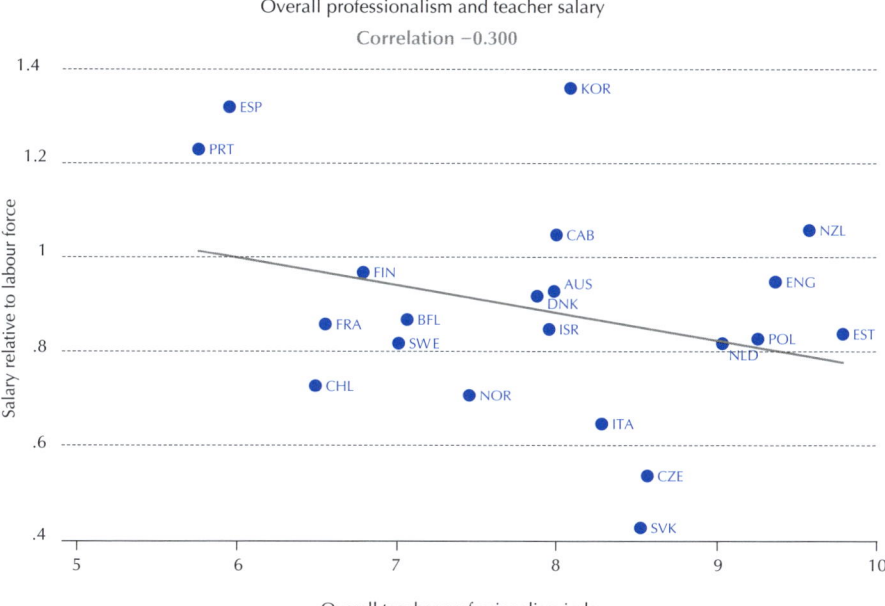

Source: OECD (2013), *Teaching and Learning International Survey (TALIS): 2013 complete database*, http://stats.oecd.org/index.aspx?datasetcode=talis_2013%20; OECD (2014), *Education GPS*, http://gpseducation.oecd.org/.

Figure 2.22 plots the basic relationship between overall teacher professionalism and average class size. The graph suggests that when values on the teacher professionalism index are higher, average class sizes tend to be slightly lower. This relationship could be driven by larger policy decisions in the education system to both invest in teachers and their working conditions, or it could reflect teachers' ability to participate more in decision making concerning the conditions governing their work. However, this relationship could work both ways: it is possible that teacher professionalism improves working conditions, but it is also possible that improvements in working conditions could improve teacher professionalism by freeing up time for other activities, for example. Again, because it is based on a small number of systems, the relatively weak negative correlation (r = -0.2) observed here should be considered with caution.

THE NATURE AND EXTENT OF TEACHER PROFESSIONALISM

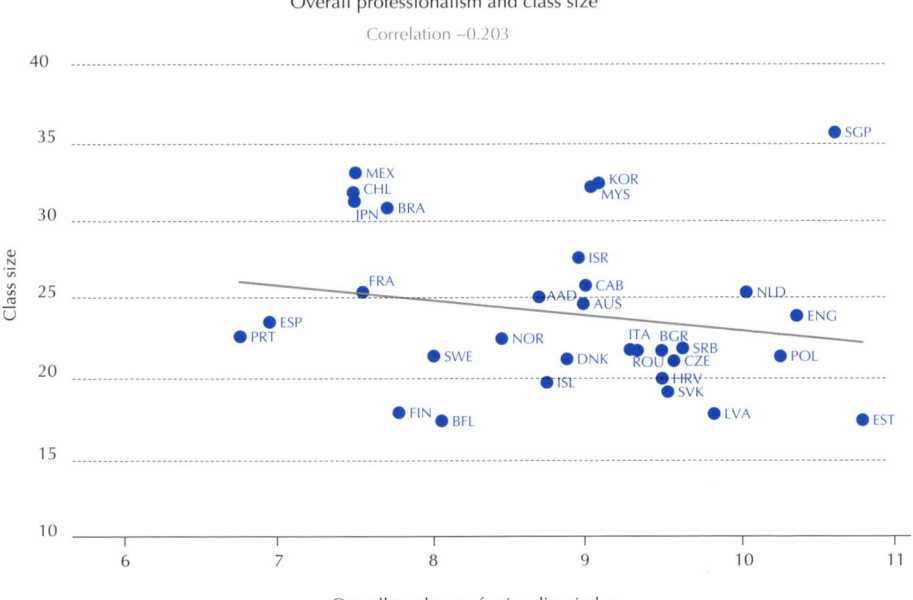

■ Figure 2.22 ■
Overall teacher professionalism and average class size (ISCED 2)

Source: OECD (2013), *Teaching and Learning International Survey (TALIS): 2013 complete database*, http://stats.oecd.org/index.aspx?datasetcode=talis_2013%20; OECD (2014), *Education GPS*, http://gpseducation.oecd.org/.

Learning outcomes

While the analyses presented above focus on the level of the teacher, the ultimate policy question is whether higher teacher professionalism will translate into better teaching, and consequently into better student learning outcomes. Figure 2.23 provides an initial gauge of whether this relationship may be true, by plotting system-level values on the overall teacher professionalism index against their scores on the most recent PISA math assessment. The trend line suggests that there is a slight positive relationship between overall values on the overall teacher professionalism index and education systems' average PISA scores (the relationship is significant at the 10% level). Because teacher professionalism is not closely related to expenditure on education (see Figure 2.20), this finding does not appear to be driven only by the level of resources, but rather it may suggest that investing in policies to promote teacher professionalism may be related to student learning through means other than simply higher levels of resources. However, as with class size, the correlation here is relatively weak and sensitive to the inclusion or exclusion of particular countries. A deeper analysis will be necessary to better understand how teacher professionalism may be related to policy-relevant outcomes for both teachers and students.

■ Figure 2.23 ■
PISA scores and overall teacher professionalism (ISCED 2)

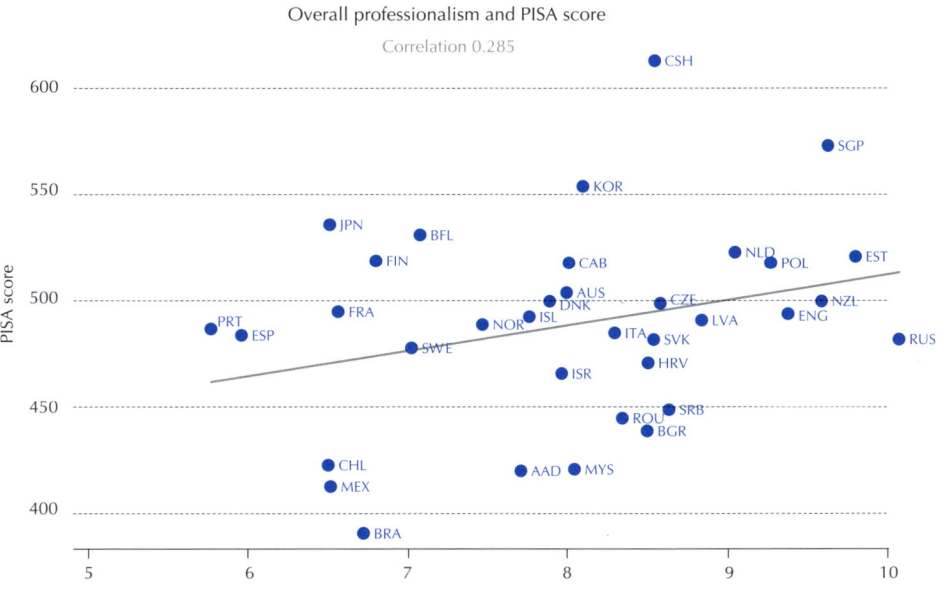

Source: OECD (2013), *Teaching and Learning International Survey (TALIS): 2013 complete database*, http://stats.oecd.org/index.aspx?datasetcode=talis_2013%20; OECD (2014), "PISA 2012 results in focus: What 15-year-olds know and what they can do with what they know", PISA, OECD Publishing, www.oecd.org/pisa/keyfindings/pisa-2012-results-overview.pdf.

DISCUSSION

In summary, this chapter provides a descriptive overview of the nature and extent of teacher professionalism in TALIS-surveyed countries and economies. The analysis shows significant differences in models of teacher professionalism prevalent in different countries, regions and school levels. In general, there is substantial cross-system variation in terms of how nations approach teacher professionalism. However, there is less variation cross-systemically in the knowledge base scale, with more variation in the peer networks scale and significant variation in education systems' values on the autonomy scale. The most striking finding is the extent to which teacher autonomy is emphasised among Northern and Central European systems, while peer networks tend to be emphasised among East Asian systems. For some systems, such as those in East Asia, there appears to be a trade-off in the extent to which autonomy or peer networks is observed. Rather than conceptualising a single model for teacher professionalism, thinking about the diverse models that systems employ offers avenues for research into the advantages and disadvantages of various approaches and the generation of new policy ideas.

Additionally, there are differences in the nature of teacher professionalism across school levels. The findings suggest that autonomy is higher for teachers of upper secondary grades, while emphasis on the development of a knowledge base and building peer networks are relatively lower, suggesting that different factors become more important as teachers are responsible for older age cohorts.

THE NATURE AND EXTENT OF TEACHER PROFESSIONALISM

These findings also indicate that teacher professionalism is not closely related to a country's spending on education – suggesting it may instead reflect other factors such as cultures of teaching or national policy priorities. The next chapter addresses how teacher professionalism predicts policy-relevant outcomes, including teachers' perceived status, job satisfaction, self-efficacy and their commitment to teaching.

Notes

1. A word of caution: not all countries and economies surveyed teachers at ISCED 1 or ISCED 3. Analyses on ISCED 1 include the following systems: Denmark; Finland; Flanders, Belgium; Mexico; Norway; and Poland. Analyses on ISCED 3 include Abu Dhabi, United Arab Emirates; Australia; Denmark; Finland; Georgia; Iceland; Italy; Mexico; Norway; Poland; and Singapore. The analyses were replicated using the subset of five countries that surveyed all three school levels and similar results were obtained.

2. Among teachers that reported receiving professional development in the last 12 months. The proportion of teachers participating in professional development in the last 12 months varies for different countries and economies, between 71.7% and 98.0% (Table 4.6, OECD, 2014d).

3. Please note that the variables that this report uses to indicate access or exposure to a mentoring programme are different from those used to indicate participation in a mentoring programme in the TALIS 2013 results report (OECD, 2014d). See Annex A for more information on which variables were used.

4. Annex B: System-Specific Profiles has all country and economy profiles.

> **A note regarding Israel**
> The statistical data for Israel are supplied by and under the responsibility of the relevant Israeli authorities. The use of such data by the OECD is without prejudice to the status of the Golan Heights, East Jerusalem and Israeli settlements in the West Bank under the terms of international law.

References

Akiba, M., G.K. LeTendre and J.P. Scribner (2007), "Teacher quality, opportunity gap, and national achievement in 46 countries", *Educational Researcher*, Vol. 36/7, pp. 369-387.

OECD (2014a), *Education GPS*, http://gpseducation.oecd.org/.

OECD (2014b), *New Insights from TALIS 2013: Teaching and Learning in Primary and Upper Secondary Education*, TALIS, OECD Publishing, Paris, http://dx.doi.org/10.1787/9789264226319-en.

OECD (2014c), "PISA 2012 results in focus: What 15-year-olds know and what they can do with what they know", PISA, OECD Publishing, www.oecd.org/pisa/keyfindings/pisa-2012-results-overview.pdf.

OECD (2014d), *TALIS 2013 Results: An International Perspective on Teaching and Learning*, TALIS, OECD Publishing, Paris, http://dx.doi.org/10.1787/9789264196261-en.

OECD (2013), *Teaching and Learning International Survey (TALIS): 2013 complete database*, http://stats.oecd.org/index.aspx?datasetcode=talis_2013%20.

World Bank (The) (2015), *World Development Indicators 2015*, http://data.worldbank.org/products/wdi.

Teacher professionalism and policy-relevant outcomes

This chapter examines the relationship between the status of teaching and key policy-relevant outcomes. In this chapter, four key outcomes are examined, namely: i) perceptions of the status of teaching; ii) satisfaction with current work environment; iii) satisfaction with the teaching profession; and iv) perceptions of self-efficacy. Variations in the relationship between teacher professionalism and teachers' perceptions and satisfaction are also examined.

3. TEACHER PROFESSIONALISM AND POLICY-RELEVANT OUTCOMES

Highlights

- There are many differences across countries and economies in terms of the extent to which teacher professionalism is associated with teacher outcomes.

- In general, teacher professionalism is an important factor in teachers' job satisfaction. Supporting teachers' knowledge base and the formation of peer networks have the strongest relationship with teachers' perceptions and satisfaction.

- Teacher professionalism is also associated with greater perceptions of the status of the teaching profession in the society and self-efficacy. Teachers in schools that adopt more of the identified practices related to improving teachers' knowledge base and expanding peer networks of support and information exchange feel more capable, and perceive themselves to have higher status.

- There are differences across education levels. Among the countries and economies participating in the Teaching and Learning International Survey (TALIS) at primary and upper secondary education, teacher professionalism is likely a more important predictor of the teacher satisfaction and perceptions of the status of the teaching profession at the lower and upper secondary level than the primary level of education.

INTRODUCTION

The chapter focuses on the link between teacher professionalism and a number of policy relevant outcomes. Throughout the analyses, the primary predictors are indices of teacher professionalism, as discussed in Chapter 1 and described in-depth in Chapter 2. Drawing on the literature on teacher professionalism, the primary predictor is an index of overall of teacher professionalism and three domain-specific indices: *knowledge base, autonomy*, and *peer networks* (see Box 3.1).

> ### Box 3.1 Teacher professionalism indices
>
> **Knowledge base** – The knowledge and skills teachers need to teach effectively
>
> **Autonomy** – Teachers' level of decision making over their work
>
> **Peer networks** – Access to networks of peers who support the exchange of information and expertise

The analysis consists of multilevel regression analyses (detailed in Annex A), which are used to estimate the relationship between higher levels of teacher professionalism and identified outcomes. Strong support is found for the idea that teacher professionalism is linked to all four policy-relevant outcomes of interest. Teachers benefiting from two-thirds of all identified best practices (i.e. with a value of roughly ten on the final index) tend to express more positive perceptions of their work environment, status and satisfaction (they rank in the top half of the distribution of all teachers on outcomes of interest). In contrast, teachers who benefit from only one or two of the identified best practices express much lower rates of satisfaction, self-efficacy and status.

TEACHER PROFESSIONALISM AND POLICY-RELEVANT OUTCOMES

The analyses find that practices that both develop teachers' knowledge base and support collective peer networks have a large and consistently positive association with teachers' perceptions in nearly every surveyed country and economy. In contrast, the effect of autonomy varies substantially – it tends to have minimal association with teachers' perceptions in most countries and economies and is rarely statistically significant. From the policy perspective, this suggests that resources may be better utilised if devoted to ongoing teacher professionalism and developing peer networks more than granting teachers more autonomy.

The analysis of teacher professionalism at different education levels suggests that teacher professionalism may be more important after primary school – the relationship between teacher professionalism and various aspects of teacher job satisfaction is stronger at the lower and upper secondary levels than primary level. At the same time, it is important to keep in mind that the comparisons across education levels need to be treated with caution due to the limited number of countries participating at the primary education level (6 countries) and the upper secondary level (11 countries). Given the link between teacher professionalism and important policy-relevant outcomes, the analysis suggests that policy interventions to support teachers – particularly those that support their knowledge base and networks of peer communities – have important effects on teachers' perceptions and job satisfaction. Overall, this means that supporting teachers in these ways may help education systems recruit and retain teachers who are more satisfied, confident in their abilities and committed to teaching.

TEACHER PERCEPTIONS OF STATUS, SATISFACTION AND SELF-EFFICACY

This study investigates four policy outcomes: teachers' perceived status, satisfaction with the work environment, satisfaction with the teaching profession and self-efficacy. Each of these outcomes comes from a specific survey item or a complex scale produced by TALIS 2013 (OECD, 2014b). Table 3.1 outlines the survey items included in each outcome; each item was answered on a Likert scale of agreement (1-4), with one indicating strong disagreement and four indicating strong agreement.

Because TALIS complex scales do not reach the level of scalar invariance, caution is needed in comparing national means on the scales. The results are replicated with composite indices calculated from the mean of teacher responses on each of the items in the scales and find very similar results, which suggests that teacher professionalism seems to have an important effect on outcomes, even when those outcomes are operationalised and measured in slightly different ways.

Table 3.1 **Overview of the TALIS questions used in the teacher perceptions of status, satisfaction and self-efficacy**

Concept	Indicators
Status	I think that teaching is valued in society
Satisfaction with profession	The advantages of being a teacher clearly outweigh the disadvantages. I regret that I decided to be a teacher. If I could decide again, I would still choose to work as a teacher. I wonder whether it would have been better to choose another profession.
Satisfaction with work environment	I would recommend my school as a good place to work. I would like to change to another school if that were possible. I enjoy working at this school. All in all, I am satisfied with my job.
Self-efficacy	To what extent do you believe that you can: • Control disruptive behaviour in the classroom • Make my expectations about student behaviour clear • Get students to follow classroom rules • Calm a student who is disruptive or noisy • Craft good questions for my students • Use a variety of assessment strategies • Provide an alternative explanation or example when students are confused • Implement alternative instructional strategies in my classroom • Get students to believe they can do well in school work • Help my students value learning • Motivate students who show low interest in school work • Help students think critically

TEACHER PROFESSIONALISM AND POLICY-RELEVANT OUTCOMES

Because the four outcomes have different scales, we standardise the variables to a mean of zero and standard deviation of one for the regression analyses. This allows for comparison across all four dependent variables and also simplifies the interpretation of the coefficients – the coefficients can be interpreted as finding that each one-unit increase on the professionalism indices, which corresponds to an additional best practice on the autonomy and peer networks scale or two best practices on the knowledge base scale, is associated with a *B* standard deviation change in the dependent variable.

> ### Box 3.2 **Technical notes on regression analysis**
>
> **Predictor variable:** The primary predictor variable is a teacher's value on the overall teacher professionalism index, which ranges from 0-15. The unit of analysis is the teacher.
>
> **Regression model:** Pooled two-level random intercepts model, with teachers grouped within schools and random intercepts for each school. All countries and economies are combined.
>
> **Survey weights:** The analysis takes into account the complex survey design of TALIS 2013, employing final teacher weights for the fixed part of the model and final school weights at the school level. The dataset is set to use balanced repeated replicate weights.
>
> **Controls:** At the individual teacher level, controls include teacher gender, years of teaching experience and subject taught. At the school level, controls include whether the school is public or private, the percentage of students who are socio-economically disadvantaged and an index of school climate, created by TALIS 2013, which captures the nature of student-teacher relations.

The analysis consists of multilevel regression models (detailed in Annex A) to estimate the relationship between increases in teacher professionalism and identified outcomes, with teachers nested within schools (see Box 3.2). Recognising that within the same system, teachers' own perceptions vary significantly based on where they work, what subject they teach and their school cultures, we control for key individual- and school-based characteristics to isolate the independent role of teacher professionalism. The analysis finds that teacher professionalism is a robust predictor of teachers' perceptions and satisfaction, even after controlling for other individual and school-level characteristics. The next section provides an overview of the findings.

OVERALL TEACHER PROFESSIONALISM

Overall teacher professionalism shows a positive and statistically significant relationship to each of the four outcome variables. Table 3.2 shows coefficients on regression models at the lower secondary level of education, with a teacher's total professionalism index as the key predictor. The table indicates that as a teacher's value on the overall professionalism index increases by one unit, his or her perceived status will increase by 6.1% of a standard deviation, satisfaction with work environment will increase by 11.3% of a standard deviation, satisfaction with the teaching profession by 9.6% of a standard deviation and perceived self-efficacy by 9.7%. This finding suggests that even after accounting for important factors, such as a teachers' gender, years of experience and the school context, teacher professionalism has an independent effect on teachers' perceived status, satisfaction and efficacy.

Table 3.2   Relationship between teacher professionalism and teacher outcomes (ISCED 2)

Teacher professionalism	Perceived status	Satisfaction with profession	Satisfaction with work environment	Perceived self-efficacy
	6.1% ***	9.6% ***	11.3% ***	9.7% ***

Notes:

1. Cell entries represent the change in standard deviation associated with one unit increase on the teacher professionalism scale. Regression models include controls for teacher gender, years of experience, subject taught, school sector and school climate.

2. Statistical significance: *** = p < 0.001

Source: OECD (2013), *Teaching and Learning International Survey (TALIS): 2013 complete database*, http://stats.oecd.org/index.aspx?datasetcode=talis_2013%20.

To make the findings interpretable, the regression coefficients are translated into the predicted percentile rank on each of the outcome variables (i.e. satisfaction, self-efficacy, perceived status) depending on the number of best practices to which the teacher has access. The regression output is used to predict where a given teacher would fall in the overall distribution of teachers in terms of their satisfaction or perceived self-efficacy or status. Because the distributions of each outcome differ somewhat, higher regression coefficients between outcomes does not necessarily indicate a higher predicted percentile.

Figure 3.1 shows a teacher's predicted percentile in the distribution of all teachers, estimated by his or her overall score on the teacher professionalism index. The figure indicates where in the distribution of all teachers a given teacher would be expected to rank if she benefited from only one support, compared to those benefiting from five or ten best practices. As the figure shows, teachers with a value on the overall index of only one are expected to fall in the bottom third of all teachers in terms of their perceived status and self-efficacy and their satisfaction with their profession and work environment. In contrast, teachers with a value of five on the overall professionalism index are in the 40-51st percentile of all teachers in terms of all outcomes. At the top end of the spectrum, teachers with values of ten on the overall index, which corresponds to benefiting from two-thirds of the identified best practices, are likely to rank in the top half of the distribution of all teachers.

In concrete terms, it appears that gains in support for teacher professionalism matter more at the lower end of the spectrum, such that implementing a few additional best practices matters more for teachers' perceptions of status and self-efficacy and satisfaction with profession and work environment if they are not benefiting from any. At the top end, additional best practices do not have the same additional effect on teachers' perceptions and satisfaction. As Figure 3.1 shows, teachers benefiting from less than two best practices for teacher professionalism are likely to rank in the bottom third of all teachers in terms of their perceived status and satisfaction – they are much less likely to state that they believe teaching is valued in society and that they are satisfied in their work environment and with their profession in general. Additionally, they are less likely to be confident about their teaching (self-efficacy), although the impact is less pronounced, as even teachers in schools with less than two best practices fall in roughly the 40th percentile of all teachers. In contrast, those benefiting from roughly two-thirds of all practices are likely to be in the top half of the distribution, all other factors held constant.

TEACHER PROFESSIONALISM AND POLICY-RELEVANT OUTCOMES

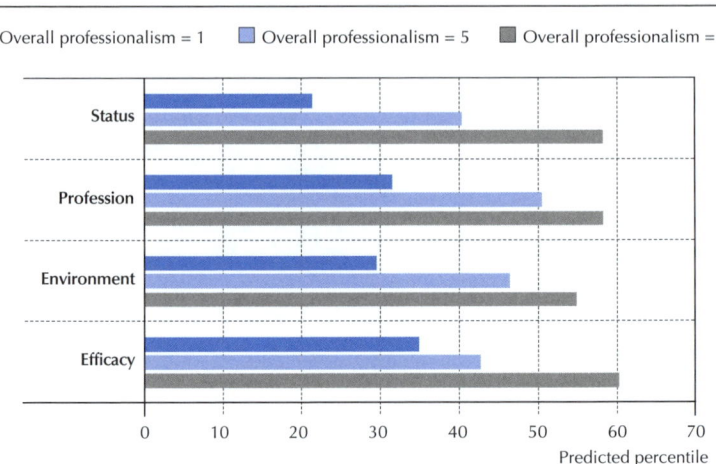

■ Figure 3.1 ■
The relationship between overall teacher professionalism and teacher outcomes (ISCED 2)

Note: The baseline is set as one best practice on the total professionalism index because very few teachers in the dataset had a value of 0 on the overall index. The small sample made predictions on that population unreliable. In subsequent domain-specific analyses with sub-indices, the baseline is set at 0.

Source: OECD (2013), *Teaching and Learning International Survey (TALIS): 2013 complete database*, http://stats.oecd.org/index.aspx?datasetcode=talis_2013%20.

TEACHER PROFESSIONALISM, BY DOMAIN

Recognising that teachers' professionalism is composed of three domains – knowledge base, autonomy and peer networks – and that teachers may have different levels of support for each, it is important to examine whether teachers' perceptions and satisfaction are associated more strongly with one domain than the others. This section presents results from regression models examining the relationship between each of the three domains separately and teachers' perceptions and satisfaction (see details in Box 3.3). Teacher professionalism is measured at the level of the individual teacher for the knowledge base and peer networks scales and as a school mean, reported by the principal, for the autonomy scale. This means that for the knowledge base and peer networks analyses, the findings link the individual teachers' experiences with their perceptions and satisfaction, whereas for the analyses for autonomy, it links the principal's reports of teachers' level of decision-making at the school level to individual teachers' perceptions and satisfaction.

Table 3.3 shows the coefficients from the models on each teacher professionalism domain – the coefficients indicate the size of the relationship between a teacher's value on each of the domain scales and the teachers' perceptions and satisfaction, in terms of a standard deviation. The table shows that the coefficients are positive and statistically significant for the knowledge base and peer networks indices, ranging from a low of 5.6% of a standard deviation for the change in the knowledge base scale to a high of 14.5% of a standard deviation when examining the change in a teacher's satisfaction with the work environment associated with each additional support for peer networks.

TEACHER PROFESSIONALISM AND POLICY-RELEVANT OUTCOMES

> **Box 3.3 Technical notes on domain specific analyses**
>
> **Predictor variables:** The domain-specific analyses utilise three primary predictor variables: the knowledge base index (0-5) and peer networks index (0-5) are measured at the individual teacher level, and the autonomy index (0-5) is measured at the school level.
>
> **Regression models:** Pooled two-level random intercepts model, with teachers grouped within schools and random intercepts generated for each school. All countries and economies are pooled.
>
> **Survey weights:** The analysis takes into account the complex survey design of TALIS 2013, employing final teacher weights for the fixed part of the model and final school weights at the school level. The dataset is set to use balanced repeated replicate weights.
>
> **Controls:** At the individual teacher level, controls include teacher gender and years of teaching experience. At the school level, controls include whether the school is public or private, the percentage of students who are socio-economically disadvantaged and an index of school climate, created by TALIS 2013, which captures the nature of the relations.

The coefficients on the autonomy scale are much smaller in all four analyses than are those on the overall teacher professionalism index – the coefficients on models of autonomy are close to zero and not consistently statistically significant. This means that, as teachers benefit from more areas of decision making in their schools, they do not necessarily experience higher levels of satisfaction or perceive greater status or self-efficacy. In fact, results show that, across the entire sample, the coefficient on the autonomy scale is actually negative when modelling perceived status and self-efficacy, suggesting that more decision making at the school level may actually make teachers feel less capable in their abilities to do their job. This relationship combines teachers from all countries and economies and may be different within each education system; however, it also suggests that more autonomy does not necessarily lead to greater perceived self-efficacy – in fact, it might indicate that teachers need other forms of support, such as time release, in order to feel empowered by opportunities for decision making. Additionally, the table shows that the coefficient is positive for both of the satisfaction indices, suggesting a positive relationship between teachers' level of autonomy and their satisfaction with both the teaching profession and their work environment; however, the size of the relationship is very small, ranging from less than 0.3% - 2.8% of a standard deviation change for each additional area of school-based decision making.

In terms of variations across teachers' perceptions and satisfaction, the analysis finds that teacher professionalism is least associated with teachers' beliefs about the status of teaching in society, and more strongly linked to their perceptions of their own teaching and their satisfaction. As the table shows, the coefficients on status are only 0.06 of a standard deviation for the knowledge base scale – while coefficients for all other outcomes are above 0.10. The status outcome specifically asks teachers to what extent they believe that teaching is a valued profession in society, which may reflect larger structures of educational requirements and pay than the other three outcomes, which are more personal perceptions of satisfaction and teaching abilities. Nonetheless, we do find that higher values on the knowledge base and peer networks indices are both positively associated with perceived status.

However, we do not know the directionality of this relationship – it may be that as teachers engage in a greater number of best practices, the higher they perceive the status of their profession. Alternatively, it may be that the more status the teaching profession enjoys in society, the more support exists for investing in practices that support teachers.

TEACHER PROFESSIONALISM AND POLICY-RELEVANT OUTCOMES

Table 3.3 **Table of coefficients on teacher professionalism indices (ISCED 2)**

Domain	Perceived status	Satisfaction with profession	Satisfaction with work environment	Perceived self-efficacy
Knowledge base	0.056***	0.123***	0.121***	0.128***
Autonomy	-0.028***	0.003	0.011***	-0.020***
Peer networks	0.084***	0.112***	0.145***	0.112***

Notes: Regression analyses are run for each domain separately.

Significance stars: * p<0.05, ** p<0.01, *** p<0.001.

Controls for teacher gender, years of experience, subject taught, school SES, school sector and school climate.

Source: OECD (2013), *Teaching and Learning International Survey (TALIS): 2013 complete database*, http://stats.oecd.org/index.aspx?datasetcode=talis_2013%20.

Meanwhile, the knowledge base scale is most strongly linked to perceived self-efficacy, which suggests that supporting teachers' professional development and learning is associated with higher levels of confidence in their teaching abilities. In contrast, practices supporting peer networks are more strongly linked to teachers' satisfaction with their current work environment, which suggests that the collaborative and mentoring practices that provide supportive communities in which teachers can learn and refine their teaching has a positive relationship with their satisfaction with their jobs.

Figure 3.2 shows the predicted percentile of teachers for each outcome based on whether they are in a school with zero best practices identified, or a school with all ten included (a value of 5 on the scale). As with the overall index, we present results in terms of a teachers' percentile rank, using regression coefficients to predict how a given teacher would compare with other teachers on each of the four outcomes.

It is clear that teachers in schools with a high level of support for knowledge are much more likely to state that they are satisfied in their jobs and able to be effective teachers. For example, Figure 3.2 shows that teachers' mean predicted percentile ranks are in in the bottom 44% in terms of all outcomes when they do not benefit from any of the best practices identified in the literature.

■ Figure 3.2 ■
The role of the knowledge base on teachers' perceptions and satisfaction (ISCED 2)

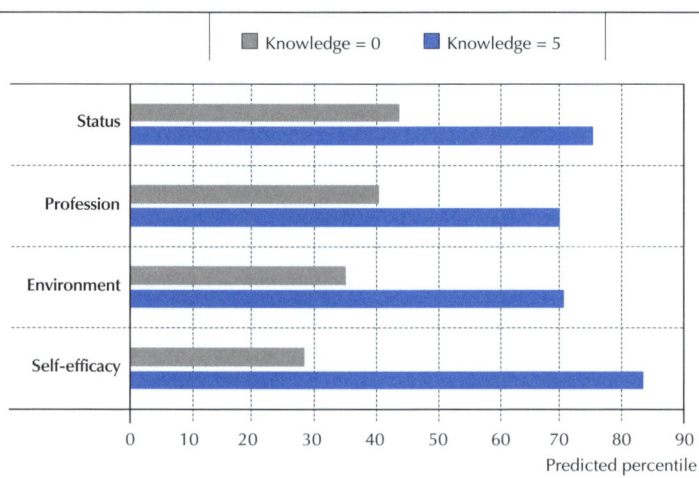

Source: OECD (2013), *Teaching and Learning International Survey (TALIS): 2013 complete database*, http://stats.oecd.org/index.aspx?datasetcode=talis_2013%20.

TEACHER PROFESSIONALISM AND POLICY-RELEVANT OUTCOMES

• Figure 3.3 •
The role of autonomy on teachers' perceptions and satisfaction (ISCED 2)

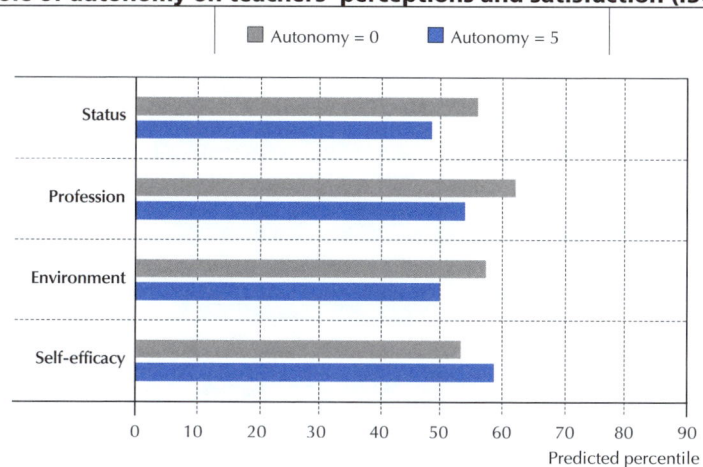

Source: OECD (2013), *Teaching and Learning International Survey (TALIS): 2013 complete database*, http://stats.oecd.org/index.aspx?datasetcode=talis_2013%20.

Figure 3.3 shows mean predicted percentiles for teachers based on their value on the autonomy scale. As the figure shows, teachers' predicted satisfaction and perceptions on each of the outcomes are relatively unaffected – mean percentile ranks range between the 48th and 62nd percentile of the distribution regardless of whether the teachers in the school participate in zero or five areas of decision making.

The weak coefficients on the autonomy scale suggest that giving teachers more decision-making power is not strongly linked to improved outcomes. It is unclear why autonomy is not more positively linked to outcomes of interest. Measurement error may play a role: the measure for autonomy is reported by principals at the school-wide level and not by teachers. This could introduce error, as principals' ideas about decision making may not reflect the experiences of their teachers precisely enough. In addition, we may need more alternate measures of what autonomy looks like for teachers, apart from domains of decision making. Prior studies suggest that teachers vary in their desire to participate in school-based management, yet most want to retain autonomy over classroom affairs (Frase and Sorenson, 1992). If teachers are not interested in taking on management responsibilities in schools, then measures of autonomy may need to approximate teachers' perceptions of choice, rather than decision making.

Figure 3.4 shows the mean predicted percentile of the distribution of teachers based on their value on the peer networks index. Similar to the findings related to the knowledge base scale, as depicted in Figure 3.2, it is clear that higher values on the peer networks scale are associated with an average percentile rank above the 60th percentile of the distribution for all four outcomes, while those with lower scores on the peer networks scale have mean percentiles lower than the 47th percentile. This suggests that teachers who benefit from more of the best practices related to peer networks, including induction and mentoring programmes, tend to place in the upper half of the distribution in terms of satisfaction with both their work environment and profession in general, perception of status and self-efficacy, while those benefitting from none of the best practices place between the 26th and 47th percentiles, on average. This finding holds true for all four outcomes.

3 TEACHER PROFESSIONALISM AND POLICY-RELEVANT OUTCOMES

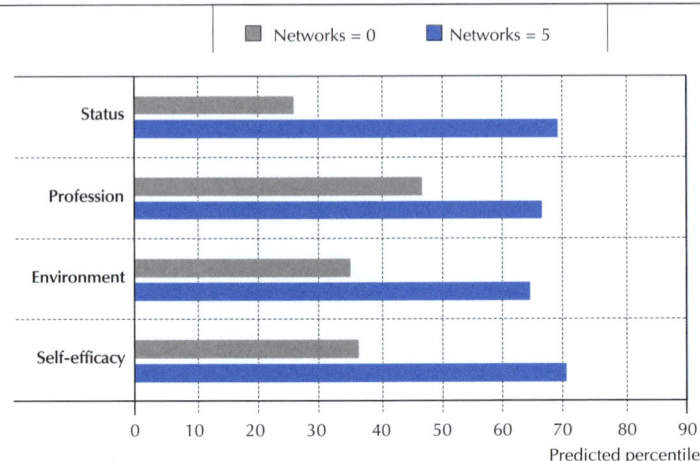

■ Figure 3.4 ■
The role of peer networks on outcomes (ISCED 2)

Source: OECD (2013), *Teaching and Learning International Survey (TALIS): 2013 complete database*, http://stats.oecd.org/index.aspx?datasetcode=talis_2013%20.

In sum, the domain-specific analyses suggest that across the entire sample of countries and economies, policies to support the development of teachers' knowledge base and the formation of peer networks are most predictive of policy-relevant outcomes, while autonomy is not strongly related to the outcomes of interest. Chapter 2 showed that education systems' models of teacher professionalism vary quite a bit in terms of how teacher professionalism is expressed. The chapter found that there is significant cross-system variation in both the extent of teacher professionalism and the domain that systems emphasise. The chapter identified various models of teacher professionalism, including some countries and economies that have high levels of professionalism on all three domains, in contrast to other nations that tend to emphasise one domain. As such, we recognise that due to differences in country contexts and teaching policies, teacher professionalism may also affect outcomes differently across systems. In the next section, we examine how teacher professionalism varies across countries and economies.

VARIATION ACROSS EDUCATION SYSTEMS

This section examines the extent to which the relationship between teacher professionalism and outcomes of interest varies cross-nationally. The analysis technique consists of country specific regressions (detailed in Box 3.4), carried out for all four outcomes, with overall teacher professionalism and each of the domains as the predictor variables.

Findings indicate that there is substantial cross-system variation: in certain countries and economies, teacher professionalism generally seems to have a small effect on all four outcomes; in others, its impact on outcomes is very strong. Figure 3.5 shows regression coefficients for each dependent variable for selected countries and economies – these education systems show different models for the effects of teacher professionalism on outcomes. It is important to note that coefficients for all countries and economies are positive – suggesting that in every participating country, teacher professionalism is positively associated with policy-relevant outcomes. Nonetheless, there are significant cross-national differences – for example, the coefficient on teacher professionalism when predicting a teacher's perceived self-efficacy is below 0.047 in the Netherlands and France, while it almost three times as large, at 0.139, in Malaysia. Coefficients for status range from 0.020 to 0.115 – indicating that teacher professionalism has a much greater impact on how teachers perceive their status in some countries or economies than in others.

> Box 3.4 **Analysis of system variation**
>
> **Predictor variables:** Four predictor variables are used: overall teacher professionalism index, scaled (0-15) and the three domain-specific indices: the knowledge base index (0-5), the peer networks index (0-5), and the autonomy index (0-5). The overall teacher professionalism index and the knowledge base and peer networks indices are all measured at the individual teacher level. The autonomy index is measured at the school level.
>
> **Regression model:** The country-specific analysis employs two-level country-specific models, which group teachers within schools, creating separate intercepts for each school. The analyses generate country-specific coefficients for each outcome.
>
> **Survey weights:** The analysis takes into account the complex survey design of TALIS 2013, employing final teacher weights for the fixed part of the model and final school weights at the school level. The dataset is set to use balanced repeated replicate weights.
>
> **Controls:** At the individual teacher level, controls include teacher gender and years of teaching experience. At the school level, controls include whether the school is public or private, the percentage of students who are socio-economically disadvantaged and an index of school climate, created by TALIS 2013, which captures the nature of the relationships between teachers.

As the figure shows, some countries and economies, such as Shanghai, China have relatively high coefficients (above 0.115) on all four dependent variables. In contrast, others, such as France, Japan, and the Slovak Republic, have relatively low coefficients on all four outcomes, suggesting that teacher professionalism is simply not as important a predictor of teachers' satisfaction and perceptions in those education systems as it is in other contexts. It is possible that other factors of national labour markets may be mediating the role that teacher professionalism has on teachers' perceptions and satisfaction.

In addition, there are other patterns among countries and economies – for example, in some countries, like Australia and the Netherlands, teacher professionalism seems to have a significant and relatively large impact on satisfaction with the profession and current work environment, but it has only a small association with perceptions of self-efficacy or status. In contrast, there are countries like Korea and Malaysia, where, when compared to other contexts, teacher professionalism seems to have a significant impact on perception outcomes – status and self-efficacy – but a more moderate impact on the satisfaction outcomes.

3. TEACHER PROFESSIONALISM AND POLICY-RELEVANT OUTCOMES

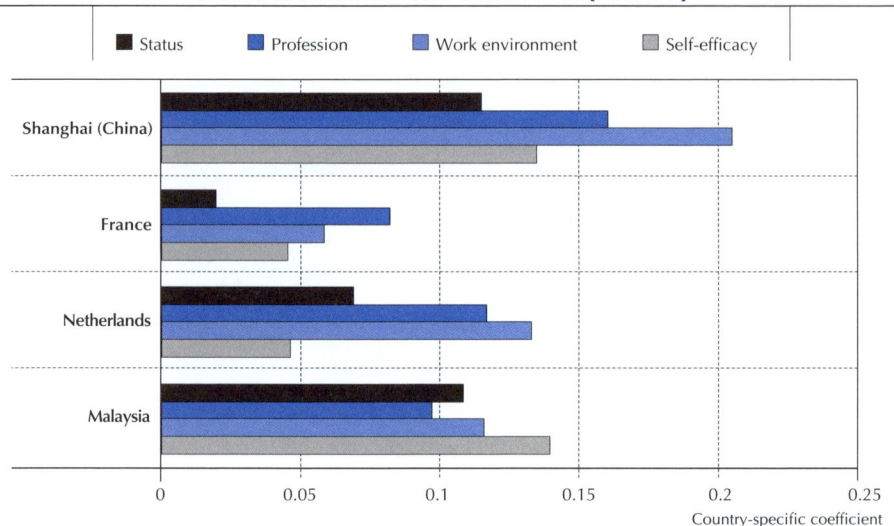

■ Figure 3.5 ■
Patterns of relationships between professionalism and outcomes in select countries and economies (ISCED 2)

Source: OECD (2013), *Teaching and Learning International Survey (TALIS): 2013 complete database*, http://stats.oecd.org/index.aspx?datasetcode=talis_2013%20.

The country/economy-specific patterns identified in Figure 3.5 are not necessarily linked to the various models of teacher professionalism identified in Chapter 2.

To further examine the nature of cross-system variation, Figure 3.6 and Figure 3.7 present the size and significance of system-specific regression coefficients. The coefficients are a measure of how much the adoption of an additional best practice is associated with a change in outcomes, measured as a standard deviation. Figure 3.6 and Figure 3.7 show the size of the relationship between teacher professionalism and two outcomes of interest. The report focuses on the coefficients for self-efficacy and satisfaction with work environment, because these two seem to have the most immediate policy relevance – job satisfaction as it pertains to retention and turnover, and self-efficacy as it pertains to teacher quality.

As can be seen, coefficients for self-efficacy range from a low of about 0.045 in France to highs of about 0.139 in Malaysia and 0.135 in England, United Kingdom. In these latter two systems there is a pronounced relationship between professionalism and the degree to which teachers feel able to carry out their jobs. The coefficient on teacher perceptions of satisfaction with their work environment tends to be higher across the board, with Abu Dhabi, United Arab Emirates; England, United Kingdom; and Shanghai, China standing out as having the strongest relationship. Compared to self-efficacy, the impact of measures of professionalism on satisfaction with work environment is much stronger.

Additionally, the analysis finds positive and statistically significant coefficients on the scales for knowledge and peer networks – in most surveyed systems, these two indicators are positively associated with all four outcomes. In contrast, Figure 3.7 shows coefficients on regressions with autonomy as the predictor. The coefficients on the index of autonomy are both negative and positive and most are actually not statistically significantly different from zero – suggesting no relationship. The figure shows that coefficients across all TALIS countries and economies range from about 0.036 to 0.034 of a standard deviation for the self-efficacy outcome and range from -0.027 to 0.072 for the work environment outcome.

TEACHER PROFESSIONALISM AND POLICY-RELEVANT OUTCOMES

For example, in Abu Dhabi, United Arab Emirates, it is clear that teacher professionalism is strongly linked to certain outcomes of interest, even while its education system has comparatively moderate levels of teacher professionalism. Additionally, countries and economies with both the highest (i.e. England, United Kingdom) and lowest levels (i.e. Mexico) of overall professionalism show up among the countries and economies with the strongest relationships between professionalism and outcomes. The lack of systematic relationships suggests that it is not only those systems with high levels of teacher professionalism where professionalism matters for teacher outcomes. Instead, the findings suggest that teacher professionalism might interact with other system-level factors or specific educational cultures such that professionalism matters more in terms of predicting outcomes in certain contexts than others.

■ Figure 3.6 ■
Country/economy-specific regression coefficients – overall professionalism index (ISCED 2)

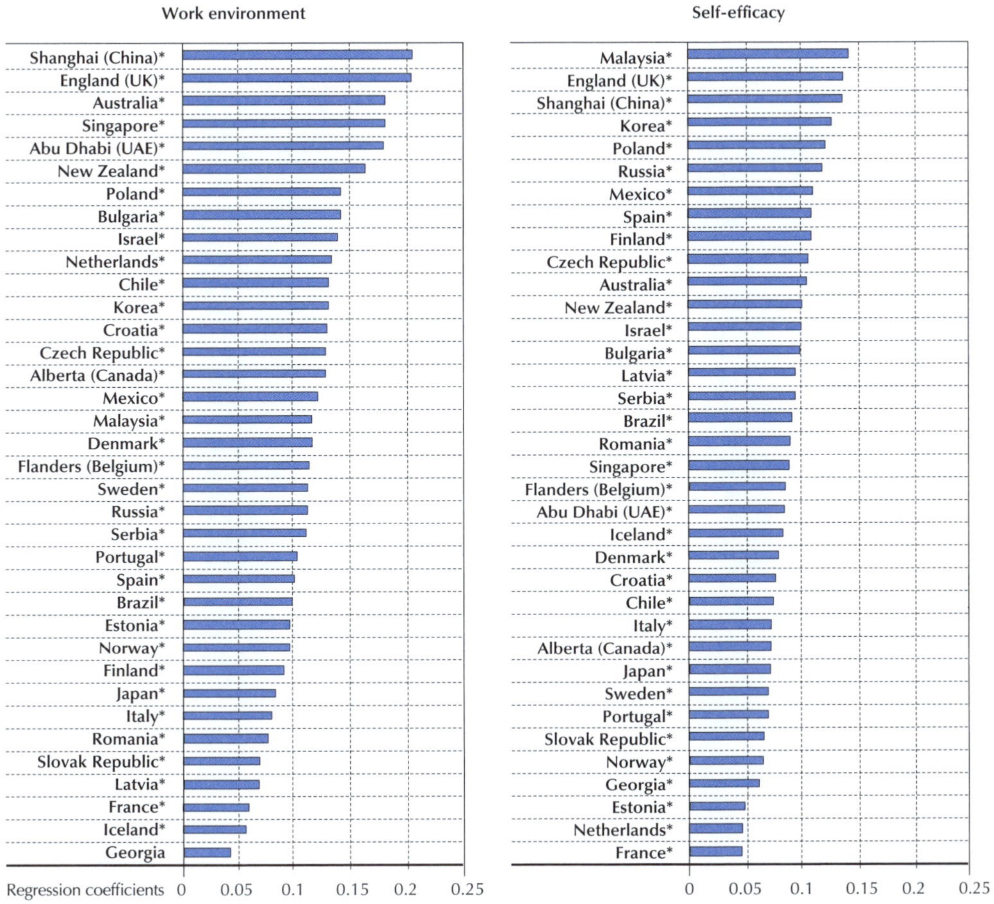

Notes:
1. * Designates coefficient is statistically significantly different than zero (p<0.05).
2. Countries/economies listed in descending order by the size of the coefficient.

Source: OECD (2013), *Teaching and Learning International Survey (TALIS): 2013 complete database*, http://stats.oecd.org/index.aspx?datasetcode=talis_2013%20.

3. TEACHER PROFESSIONALISM AND POLICY-RELEVANT OUTCOMES

• Figure 3.7 •
Country/economy-specific regression coefficients for autonomy scale (ISCED 2)

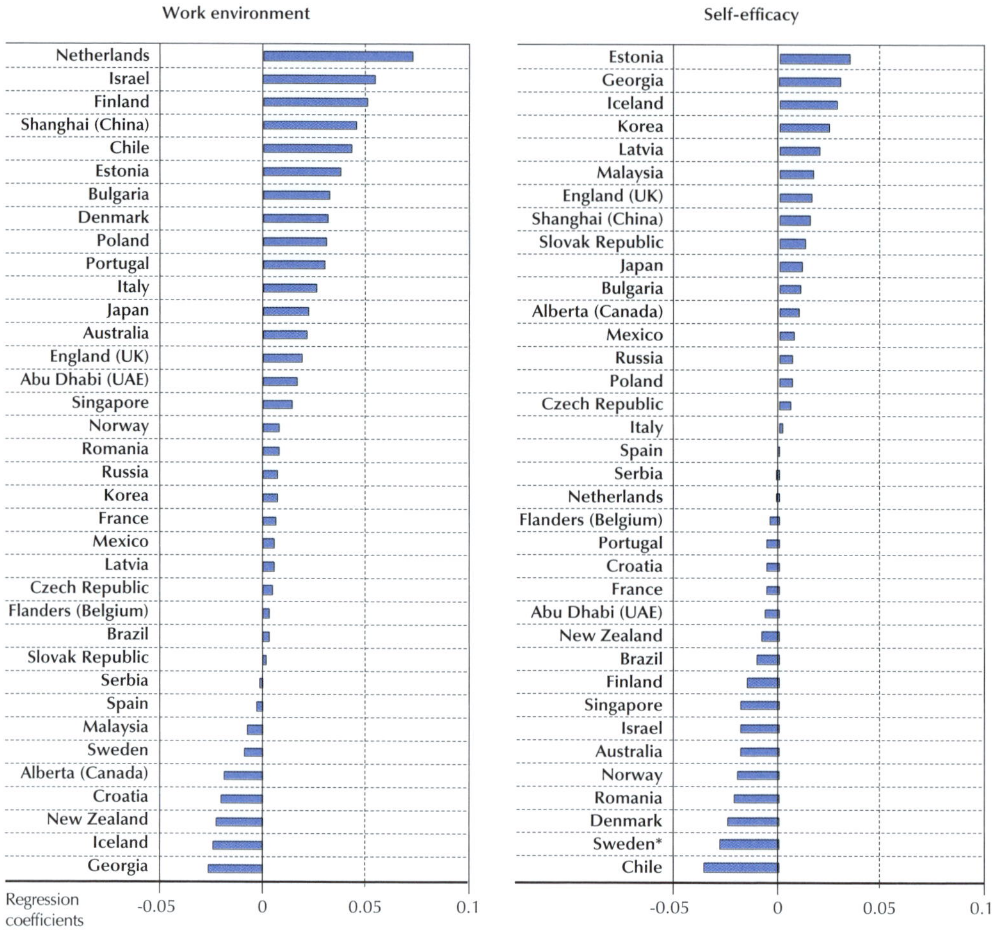

Work environment

Netherlands	
Israel	
Finland	
Shanghai (China)	
Chile	
Estonia	
Bulgaria	
Denmark	
Poland	
Portugal	
Italy	
Japan	
Australia	
England (UK)	
Abu Dhabi (UAE)	
Singapore	
Norway	
Romania	
Russia	
Korea	
France	
Mexico	
Latvia	
Czech Republic	
Flanders (Belgium)	
Brazil	
Slovak Republic	
Serbia	
Spain	
Malaysia	
Sweden	
Alberta (Canada)	
Croatia	
New Zealand	
Iceland	
Georgia	

Self-efficacy

Estonia	
Georgia	
Iceland	
Korea	
Latvia	
Malaysia	
England (UK)	
Shanghai (China)	
Slovak Republic	
Japan	
Bulgaria	
Alberta (Canada)	
Mexico	
Russia	
Poland	
Czech Republic	
Italy	
Spain	
Serbia	
Netherlands	
Flanders (Belgium)	
Portugal	
Croatia	
France	
Abu Dhabi (UAE)	
New Zealand	
Brazil	
Finland	
Singapore	
Israel	
Australia	
Norway	
Romania	
Denmark	
Sweden*	
Chile	

Regression coefficients: -0.05, 0, 0.05, 0.1

Notes:
1. * Designates coefficient is statistically significantly different from zero (p<0.05).
2. Countries/economies listed in descending order by the size of the coefficient.

Source: OECD (2013), *Teaching and Learning International Survey (TALIS): 2013 complete database*, http://stats.oecd.org/index.aspx?datasetcode=talis_2013%20.

Nonetheless, there are also exceptions. In five of the surveyed countries and economies – Finland; Israel; the Netherlands; Poland; and Shanghai, China – autonomy is positive and a statistically significant predictor of satisfaction with the current work environment. Autonomy also seems to be a statistically significant and positive predictor of status in Estonia and satisfaction with the teaching profession in Israel. It is possible that in these countries and economies, many of which have high values on teacher professionalism overall (e.g. Estonia and Poland), there is a virtuous cycle whereby autonomy is an important part of teacher professionalism and contributes to enhanced satisfaction and status. Additionally, Estonia; Poland; the Netherlands and Shanghai, China also tend to have high values on the knowledge base scale and peer networks scale. It is possible that autonomy may be important in teachers' satisfaction with their work environment, but only when supported by a strong knowledge base and peer networks. This would suggest that the role of autonomy requires a foundation of other supports for it to translate into outcomes. However, more research is needed to fully understand the effect of autonomy in these systems.

Nonetheless, these are the only contexts for which autonomy seems to affect outcomes. Additionally, although coefficients on the pooled regressions are negative, there are no statistically significant negative coefficients in the country-specific analyses. This suggests that although the analysis does not find a strong positive relationship for autonomy on outcomes, there is no reason to believe that additional autonomy negatively impacts teachers' satisfaction, status or self-efficacy either. Moreover, across all countries, autonomy seems to have the strongest relationship with teachers' perceptions of their current work environments and much less with status or satisfaction.

THE ROLE OF SYSTEM-LEVEL FACTORS

This report has found that teacher professionalism is positively associated with teachers' perceptions and satisfaction with their work environment and profession. However, teachers' perceptions and satisfaction may also vary based on other system-wide characteristics, such as relative salaries and accountability systems. For example, education systems may adopt policies such as attempting to attract better teachers through higher pay, or by making teachers accountable for student outcomes as a way of improving teaching. System-level policies such as these may bias the analysis of teacher professionalism if they are associated with both teacher professionalism and teacher-level outcomes. As such, the chapter also examines the role of other important system-level factors in a subsequent section to understand how and whether teacher professionalism is associated with other policies aimed at improving teacher quality (see Box 3.5 for more details).

Box 3.5 **Technical notes on system-level analysis**

Predictor variables: The primary predictor variable is a teacher's value on the overall teacher professionalism index, which ranges from 0-15. The unit of analysis is the teacher.

Regression model: The country-specific analysis employs two-level country-specific models, which group teachers within schools, creating separate intercepts for each school. The analyses generate country-specific coefficients for each outcome.

Survey weights: The analysis takes into account the complex survey design of TALIS 2013, employing final teacher weights for the fixed part of the model and final school weights at the school level. The dataset is set to use balanced repeated replicate weights.

Control variables: At the system level, the regression models include an indicator variable in regression models for whether a country has a testing-for-accountability policy and a continuous variable indicating average teacher salary relative to the salaries of tertiary educated individuals in the labour force.

At the individual teacher level, controls include teacher gender and years of teaching experience. At the school level, controls include whether the school is public or private, the percentage of students who are socio-economically disadvantaged and an index of school climate, created by TALIS 2013, which captures the nature of the relations.

3
TEACHER PROFESSIONALISM AND POLICY-RELEVANT OUTCOMES

This section examines whether the relationships noted between policy-relevant outcomes and teacher professionalism, as measured by implementation of best practices, hold after other measures of teacher professionalism are taken into consideration. Specifically, it explores two system-level factors that can be considered alternative ways of professionalising teaching – relative pay and policy frameworks that pay teachers for students' performance. Teacher pay can be considered one policy designed at recruiting and retaining high-quality teacher labour, with the goal of improving teacher quality. Cross-national research into teacher recruitment and retention has found that in countries such as the United States, where teachers' salary ladders are relatively flat, leading to only small increases over time, "...teaching is not a financially attractive profession...", and that low relative salaries are one reason many teachers leave the profession (Akiba and LeTendre, 2009: 22). As such, policies that pay teachers well can be considered one approach to improving the recruitment and retention of high-quality teachers.

Second, in some education systems, policies tying formal evaluations, pay or sanctions to student performance as a form of test-based accountability have been adopted on the grounds that they would incentivise good teaching. There has been a large increase in testing for accountability over the past three decades around the world, including in those countries and economies participating in TALIS (Smith, forthcoming). When testing for accountability, education systems aggregate student scores to the level of the teacher or school, and use these aggregates for assessing teacher quality. The adoption of testing for accountability policies has been one of the most powerful and pervasive trends in global educational policy in the past two decades (Smith, forthcoming: 13). Nonetheless, such policies can be controversial, as they hold teachers accountable for student performance when aspects of performance are outside their control (Smith, forthcoming).

This section also examines whether teacher pay, or testing for accountability affect the relationship between teacher professionalism and outcomes. Because these policies are system-level factors, the analysis uses three-level models that account for the fact that teachers are grouped in schools in education systems, which share the same pay and accountability policies. Table 3.4 shows coefficients for these models. As in previous analyses, the coefficients can be interpreted as indicating the change in the standard deviation of the outcome – teachers' perceptions and satisfaction – resulting from implementing one additional best practice. The first row of the table shows teacher professionalism coefficients without the system controls, as a basis of comparison. The second row includes a model with the two system controls – as is clear, the coefficients change only slightly. Their sign, significance and magnitude change very little for most outcomes. This suggests that the inclusion of these other system-level controls does not substantively alter the relationship noted between teacher professionalism and outcomes. This means that teacher professionalism is positively associated with teachers' perceptions and satisfaction, even after accounting for teachers' relative salary and whether they work in a system of high accountability.

The third and fourth rows of the table show that other measures of teacher professionalism also seem to be important predictors of teachers' perceptions and satisfaction and should be studied in their own right, although they are outside the scope of the analysis. The table shows that, in general, teachers that work in countries with evaluative or incentive-based environments tend to have lower satisfaction and perceived efficacy, although they may also perceive higher status. Additionally, not unexpectedly, teachers who are paid higher salaries tend to state that teaching is more highly valued in society than those with lower relative salaries.

TEACHER PROFESSIONALISM AND POLICY-RELEVANT OUTCOMES

Table 3.4   **The relationship between outcomes and alternate educational policies**

	Perceived status	Satisfaction with profession	Satisfaction with work environment	Perceived self-efficacy
Standardised coefficients on teacher professionalism				
Teacher professionalism – without system-level factors	0.061***	0.096***	0.113***	0.097***
Teacher professionalism – with system level factors	0.059***	0.098***	0.117***	0.090***
Standardised coefficients on selected system-level teacher professionalism factors				
High stakes testing policy (0/1)	0.034*	-0.336***	-0.197***	-0.167***
Higher relative salary	0.248***	0.091***	0.070*	0.034

Notes:

1. All regression models control for teacher gender, years of experience, subject taught, school SES, school sector and school climate.

2. Significance stars: * p<0.05, ** p<0.01, *** p<0.001.

Source: Smith, W. (forthcoming), "Exploring educator based testing for accountability: National testing policies and student achievement", in T. Burns (ed.), *Modern Governance in Education: The Challenge of Complexity*, OECD Publishing, Paris; OECD (2014a), *Education GPS*, http://gpseducation.oecd.org/.

These findings suggest that teacher professionalism is an important predictor of outcomes, above and beyond other policies to promote professionalism – pay and testing. This finding supports arguments for the importance of investing in teachers and their professionalism as a preferred approach to educational reform.

DIFFERENCES BY SCHOOL LEVEL

As we noted in Chapter 2, teacher professionalism differs by school level. This section examines differences across school levels. In order to maximise the number of observations, the analysis compares countries with data on two school levels at a time – comparing primary to lower secondary and lower secondary to upper secondary. This method allows us to look into potential differences across levels, but it applies only to the specific subset of countries that participated in the data collection at particular comparison levels. This means that generalisations to other countries should be made with care.

Figure 3.8 shows the coefficient on regression models predicting total professionalism on outcomes of interest at each level of schooling. The bars represent the change in the outcome, measured as a percent of a standard deviation, resulting from implementing one additional best practice. The figure suggests that teacher professionalism might matter more in the secondary levels than in primary – at least with respect to teachers' perceived status, their satisfaction with the teaching profession and their current work environment. In contrast, the coefficients modelling the effect of professionalism on self-efficacy appear to be both large and similar at all levels of schooling.

Increasing support for teacher professionalism appears to have a stronger and larger association with teachers' perceptions and satisfaction at higher levels of schooling – this may reflect differences in the nature of teaching at different educational levels, such that teachers may need more or different types of supports at higher levels of schooling. For example, it is possible that environmental factors not related to teacher professionalism – such as the composition of the student body or administrative decisions – may be more important predictors of teachers' satisfaction and self-efficacy at the primary level due to less curricular specialisation and other factors.

TEACHER PROFESSIONALISM AND POLICY-RELEVANT OUTCOMES

It is also important to note that descriptive analysis in Chapter 2 found that teachers at the primary level enter the profession with more exposure to pedagogy and practice prior to teaching. In contrast, teachers at the upper secondary level were the most likely to have no exposure to pedagogy and practice prior to entering teaching, and simultaneously were granted the most autonomy.

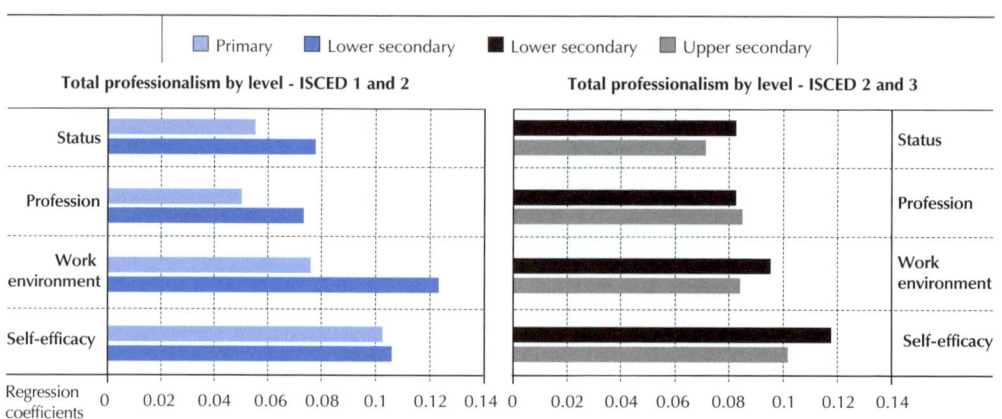

■ Figure 3.8 ■
Teacher professionalism and outcomes by educational level

Source: OECD (2013), *Teaching and Learning International Survey (TALIS): 2013 complete database*, http://stats.oecd.org/index.aspx?datasetcode=talis_2013%20.

The findings concerning the relationship between teacher professionalism and outcomes are robust to various robustness checks, including checks for biases due to missing variables, and various samples. Additionally, school-level means for the knowledge base and peer networks indices are also used as predictor variables; the models find similarly large and significant coefficients for most outcomes (see Annex A for more information on robustness checks). These robustness checks all find strong statistically significant coefficients on overall teacher professionalism, as well as the knowledge base scale and the peer networks index, even after testing for various possible biases and model specifications.

DISCUSSION

Teacher professionalism linked with perceptions of status and job satisfaction. The findings suggest that teacher professionalism is an important factor in teachers' job satisfaction and their perceptions of status and self-efficacy. More specifically, supporting teachers' knowledge base and the formation of their peer networks have the strongest relationship with their perceptions and satisfaction. In contrast, teacher autonomy, as measured by opportunities for decision making, seems to have little impact in most systems. In general, the findings indicate that teachers in schools that adopt more of the identified best practices related to improving teachers' knowledge base and expanding peer networks of support and information exchange tend to be more satisfied, feel more capable and perceive themselves to have higher status. This suggests that schools will benefit from implementing identified best practices, as well as by designing novel approaches to supporting teachers' knowledge base and peer networks.

Results consistent with prior research. These findings build on previous studies that find best practices are important predictors of teacher quality and satisfaction. Prior research has found that teachers desire feedback on their teaching, and that this feedback is a strong predictor of their job satisfaction (Frase and Sorenson, 1992). The large and statistically significant relationship between teachers' job satisfaction and their participation in peer networks, which includes a measure of whether teachers receive feedback, supports this finding. Moreover, this study finds that participation in peer networks is linked not only to satisfaction, but also to other important teacher-level outcomes, including their perceived status and self-efficacy.

Additionally, with respect to teachers' self-efficacy, the findings suggest that supporting teacher professionalism is positively linked to teachers' perceptions of their own abilities. This finding can be interpreted in light of prior research, which has found that participation in professional development is linked to improved teacher practice (Cohen and Hill, 2008; Wallace, 2009). In other words, teachers think that they are more capable teachers because through their knowledge requirements and participation in peer networks, they actually are more knowledgeable of best practices, making them more capable overall.

In terms of teachers' perceived status, the findings suggest that teachers perceive their profession to have higher status not only when they enjoy higher relative salaries, but also when they receive more support for professionalism.

Findings on teacher autonomy are inconclusive. Although the analyses suggest there is no clear or systematic relationship between autonomy and teacher perception and satisfaction, a couple of caveats are necessary. While teacher decision making is not related to teacher overall satisfaction in most countries, there is a subset of countries for which autonomy is an important part of overall professionalism. Prior studies have also found mixed findings with respect to autonomy, many of which stem from a lack of clear interpretation of the meaning of autonomy. For example, one survey of teachers in the United States found that autonomy "...means different things to different people. Some see it as the chance to have substantial freedom and independence in the classroom...," while others "...view autonomy as the freedom to develop collegial relations to accomplish tasks that extend beyond the classroom." (Frase and Sorenson, 1992: 40) Similarly, others have explained that the concept of teacher empowerment "...has been elusive as both a theoretical and empirical construct..." (Hoy and Sweetland, 2001: 710) As such, this study is not the first to find little conclusive evidence supporting the importance of autonomy in teachers' satisfaction, status and self-efficacy.

Nonetheless, more research – with different measures and specifications of autonomy – is needed, particularly research that asks teachers directly about their experiences with decision making in and out of the classroom. In particular, Hoy and Sweetland suggest that teacher autonomy should capture not only objective domains of decision making, but also teachers' attitudes and perceptions of their level of decision-making power, stating that teacher empowerment is "...not simply to the amount of teacher participation in classroom decisions but to the extent to which teachers believe they are involved in important instructional and classroom decisions." (2001: 711)

Cross-system differences. In addition to differences by domain of teacher professionalism, system differences also exist. The findings point to significant differences between countries – both in terms of what professionalism looks like, and how it affects outcomes. The descriptive analysis conducted in Chapter 2 shows that the nature and extent of teacher professionalism varies significantly

TEACHER PROFESSIONALISM AND POLICY-RELEVANT OUTCOMES

across systems. The findings in Chapter 3 extend those in Chapter 2 to suggest that teacher professionalism matters more in terms of predicting outcomes in some countries and economies than in others, indicating the need for additional research into how specific contexts mediate the relationship between professionalism practices and outcomes.

While the analysis finds less support for autonomy on its own, it is important to note that some education systems that are recognised as particularly effective (Scandinavian countries) also rate highly on teacher autonomy, and it may be the way that this factor interacts with knowledge and peer networks that produces the desired outcomes in these countries. Additionally, the system-specific analysis finds that autonomy matters for teachers' outcomes in a few select contexts, meaning that country- or economy-specific teacher labour markets are important mediators of whether professionalism affects outcomes.

Differences by level of education. The analyses also find that education level may matter: teacher professionalism is likely a more important predictor of teacher satisfaction and perceptions at the lower and upper secondary level than the primary level of education. We do not know whether this is related to the nature of secondary schooling or the teachers recruited at the secondary level; however, it does suggest that secondary teachers may benefit more from investments in teacher professionalism. This is important as governments have the incentive to invest resources more heavily where they are most needed. While it would be a mistake to abandon the idea of support for professionalism at the primary level, this research suggests that it is at the point at which curricula become more specialised and teachers need more subject-specific knowledge that support for professionalism becomes more crucial. We also note that secondary teachers tend to have less exposure to pedagogy and practice than teachers at lower levels – this may be one area where secondary teachers could benefit.

A note regarding Israel
The statistical data for Israel are supplied by and under the responsibility of the relevant Israeli authorities. The use of such data by the OECD is without prejudice to the status of the Golan Heights, East Jerusalem and Israeli settlements in the West Bank under the terms of international law.

References

Akiba, M. and G. LeTendre (2009), *Improving Teacher Quality: The US Teaching Force in Global Context*, Teachers College Press.

Cohen, D.K. and H.C. Hill (2008), *Learning Policy: When State Education Reform Works*, Yale University Press.

Frase, L.E. and L. Sorenson (1992), "Teacher motivation and satisfaction: Impact on participatory management", *NASSP Bulletin*, Vol. 76/540, pp. 37-43.

Hoy, W.K. and S.R. Sweetland (2001), "Designing better schools: The meaning and measure of enabling school structures", *Educational Administration Quarterly*, Vol. 37/3, pp. 296-321.

OECD (2014a), *Education GPS*, http://gpseducation.oecd.org/.

OECD (2014b), *TALIS 2013 Results: An International Perspective on Teaching and Learning*, TALIS, OECD Publishing, Paris, http://dx.doi.org/10.1787/9789264196261-en.

Smith, W. (forthcoming), "Exploring educator based testing for accountability: national testing policies and student achievement", in T. Burns (ed.), *Modern Governance in Education: The Challenge of Complexity*, OECD Publishing, Paris.

Wallace, M.R. (2009), "Making sense of the links: Professional development, teacher practices, and student achievement", *The Teachers College Record*, Vol. 111/2, pp. 573-596.

4

Equity and teacher professionalism

> This chapter examines differences in teacher professionalism support within an individual country. The analyses focus on differences between high-needs schools – that is, schools where at least 30% of student body belongs to one of the categories: second-language learners, students with special needs, or students that are socio-economically disadvantaged – as compared to low-needs schools with less than 11% of the student body in one of the three high-needs categories. It explores teacher professionalism support patterns within a given country/economy, providing policy makers with the information necessary to target interventions.

4
EQUITY AND TEACHER PROFESSIONALISM

Highlights

- There are differences in the level of teacher professionalism across high- (with at least 30% of the student body in one of the three high-needs categories: second-language learners, students with special needs, socio-economically disadvantaged students) and low-needs schools (with less than 11% of the student body in one of the high-needs categories).

- Across all high-needs groups (socio-economically disadvantaged, special-needs, or second-language), the greatest amount of within-country diversity in teacher support is found in the autonomy domain.

- Across all high-needs groups, the five most equitable economies (where average scores are higher for teachers in high-needs schools in at least one teacher professionalism domain) are: England (United Kingdom), Korea, Latvia, Spain, and Sweden.

- The positive association between teacher professionalism practices and teacher job satisfaction is largely amplified in high-needs schools.

INTRODUCTION

While Chapters 2 and 3 focused on comparisons between systems, providing important information on global trends and potential areas for national policy application, this chapter explores patterns of teacher professionalism support within a given system, providing policy makers with the information necessary to target interventions.

Having high-quality, well-trained and supported teachers is essential for student well-being and achievement. However, the support teachers receive in high-needs schools often lags behind that of their peers who teach in relatively lower-needs schools (see Darling-Hammond et al., 2009; Johnson et al., 2004). In this chapter, high-needs schools are those schools which self-identify as having at least 30% of their student body in one of three high-needs categories: second-language learners, student with special needs or students that are socio-economically disadvantaged (see Box 4.1 for more information). The difference between the amount of support provided to teachers in high-needs schools and to teachers in low-needs schools (less than 11% of their student body in one of the three high-needs categories) is referred to as the teacher professionalism support gap.

Teacher professionalism support gaps can be identified in each teacher professionalism domain: (1) *professional knowledge base* – the presence of teaching credentials and support for continued professional development; (2) *autonomy* – the decision-making power teachers have over aspects of their teaching; and (3) *peer networks* – the role teachers play in regulating their own standards, including measures of peer socialisation, guidance and feedback. Teacher support gaps in any of the professionalism domains may help explain the discrepancies in teacher quality common in high-needs schools in many countries (Imazeki and Goe, 2009; Jacob, Vidyarthi and Carroll, 2012; Kertesi and Kézdi, 2011; Mulkeen, 2006; OECD, 2005). Addressing the teacher professionalism support gap, therefore, is an important step in ensuring that students' in high-needs schools have access to high-quality teachers. In addition to providing the tools necessary to deal with the diverse student body found in high-needs schools, teacher support, such as providing comprehensive induction programmes

(Smith and Ingersoll, 2004), or providing teachers with greater decision-making authority (Guarino, Sanibañez and Daley, 2006), has been shown to decrease teacher attrition, essential to the stability of high-needs schools that traditionally are faced with greater teacher turnover.

To remedy the teacher professionalism support gap, it is important to move beyond equality and towards equity. While equality indicates that all teachers have access to the same amount of support, equity suggests that all teachers have access to the supports they need to successfully complete their work. In high-needs schools, equity comes when teachers have greater access to practices that support their teacher professionalism. Essentially, with the diversity in socio-economic background and academic ability present in high-needs schools, teachers must take on multiple roles, moving well beyond traditional teaching roles, and be equipped to fully differentiate their instruction while diversifying their instructional approaches. This requires a teacher professionalism support advantage where teachers in high-needs schools have greater access to the supports necessary to thoroughly meet this challenging task.

In exploring the teacher professionalism support gap and surrounding equity concerns, this chapter focuses on teachers in lower secondary schools (ISCED 2) and addresses two important questions. First, how do each country's teacher professionalism support gaps (i.e. knowledge, autonomy, and peer networks) differ by high-needs category (second language, special needs, and socio-economically disadvantaged)? Second, how does the relationship between teacher professionalism support and teacher's satisfaction with their current work environment differ between teachers that work in a high-needs school and those that work in relatively low-needs schools? This chapter starts by exploring high needs categories, leading to a discussion of teacher professionalism support gaps in the complete sample of 2013 TALIS participants, as well as by individual countries. Following the approach of Chapter 2, triangle graphs are then used to identify cross-national equity patterns, distinguishing between those countries that provide more equitable teacher support, less equitable support, or replace one type of teacher professionalism practice with another. The association between each teacher professionalism domain and teacher satisfaction with their current work environment is addressed in the next section. Moving one step beyond the multilevel analysis provided in Chapter 3, this section provides estimates for teachers working in high and low socio-economically disadvantaged schools for each country and economy.[1] The concluding summary provides policy-relevant suggestions for countries looking to bolster their teacher workforce and, ultimately, benefit students in high-needs schools.

IDENTIFYING HIGH-NEEDS SCHOOLS

To examine differences between teacher professionalism support practices across schools, three high-needs student groups are used: second-language learners, students with special needs and students that are socio-economically disadvantaged (see Box 4.1). As detailed in Table 4.1, these three student groups are then divided based on the concentration of students in a given school into high, medium, and low categories.

Table 4.1 **Identifying high-needs schools**

School categorisation	Low-needs	Medium-needs	High-needs
Percentage of students in high-needs group	Less than 11% of students	11 to 30% of students	Greater than 30% of students

Source: Authors' categorisation from 2013 TALIS principal questionnaire.

4. EQUITY AND TEACHER PROFESSIONALISM

Box 4.1 **Defining high-needs student groups**

High-needs student groups are classified using responses from the 2013 TALIS Principal Questionnaire. Question 15 asks principals to identify the broad percentage of students in their school that have the following characteristics:

- Students whose first language is different from the language of instruction or from a dialect of this/these language(s).
- Students with special needs.
- Students from socio-economically disadvantaged homes.

Potential response categories included none, 1% to 10%, 11% to 30%, 31% to 60%, and more than 60%. As few schools have more than 60% of students in any of the high-needs student groups, the top two categories (31% to 60% and more than 60%) were combined into a high-needs category. A high socio-economically disadvantaged school, for example, is a school with more than 30% of its students coming from socio-economically disadvantaged homes.

Although some past research (for example, see Alberta Education, 2014) has classified a high concentration of students with special needs or second-language students as anything greater than 1 in 10 students, this study uses the 30% threshold for all high-needs student groups to allow for easy comparison and interpretation.

Figure 4.1 shows the breakdown of the complete teacher sample of the Teaching and Learning International Survey (TALIS) countries/economies by second-language student concentration. It indicates that approximately eight in ten teachers in the total sample teach in a school where less than 11% of students are second-language students. Approximately one in ten teachers teach in medium second-language concentration schools with a roughly equal amount in high concentration schools.

■ Figure 4.1 ■
Percentage of teachers, by second-language student concentration

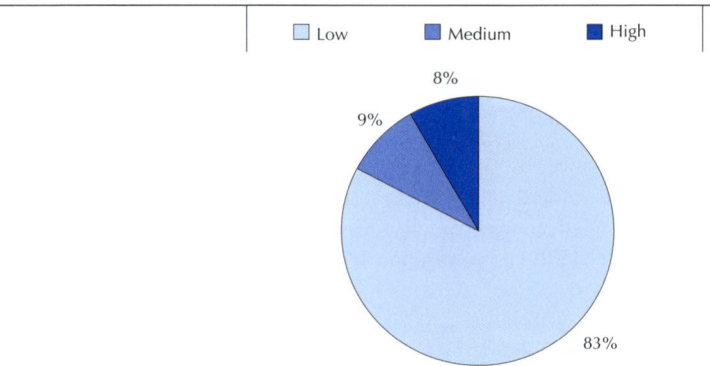

Source: OECD (2013), *Teaching and Learning International Survey (TALIS): 2013 complete database*, http://stats.oecd.org/index.aspx?datasetcode=talis_2013%20.

EQUITY AND TEACHER PROFESSIONALISM | 4

Figure 4.2 illustrates that a very small portion (3%) of teachers teach in schools with a high concentration of students with special needs. Similar to the overall breakdown for second language, eight in ten teachers teach in a school in the low concentration category.

▪ Figure 4.2 ▪
Percentage of teachers, by concentration of students with special needs

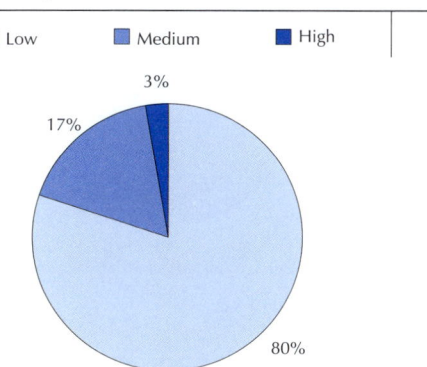

Source: OECD (2013), *Teaching and Learning International Survey (TALIS): 2013 complete database*, http://stats.oecd.org/index.aspx?datasetcode=talis_2013%20.

Traditionally, high-needs schools are associated with the socio-economic status of their students. Figure 4.3 illustrates the vast differences between the concentration of socio economically disadvantaged students and the other high-needs categories. The figure shows that just under half of teachers teach in a school with a low concentration of socio economically disadvantaged students. In contrast, approximately two in ten teachers work at a school with a high concentration of socio-economically disadvantaged students. In comparison with the other high-needs categories, a greater percentage of teachers work in high socio-economically disadvantaged schools (22%) than in medium or high special-needs schools (20% in total) or second-language schools (17% in total). As teachers in each of the high concentration categories face unique challenges and opportunities requiring additional support and training, teachers in schools that have large concentrations of all three student groups face an especially demanding task. Following the 2014 OECD report covering initial results from 2013 TALIS (OECD, 2014b), these most challenging schools include high socio-economically disadvantaged student concentrations, as well as medium or high concentrations of second-language students and students with special needs. In the complete sample of TALIS countries/economies, approximately 2.5% of teachers work in the most challenging schools. In the remainder of this chapter, the different high-needs groups will be considered alternatively to help identify which sub-population should be targeted for the relevant teacher professionalism support policy.

4
EQUITY AND TEACHER PROFESSIONALISM

■ Figure 4.3 ■
Percentage of teachers, by socio-economically disadvantaged student concentration

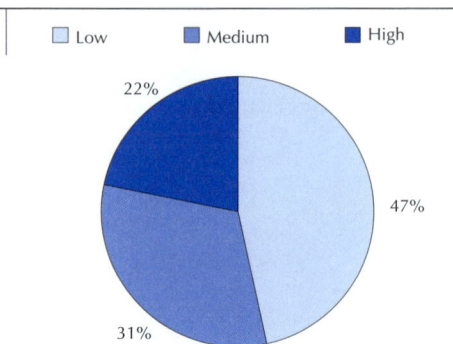

Source: OECD (2013), *Teaching and Learning International Survey (TALIS): 2013 complete database*, http://stats.oecd.org/index.aspx?datasetcode=talis_2013%20.

TEACHER PROFESSIONALISM DOMAINS, BY HIGH-NEEDS CATEGORIES

Teacher professionalism support practices may vary across schools with different student compositions as teachers and schools attempt to meet their specific student needs. Figure 4.4 shows the mean value of each teacher professionalism domain by second-language and special-needs categories, respectively. In both graphs it is apparent that the combination of teacher professionalism support practices differs by concentration category (low, medium, high), with the highest average score consistently found in the peer networks domain. High-needs second-language schools seem to especially prefer teacher professionalism practices associated with peer networks, while greater autonomy is present in high-needs special-needs schools. The high level of autonomy in high and middle special-needs schools is particularly interesting as these schools are the only subgroups across all categories to have a value on the autonomy scale of at least 2.5. This suggests that teachers in middle and high special-needs schools have greater decision-making authority on aspects of their teaching. With proper support this allows teachers to adjust curriculum and instruction to meet the special needs of students in their classroom. Alternatively, the high score could indicate that standards and curriculum for students with special needs, and hence teachers of students with special needs, is less developed, or that students with special needs as a group are exempt from following the typically mandated guidelines.

Unlike second-language and special-needs categories, an obvious trend is present across socio-economically disadvantaged categories (see Figure 4.5). As the percentage of socio-economically disadvantaged students increases, there is a decrease in teacher professionalism support across all domains. In all domains, the greater support for teachers is found in relatively low-needs schools, while the least amount of support is found in high-needs schools with a high concentration of socio-economically disadvantaged students. This pattern is starkly illustrated in the autonomy domain, where the average autonomy score for teachers in the low socio-economically disadvantaged category is over 0.5 point higher than those in high socio-economically disadvantaged schools. In this latter category, teachers have less decision-making authority, with access to less than two in five of the best practices associated with autonomy. Overall, this indicates that teachers in the most socio-economically disadvantaged schools have access to the least teacher professionalism support. Given the challenges and low student achievement in the most socio-economically disadvantaged schools, continuing to underinvest in teachers in these schools can exasperate the already large achievement gaps present in many countries.

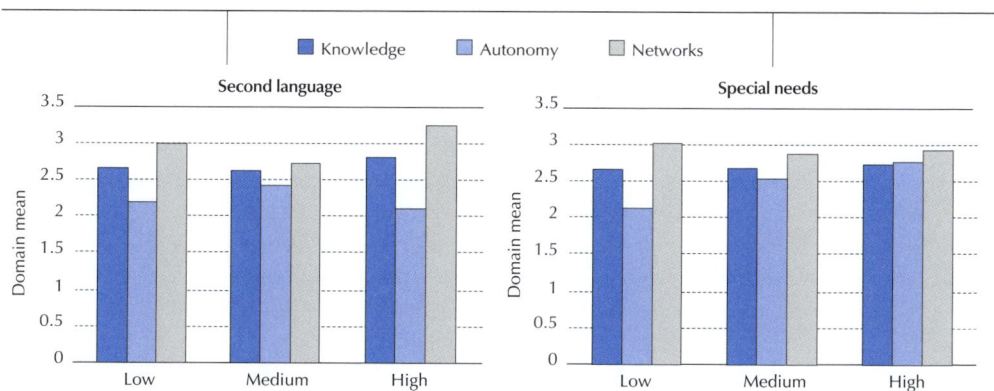

■ Figure 4.4 ■
Domain means, by second-language and special-needs concentration

Source: OECD (2013), *Teaching and Learning International Survey (TALIS): 2013 complete database*, http://stats.oecd.org/index.aspx?datasetcode=talis_2013%20.

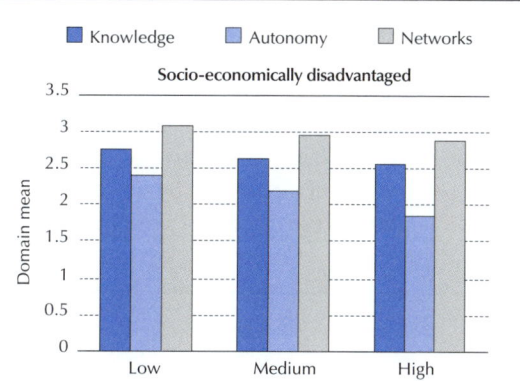

■ Figure 4.5 ■
Domain means, by socio-economically disadvantaged concentration

Source: OECD (2013), *Teaching and Learning International Survey (TALIS): 2013 complete database*, http://stats.oecd.org/index.aspx?datasetcode=talis_2013%20.

TEACHER PROFESSIONALISM SUPPORT GAP

Cultural and historical differences between countries may lead some countries to a preference for one teacher professionalism domain (knowledge, autonomy, peer networks) or one special-needs group (second-language, special-needs, socio-economically disadvantaged) over another. Looking at teacher professionalism support gaps (see Box 4.2) within a country can help identify inequitable patterns of teacher support, given the country's unique history and culture. Large support gaps indicate that teachers in high-needs schools are receiving substantially less teacher professionalism support than their peers in relatively lower-needs schools. Support advantages indicate that a more equitable

4 EQUITY AND TEACHER PROFESSIONALISM

pattern is present with teachers in high-needs schools receiving more support, providing them with the additional resources necessary given their high-needs student population. In comparing teachers in high and low second-language schools, a significant teacher professionalism advantage is present, with the average scores on the knowledge and peer networks domains for teachers in schools with a high concentration of second-language learners greater than their peers in lower-needs schools (see Annex C). Across the TALIS participants, each teacher professionalism domain has approximately the same number of systems exhibiting a significant gap as a significant advantage – knowledge (4 gaps, 3 advantages), autonomy (11 gaps, 10 advantages), and peer networks (6 gaps, 9 advantages) – indicating that there is no universal pattern across all systems. The largest fluctuation across countries, with a high number of gaps and advantages, is found in the autonomy domain.[2] In the Czech Republic, teachers in high second-language schools had an average autonomy score ($\bar{x} = 1.10$) almost 2.5 points below their peers in low second-language schools ($\bar{x} = 3.52$), indicating that teachers in high second-language schools have access to approximately one in five best autonomy practices, while those in low second-language schools have access to between three and four best practices for autonomy. Gaps of at least one best practice were also present in Brazil, Finland, the Russian Federation and Serbia. The largest autonomy advantage is found in Chile, where teachers in high second-language schools score, on average, 1.81 points above teachers in low second-language schools. Schools in Abu Dhabi, United Arab Emirates and Latvia also provide at least one more autonomy best practice to teachers in high second-language schools.

Box 4.2 Calculating the teacher professionalism support gap

To calculate the teacher professionalism support gap, the difference in domain score between high and low concentration schools is calculated ($\bar{x}_{high} - \bar{x}_{low}$). Negative scores indicate a gap is present, with teachers in higher-needs schools less likely to have access to teacher professionalism practices. A positive score indicates an advantage is present, with teachers in higher-needs schools more likely to have access to teacher professionalism practices. Annexes C, D and E provide the teacher professionalism support gap by each high-needs student group, with dark blue identifying a significant gap is present and dark grey indicating a significant advantage is present.

In comparing high and low special-needs schools, the complete sample indicates that schools with a high concentration of students with special needs provide teachers with greater autonomy, knowledge-base support and peer-networks support than their peers in low special-needs schools (see Annex D).[3] Similar to the differences between teachers in high and low second-language schools, when exploring special-needs schools across TALIS participants there are an approximately equal number of systems with significant gaps and significant advantages: knowledge (2 gaps, 1 advantage), autonomy (8 gaps, 9 advantages), peer networks (3 gaps, 4 advantages). The presence of few gaps or advantages in the knowledge base and peer networks scales suggests that, in general, the support for teachers' professional knowledge and peer networks is similar for high and low special-needs schools in most systems. In the autonomy domain, the largest gaps are found in the Netherlands and the Russian Federation, where differences between high and low special-needs schools are at least 0.8 point. Large autonomy advantages of over one point are found in Alberta, Canada; England, United Kingdom; Korea; New Zealand; and Romania.

As hinted at in Figure 4.5 (see above), teachers in high socio-economically disadvantaged schools receive less support than teachers in any other high-needs context. Additionally, teachers in high socio-economically disadvantaged schools receive significantly less support in all three teacher professionalism domains, compared to their peers in relatively low socio-economically disadvantaged schools (see Annex E). The greatest fluctuation in support is once again found in the autonomy domain, where an autonomy gap is present in more than a third of TALIS participants. However, unlike the exploration of teacher support in second-language and special-needs schools, a more prominent trend is present for teacher support in socio-economically disadvantaged schools across countries. Specifically, nearly two times as many systems exhibit an autonomy gap (13) than an autonomy advantage (7), suggesting that reducing the decision-making authority of teachers in high socio-economically disadvantaged schools is a relatively accepted practice. Looking at individual systems, significant autonomy gaps above 0.8 point are present in Abu Dhabi, United Arab Emirates and Israel. In the opposite direction, Finland has an autonomy advantage, with teachers in high socio-economically disadvantaged schools scoring, on average, 0.83 points higher in the autonomy domain.

WITHIN-SYSTEM EQUITY PATTERNS

To explore how countries support teachers differently depending on the high-needs environment in which they teach (high, medium, low), the following section uses triangle graphs to identify equity patterns. Looking at patterns of support across all three teacher professionalism domains can help systems identify which teacher professionalism domain they preference and what areas of support are lacking for teachers in high-needs schools. As teachers in high-needs schools often require greater support to meet the diverse needs of the student body, it is important to distinguish between equity and equality. More equitable patterns of teacher professionalism support are found in systems that have support advantages in at least one teacher professionalism domain. Equal patterns are found in systems where neither a support gap nor a support advantage is present. Less equitable patterns are found in systems that have support gaps in at least one teacher professionalism domain. Replacement patterns are present when both support gaps and support advantages are present in a system, suggesting that in high-needs schools, one teacher professionalism domain may be emphasised in place of another.

To demonstrate each of these equity patterns, triangle graphs, like those introduced in Chapter 2, are used with country average scores for knowledge (K), autonomy (A) and networks (N) plotted on a plane. Each point in the resulting triangle represents the average score of the given domain. Overlapping triangles are provided for the low (in light blue), medium (in dark blue) and high (in grey) concentration categories. Equity profiles of all systems can be found in Annex F. Equal patterns are not displayed in the examples below because it is difficult to distinguish between overlapping triangles that do not have any points that are significantly different.

Equity patterns by second-language concentration

A more equitable pattern, indicating that additional support is provided to teachers in high second-language schools, is exemplified by the Latvia triangle graph (see Figure 4.6). In Latvia, significant advantages are present for teachers in high second-language schools across all teacher professionalism domains. This is illustrated in the triangle graph by the difference between high (grey line) and low (light blue line) categories. The triangle for the low category fits entirely inside the high category, indicating that the high category has higher mean scores in all domains. The greatest advantage is found in the autonomy domain, where teachers in the high category score, on average, 1.15 points above teachers in the low second-language schools.

Other countries that display a more equitable pattern for teachers in high second-language schools include Australia, Georgia, Mexico, Spain and Sweden.

■ Figure 4.6 ■
Latvia – more equitable second-language pattern

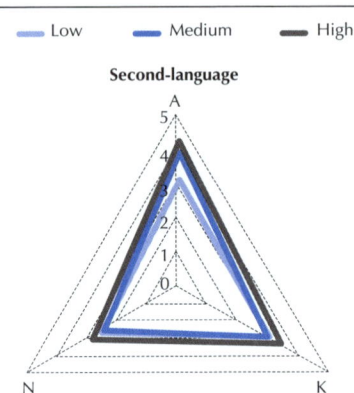

Source: OECD (2013), *Teaching and Learning International Survey (TALIS): 2013 complete database*, http://stats.oecd.org/index.aspx?datasetcode=talis_2013%20.

A less equitable pattern is illustrated by the Estonia triangle graph (see Figure 4.7), where a large autonomy gap is present. The triangle graph shows nearly equivalent scores for the peer networks and knowledge base scales, but a significant gap of nearly one point in the autonomy scale. Specifically, teachers in high second-language schools in Estonia have a mean autonomy score of 3.16 compared to teachers in low second-language schools, whose average score is 4.08, indicating that they have access to approximately one less autonomy best practice then their peers in relatively lower-needs schools. Other countries/economies displaying less equitable patterns in high second-language schools include Brazil; Croatia; Malaysia; the Netherlands; Portugal; Serbia; Shanghai, China; and the Slovak Republic.

■ Figure 4.7 ■
Estonia – less equitable second-language pattern

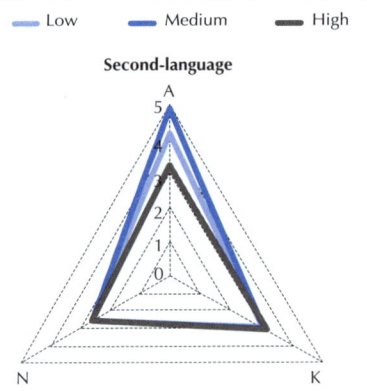

Source: OECD (2013), *Teaching and Learning International Survey (TALIS): 2013 complete database*, http://stats.oecd.org/index.aspx?datasetcode=talis_2013%20.

A replacement pattern in which a country has at least one significant gap and one significant advantage is illustrated by the Finland triangle graph (see Figure 4.8). In the graph it can be seen that teachers in high second-language schools have a mean autonomy score approximately 1.10 points below teachers in low second-language schools. At the same time, teachers in high second-language schools score, on average, 1.01 points more in the peer networks scale. Replacement patterns indicate that the environment for teachers in high second-language schools is substantially different from those in low second-language schools. Unlike more or less equitable patterns, where significant differences across teacher professionalism domains are all in the same direction, the mix of gaps and advantages in replacement pattern countries leads to schools, and teacher supports, that look distinct, depending on second-language student concentration. Other countries/economies with replacement patterns in high second-language schools include Abu Dhabi, United Arab Emirates; Alberta, Canada; Bulgaria; Chile; the Czech Republic; Italy; New Zealand; Norway; and the Russian Federation.

■ Figure 4.8 ■
Finland – replacement second-language pattern

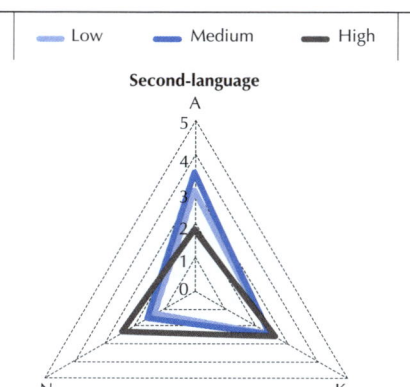

Source: OECD (2013), *Teaching and Learning International Survey (TALIS): 2013 complete database*, http://stats.oecd.org/index.aspx?datasetcode=talis_2013%20.

Equity patterns by special-needs concentration

Alberta, Canada displays a more equitable pattern in high special-needs schools, indicating that teachers in schools with the highest percentage of students with special needs receive the greatest support. As illustrated in Figure 4.9, teachers in high special-needs schools have greater autonomy than those in low special-needs schools. A difference of 1.35 points indicates that teachers in high special-needs schools have, on average, access to more than one additional best practice related to teacher autonomy. More equitable patterns in high special-needs schools are also found in Chile; England, United Kingdom; Flanders, Belgium; Japan; Korea; Latvia; and New Zealand.

EQUITY AND TEACHER PROFESSIONALISM

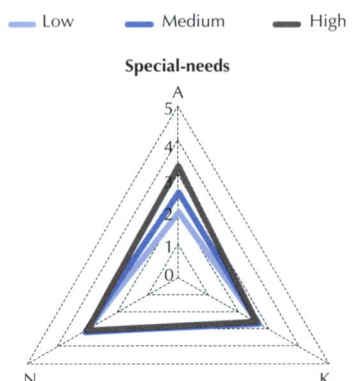

▪ Figure 4.9 ▪
Alberta (Canada) – more equitable special-needs pattern

Source: OECD (2013), *Teaching and Learning International Survey (TALIS): 2013 complete database*, http://stats.oecd.org/index.aspx?datasetcode=talis_2013%20.

The less equitable example of the Netherlands (see Figure 4.10) is nearly a mirror opposite of Alberta, Canada, displaying an autonomy gap of nearly one point between teachers in high special-needs and low special-needs schools. In addition to the Netherlands, countries/economies where less equitable patterns in high special-needs schools are found include Denmark; Malaysia; the Russian Federation; and Shanghai, China.

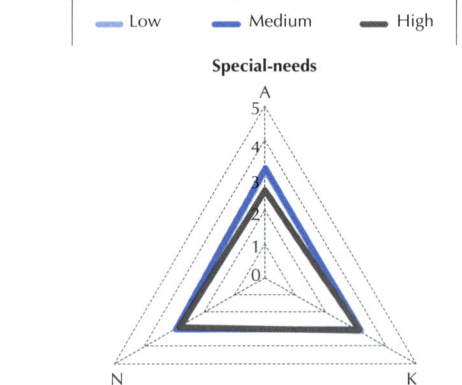

▪ Figure 4.10 ▪
The Netherlands – less equitable special-needs pattern

Source: OECD (2013), *Teaching and Learning International Survey (TALIS): 2013 complete database*, http://stats.oecd.org/index.aspx?datasetcode=talis_2013%20.

Relatively few countries demonstrate replacement patterns in high special-needs schools. The differences in teacher support in France (see Figure 4.11) suggests that high special-needs schools may be replacing autonomy support practices with peer networks support practices. Specifically, teachers in high special-needs schools have a mean autonomy scale score 0.60 point lower than their peers in low special-needs schools, but a peer networks scale score 0.38 point higher. This is illustrated in the triangle graph by a high special-needs triangle with an autonomy point nearer to zero and a peer networks point extending beyond that of the low category triangle. Other countries that display a replacement pattern for high special-needs schools include the Czech Republic, Georgia and Romania.

▪ Figure 4.11 ▪
France – replacement special-needs pattern

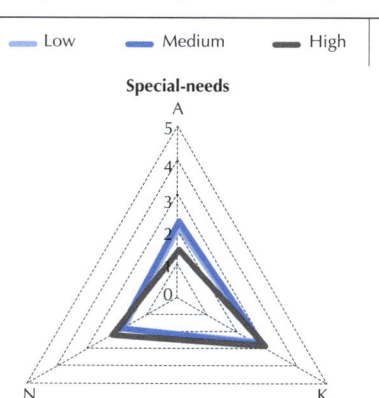

Source: OECD (2013), *Teaching and Learning International Survey (TALIS): 2013 complete database*, http://stats.oecd.org/index.aspx?datasetcode=talis_2013%20.

Equity patterns by socio-economically disadvantaged concentration

The greatest number of within-country gaps and advantages are found when comparing high and low socio-economically disadvantaged schools. Not surprising given the overall support gaps across all teacher professionalism domains for high socio-economically disadvantaged schools, more equitable patterns for this concentration category are present in fewer countries than the other concentration categories (second-language and special-needs). Figure 4.12 illustrates Georgia as an exemplary more equitable country. In Georgia, teachers in high socio-economically disadvantaged schools score, on average, approximately a half point higher on the autonomy scale than teachers in low socio-economically disadvantaged schools. Other countries with a more equitable pattern in high socio-economically disadvantaged schools include Alberta, Canada; Brazil; England, United Kingdom; Finland; Spain; and Sweden.

▪ Figure 4.12 ▪
Georgia – more equitable socio-economically disadvantaged pattern

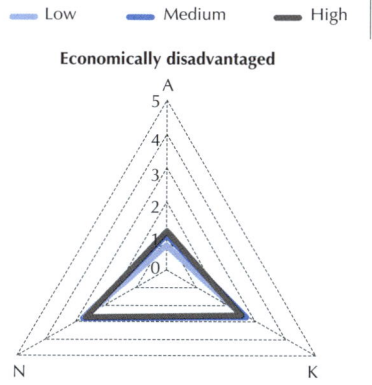

Source: OECD (2013), *Teaching and Learning International Survey (TALIS): 2013 complete database*, http://stats.oecd.org/index.aspx?datasetcode=talis_2013%20.

Given that slightly more than a third of countries have a significant autonomy gap between teachers in high and low socio-economically disadvantaged schools, it is not surprising that the most common trend for the less equitable category is a significant reduction in available autonomy best practices. For example, teachers in high socio-economically disadvantaged schools in Israel (see Figure 4.13) have an autonomy score over one point lower than teachers in low socio-economically disadvantaged schools. The 13 countries/ economies that display less equitable patterns in high socio-economically disadvantaged schools are more than the less equitable patterns present in high second-language schools (8) and high special-needs schools (6). In addition to Israel, less equitable patterns can be found in Abu Dhabi, United Arab Emirates; Australia; Estonia; Flanders, Belgium; Italy; Japan; Malaysia; Mexico; Norway; Poland; Portugal; and Shanghai, China.

■ Figure 4.13 ■
Israel – less equitable socio-economically disadvantaged pattern

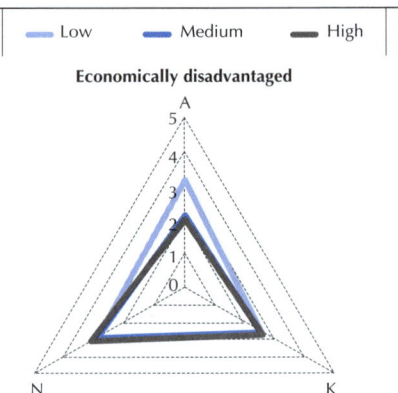

Source: OECD (2013), *Teaching and Learning International Survey (TALIS): 2013 complete database*, http://stats.oecd.org/index.aspx?datasetcode=talis_2013%20.

While the majority of the systems in the less equitable category above have significantly lower autonomy scores with non-significant differences in other domains, many countries seem to replace autonomy practices in high socio-economically disadvantaged schools with more peer knowledge support. This replacement pattern is illustrated by Singapore in Figure 4.14. Teachers in low socio-economically disadvantaged schools score, on average, approximately 2.5 points on the autonomy scale. This average score is reduced to less than 2 for teachers in high socio-economically disadvantaged schools, while the average knowledge score is concurrently 0.22 of a point higher. Other replacement patterns in high socio-economically disadvantaged schools are found in Bulgaria, Chile, Denmark and France.

The equity patterns identified in Table 4.2 and the complete equity profiles in Annex F can help countries identify areas of preference, where some teachers are supported over others. For example, in Italy, although significant gaps or advantages are only found in the autonomy domain, teachers in high second-language schools have autonomy scores higher than their peers in low second-language schools, while teachers in high socio-economically disadvantaged schools have less decision-making power than teachers in low socio-economically disadvantaged schools. Additionally, patterns across concentration categories become apparent. For example, in Chile, teachers in high-needs schools, regardless of concentration category, tend to have access to more decision-making authority, but less support for professional knowledge. A similar pattern is found in France.

Combining the equity patterns above reveal model systems that provide more support for teachers in high-needs schools. Table 4.2 presents the most equitable and least equitable systems for teacher

EQUITY AND TEACHER PROFESSIONALISM

professionalism support. The five most equitable systems have more equitable or equal patterns in all concentration categories (second-language, special-needs, socio-economically disadvantaged), while the nine least equitable systems have less equitable or equal patterns in all concentration categories. All other systems are classified as mixed equity systems. The most equitable systems are exemplars that other systems can use to explore how they may be able to more comprehensively support teachers in high-needs schools.

▪ Figure 4.14 ▪
Singapore – socio-economically disadvantaged pattern

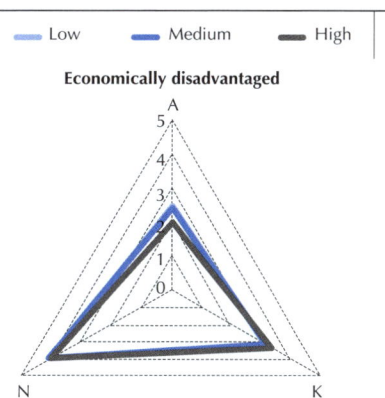

Source: OECD (2013), *Teaching and Learning International Survey (TALIS): 2013 complete database*, http://stats.oecd.org/index.aspx?datasetcode=talis_2013%20.

Table 4.2 **Most equitable, mixed equity and least equitable countries/economies for teacher professionalism support**

Most equitable	Mixed equity	Least equitable
England (United Kingdom)	Abu Dhabi (United Arab Emirates)	Croatia
Korea	Alberta (Canada)	Estonia
Latvia	Australia	Israel
Spain	Brazil	Malaysia
Sweden	Bulgaria	Netherlands
	Chile	Poland
	Czech Republic	Portugal
	Denmark	Serbia
	Finland	Slovak Republic
	Flanders (Belgium)	
	France	
	Georgia	
	Iceland	
	Italy	
	Japan	
	Mexico	
	New Zealand	
	Norway	
	Romania	
	Russian Federation	
	Shanghai (China)	
	Singapore	

Source: Based on author's calculations of 2013 TALIS data.

SUPPORTING TEACHER PROFESSIONALISM: INSIGHTS FROM TALIS 2013 © OECD 2016

4 EQUITY AND TEACHER PROFESSIONALISM

CROSS-SYSTEM DIFFERENCES IN SOCIO-ECONOMICALLY DISADVANTAGED SCHOOLS

Extending the support gap and advantage discussion, this section explores patterns in system support for teachers in high socio-economically disadvantaged schools (see Box 4.3) and two characteristics of interest: prevalence of high-needs schools and average student achievement. To examine the relationship between teacher professionalism support gaps and the prevalence of high socio-economically disadvantaged schools in a country/economy, Figure 4.15 maps the average teacher professionalism support gap[4] onto the percentage of schools that fall into the high socio-economically disadvantaged category. With both axes centred at the mean, the scatter plot illustrates which systems have a larger than average percentage of high socio-economically disadvantaged schools (above the x-axis) or provide more support than average to teachers in high socio-economically disadvantaged schools (to the right of the y-axis).

> Box 4.3 **Focus on socio-economically disadvantaged schools**
>
> To conduct more fine-tuned analysis, a large sample size is needed. As the primary aim of this chapter is to compare high and low special-needs schools, this section, and those that follow, focuses on the high-needs student category that has the requisite sample size, and therefore statistical power, to complete the analysis – socio-economically disadvantaged. Of the 36 participants in the 2013 TALIS, only the Czech Republic, Denmark, Finland and the Russian Federation have less than 5% of schools classified as high socio-economically disadvantaged schools. In contrast, 18 out of 36 participants (50%) have less than 5% of schools classified as high second-language schools and 27 out of 36 (75%) have less than 5% of schools classified as high special-needs schools.

The most important quadrant for equity purposes is the top left, where countries have an above average percentage of teachers in schools in the high socio-economically disadvantaged category, and teachers in this above average number of schools receive below average support. Especially interesting are Israel and Portugal, which have two of the highest percentages of teachers in the high socio-economically disadvantaged categories at 45.7% and 49.9%, while also having the largest average support gap at -0.31 and -0.35. As a result, in Israel, nearly 50% of their national teaching pool, and those with the higher-needs student populations, receive less support than the 22% of teachers at low socio-economically disadvantaged schools, which often have fewer obstacles in student attendance and achievement. In Portugal the 10% of teachers at low socio-economically disadvantaged schools get more support on average than the 49.9% of teachers in high socio-economically disadvantaged schools. Finland and Iceland should be noted as interesting examples. Finland has the highest average support score (0.36) with the lowest percentage of teachers in high socio-economically disadvantaged schools (2.6%). Similarly to Finland, Iceland has a high average support score (0.34) and a low percentage of teachers in high socio-economically disadvantaged schools (2.7%).

EQUITY AND TEACHER PROFESSIONALISM   4

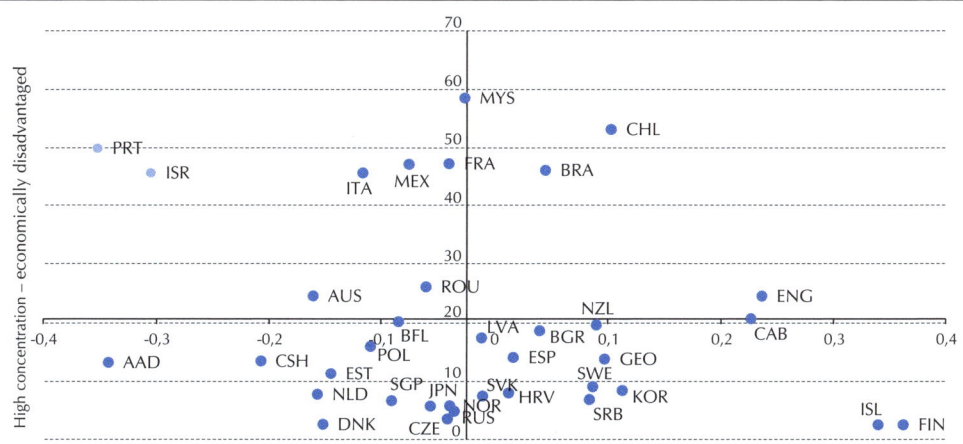

Source: OECD (2013), *Teaching and Learning International Survey (TALIS): 2013 complete database*, http://stats.oecd.org/index.aspx?datasetcode=talis_2013%20.

One of the many goals systems have when they invest in teacher professionalism is increasing student achievement. Chapter 2 revealed a positive association between the total amount of support available to teachers in a system and the system's average score on the PISA 2012 test (see Figure 2.23), suggesting that greater teacher professionalism support may be associated with student learning. Here the study explores whether large differences in teacher professionalism support within a given system are related to the system's average PISA score. In short, the answer appears to be no, as there is no correlation between the system's average teacher professionalism support gap and its average PISA score. However, this does not mean that teacher professionalism support gaps cannot teach us something about student achievement. As the support gap is a within-system measure that essentially captures inequities in teacher professionalism support for teachers in high and low socio-economically disadvantaged schools, a more accurate investigation would explore the association between teacher professionalism support gaps and within-country differences in PISA score. Figure 4.16 attempts to do this by mapping the average teacher professionalism support gap by system average PISA standard deviation, for systems with available data. The trend line indicates a very slight negative correlation is present, suggesting that more equitable teacher support is associated with smaller within-system PISA score gaps.

Figure 4.17 further limits the teacher professionalism support gap to the domain with the greatest fluctuation in scores between and within systems, autonomy, for systems with available PISA data. Mapping the average autonomy support gap for teachers in high socio-economically disadvantaged schools against system average PISA standard deviation reveals a strong negative correlation of nearly -0.38. This indicates that countries/economies that provide greater autonomy to teachers in high socio-economically disadvantaged schools have lower within-country PISA score differences, suggesting that giving teachers in high socio-economically disadvantaged schools more decision-making authority may increase equity in within-system student achievement. This pattern holds even after removing Israel as an outlier.

4
EQUITY AND TEACHER PROFESSIONALISM

▪ Figure 4.16 ▪
Mean PISA standard deviation and teacher professionalism support gap

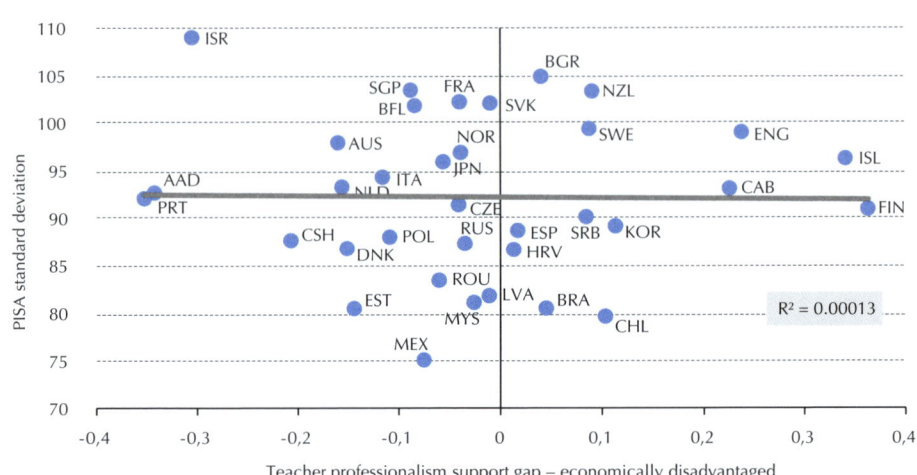

Source: OECD (2013), *Teaching and Learning International Survey (TALIS): 2013 complete database*, http://stats.oecd.org/index.aspx?datasetcode=talis_2013%20; OECD (2014a), "PISA 2012 results in focus: What 15-year-olds know and what they can do with what they know", PISA, OECD Publishing, www.oecd.org/pisa/keyfindings/pisa-2012-results-overview.pdf.

▪ Figure 4.17 ▪
Mean PISA standard deviation and autonomy support gap

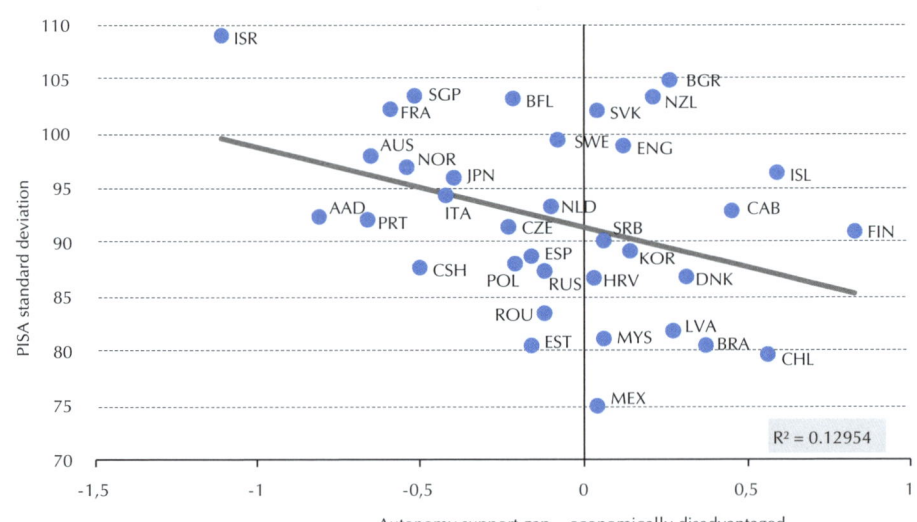

Source: OECD (2013), *Teaching and Learning International Survey (TALIS): 2013 complete database*, http://stats.oecd.org/index.aspx?datasetcode=talis_2013%20; OECD (2014a), "PISA 2012 results in focus: What 15-year-olds know and what they can do with what they know", PISA, OECD Publishing, www.oecd.org/pisa/keyfindings/pisa-2012-results-overview.pdf.

EQUITY AND TEACHER PROFESSIONALISM | **4**

PREDICTING TEACHER SATISFACTION WITH THEIR CURRENT WORK ENVIRONMENT

Recognising that systems appear to take a variety of approaches to supporting teachers in high-needs schools, the next section examines whether the association between teacher professionalism domains and measures of teacher satisfaction differ by the school environment teachers work in. The below analysis (see Box 4.4 for details) focuses on the relationship between teachers in schools with low, medium, and high concentrations of socio-economically disadvantaged students and teacher's satisfaction with their current work environment. Satisfaction with the current work environment is the preferred outcome variable, as teachers who are unsatisfied with their current employment are more likely to leave, exasperating teacher attrition issues in high-needs schools.

> **Box 4.4 Predicting teacher satisfaction with the current work environment**
>
> To predict teacher's satisfaction with the current work environment, the analysis follows a similar approach to that taken in Chapter 3. A two-level random intercept Hierarchical Linear Model (HLM) is used to capture the nested nature of teachers in schools where the level one intercept varies by j, adjusting the intercept for individual i, with u representing the level 1 error term and e representing the level two error term (see equation 1). Individual level control variables include sex (female = 1), years of experience as a teacher and subject in which a teacher's education degree was attained. School type (private = 1) is used as a school-level control. Both school level and teacher level weights were included in the analysis.
>
> **Equation 1**
>
> Teacher satisfaction$_{ij}$ = γ_{00} + β_{01} (knowledge) + β_{02} (autonomy) + β_{03} (peer networks) + β_{04} (individual level controls) + β_{10} (private) + V_{0j} + ε_{ij}

Table 4.3 provides results for the analysis from the complete sample predicting teacher satisfaction with their current work environment by teacher professionalism domain. Separate models were completed for teachers in low, medium and high socio-economically disadvantaged schools, allowing us to compare relationships across models and gauge the relative importance of teacher professionalism domains in varied school environments. Evident in the table, the autonomy domain is not significantly related to teacher satisfaction, regardless of school concentration. The knowledge base and peer networks domains are both positive and significantly related to teacher satisfaction in all concentration categories. This suggests that, when looking at the complete sample of all systems, providing teachers with more autonomy is not related to increases in teacher satisfaction[5] while greater support both for professional knowledge and peer networks is associated with more-satisfied teachers. In terms of the magnitude of the relationship, teacher professionalism practices that support peer networks appear to be more important for teachers' satisfaction in schools with a higher concentration of socio-economically disadvantaged students. This suggests that, on average, support in this teacher professionalism domain may influence the teacher satisfaction of teachers in high-needs schools more. As more-satisfied teachers are more likely to remain in their current position, investments in peer networks are investments in teacher retention, reducing the turnover that often plagues high socio-economically disadvantaged schools. It is also interesting to note the non-significant difference between private and public schools in the high concentration category, suggesting that private schools that work with a higher-needs student population are more similar to the public school counterparts, relative to the difference between more privileged private schools and privileged public schools.

Table 4.3 Association between teacher professionalism domains and teacher's satisfaction with current work environment by socio-economically disadvantaged concentration – complete sample

	Low concentration model	Medium concentration model	High concentration model
Knowledge	**0.154** (0.03)	**0.144** (0.03)	**0.153** (0.027)
Autonomy	-0.014 (0.022)	0.02 (0.025)	-0.026 (0.023)
Peer network	**0.197** (0.019)	**0.155** (0.02)	**0.261** (0.022)
Female	**0.094** (0.04)	**0.176** (0.051)	0.037 (0.049)
Years of experience	**0.005** (0.002)	0.003 (0.003)	**0.008** (0.003)
Humanities[a]	-0.122 (0.069)	**-0.149** (0.056)	-0.02 (0.055)
Social sciences[a]	0.068 (0.056)	**0.117** (0.052)	0.04 (0.054)
Other subjects[a]	-0.022 (0.057)	-0.021 (0.046)	0.062 (0.052)
Private school	**0.684** (0.142)	**1.183** (0.187)	0.166 (0.256)
Constant	10.901 (0.188)	10.903 (0.181)	11.053 (0.139)
Number of teachers	52.621	35.305	24.237

Notes:

[a] Reference category is teachers with degree in maths or science.

Unstandardised coefficients provided. Robust standard errors in parentheses. Significant results (p<.05) in bold.

Source: Based on author's calculations of 2013 TALIS data.

To explore the cross-system differences in the effects of teacher professionalism domains, Figure 4.18, Figure 4.19 and Figure 4.20 present the unstandardised coefficients by domain for each system separated by a high and low socio-economically disadvantaged concentration level (see also Annex E). Dark grey and dark blue bars represent significant effects in low socio-economically disadvantaged and high socio-economically disadvantaged schools, respectively. Although not presented, each result controls for teacher's sex, years of experience, subject degree and school type. Systems with less than 5% of teachers employed in high socio-economically disadvantaged schools are excluded from the analysis (see Annex F for a breakdown of teachers by concentration category).

Not surprisingly given the non-significant autonomy results seen in Table 4.3, autonomy is rarely associated with teachers' satisfaction with their current work environment. As demonstrated on Figure 4.18, a significant relationship between autonomy and teacher satisfaction is present in less than a third of the systems, and in no systems is the relationship significant for teachers in both low socio-economically disadvantaged and high socio-economically disadvantaged schools. This finding reinforces the results shown in Table 4.3, which suggest greater levels of teacher autonomy are not associated with greater levels of teacher satisfaction.

EQUITY AND TEACHER PROFESSIONALISM

- Figure 4.18 -
The association between the autonomy scale and teacher satisfaction with their current work environment

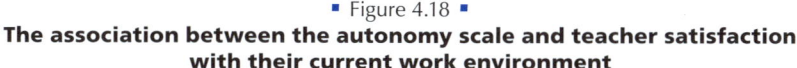

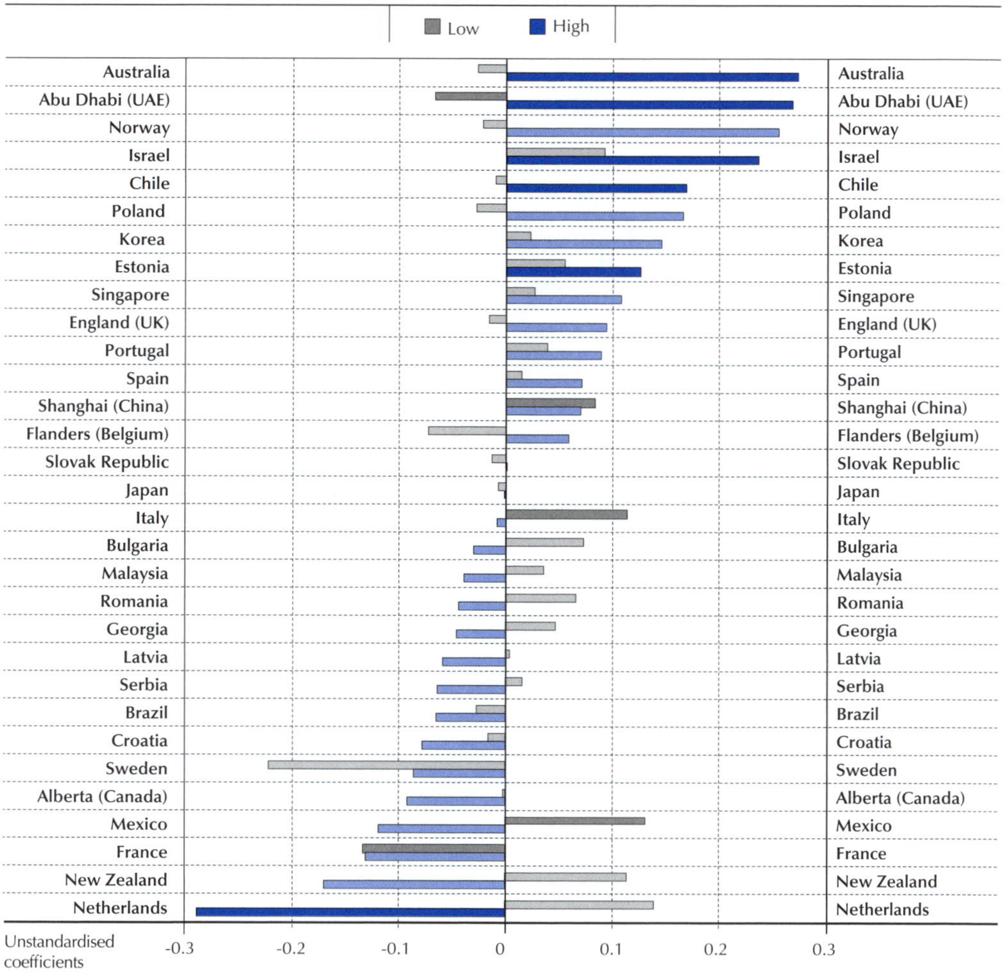

Notes: Dark grey and dark blue indicate significant effect (p<.05).
Systems with less than 5% high socio-economically disadvantaged schools are not included in the figure.

Source: OECD (2013), *Teaching and Learning International Survey (TALIS): 2013 complete database*, http://stats.oecd.org/index.aspx?datasetcode=talis_2013%20.

In both the knowledge base and peer networks domain there is a positive association between greater levels of teacher support and more teacher satisfaction. In looking at the differences in this association with the knowledge base domain between teachers in low and high socio-economically disadvantaged schools, it can be seen that in 8 of the 32 countries/economies included, the size of the relationship decreases significantly as the concentration of socio-economically disadvantaged students increases (see Figure 4.19). For example, in Malaysia, the size decreases from 0.51 in the low concentration category to 0.24 in the high concentration category, suggesting that, although still positive, the effect of increasing the knowledge base scale on teacher satisfaction for teachers in higher-needs schools in Malaysia is approximately half that of increasing the knowledge base domain for teachers in lower-needs schools. The opposite, and more common, trend of

additional support being more important for teacher satisfaction in high socio-economically disadvantaged schools is found in 11 of 32 systems. This pattern is demonstrated by Abu Dhabi, United Arab Emirates, where the size of the knowledge-teacher satisfaction association increases from 0.27 in the low concentration category to 0.51 in the high concentration category. The greatest overall association is found for teachers in high concentration schools in Norway, where a one point increase in the knowledge base domain for teachers in high-needs schools is associated with a 0.84 point increase in teacher satisfaction. The lack of an association between the knowledge base scale and teacher satisfaction in low-needs schools in Norway reinforces the importance of targeting teacher support to teachers in high-needs schools to help increase their satisfaction and reduce teacher attrition.

■ Figure 4.19 ■
The association between the knowledge scale and teacher satisfaction with their current work environment

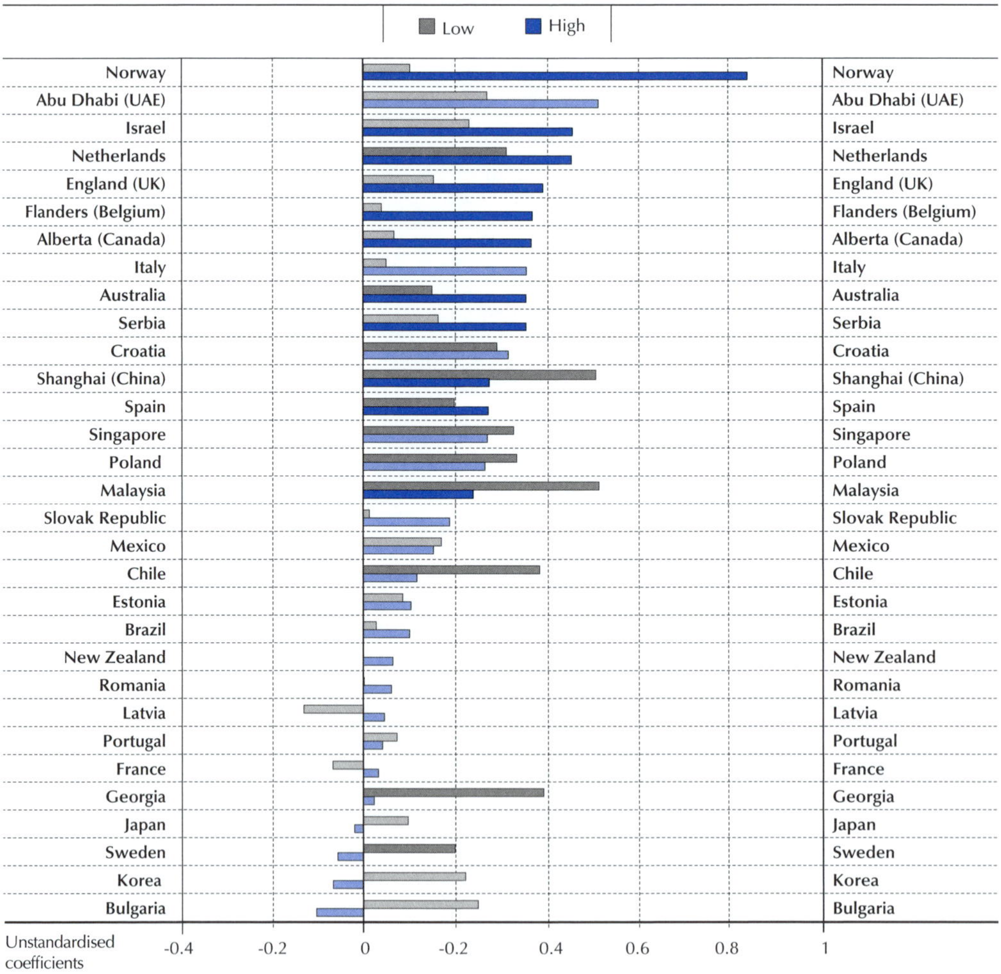

Notes: Dark grey and dark blue indicate significant effect (p<.05).
Systems with less than 5% high socio-economically disadvantaged schools are not included in the figure.

Source: OECD (2013), *Teaching and Learning International Survey (TALIS): 2013 complete database*, http://stats.oecd.org/index.aspx?datasetcode=talis_2013%20.

EQUITY AND TEACHER PROFESSIONALISM

Figure 4.20 suggests that there is a near universal positive relationship between the presence of peer networks and teacher satisfaction with their current work environment. Regardless of the concentration of socio-economically disadvantaged students, it is clear that high peer networks are important for teacher satisfaction. A more nuanced look at the numbers finds that, in approximately 60% of systems, the size of the effect is greater in high-needs schools. For example, in Bulgaria, a one point increase in the peer networks, scale is associated with a 0.22 point increase in teacher satisfaction for teachers in low concentration schools, but a 0.75 point increase for teachers in high concentration schools. Although providing additional support for peer networks appears to benefit teachers nearly everywhere, the larger relative benefit of increased support for teachers in high needs schools once again suggests that targeting teacher professionalism support programmes at teachers in high-needs schools may be an effective and important approach.

■ Figure 4.20 ■
The association between the peer networks scale and teacher satisfaction with current work environment

[Bar chart showing unstandardised coefficients from -0.4 to 1 for Low and High concentration schools across countries: Bulgaria, Australia, Netherlands, Abu Dhabi (UAE), England (UK), New Zealand, Serbia, Singapore, Estonia, Croatia, Chile, Sweden, Shanghai (China), Norway, Flanders (Belgium), Mexico, Slovak Republic, Brazil, Alberta (Canada), Poland, Portugal, Malaysia, Italy, Spain, France, Korea, Latvia, Romania, Israel, Japan, Georgia]

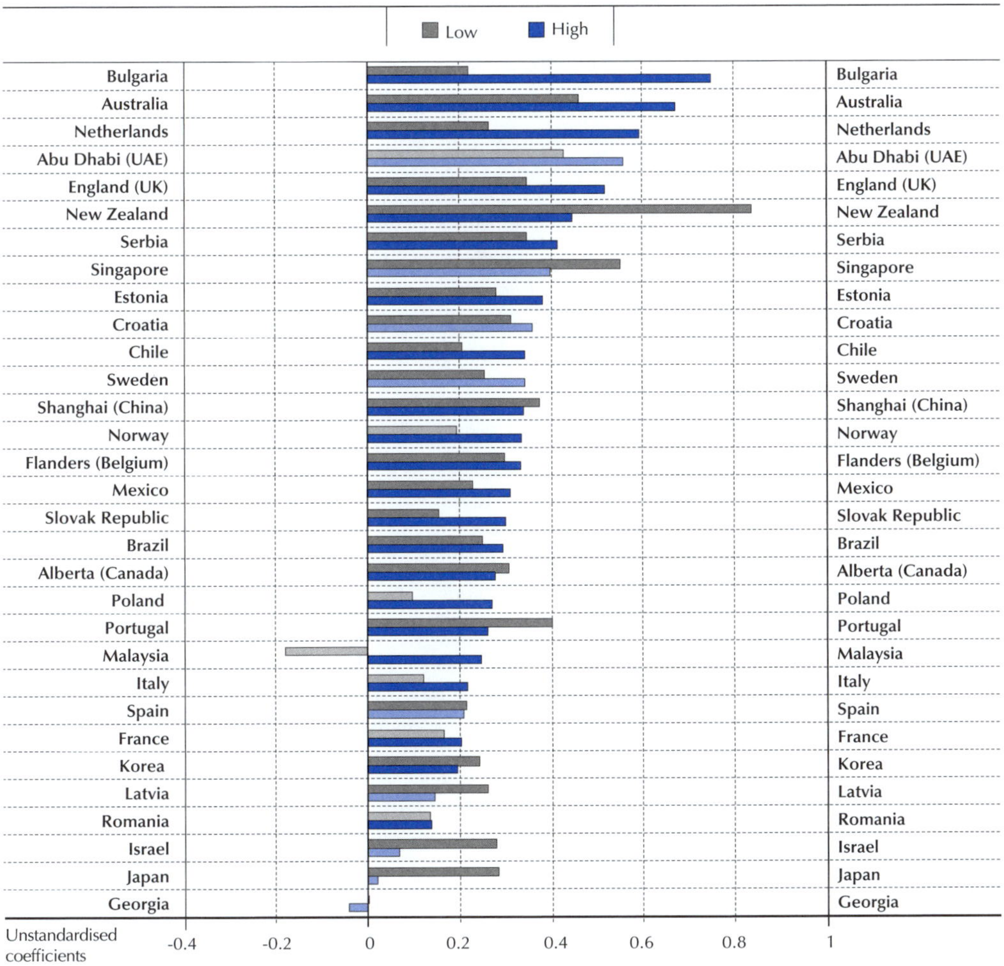

Notes: Dark grey and dark blue indicate significant effect (p<.05).
Systems with less than 5% high socio-economically disadvantaged schools are not included in the figure.

Source: OECD (2013), *Teaching and Learning International Survey (TALIS): 2013 complete database*, http://stats.oecd.org/index.aspx?datasetcode=talis_2013%20.

4 EQUITY AND TEACHER PROFESSIONALISM

In summary, teacher satisfaction is closely associated with higher scores in the knowledge base and peer networks scales in most systems. However, the size of this association is generally greater for teachers in high concentration schools. This suggests that, while improvements in practices that support teachers' professional knowledge base and teachers' peer networks may benefit all teachers, they may be an especially valuable practice in high-needs schools where they have the greatest impact on teacher satisfaction.

EXPLORING DIFFERENCES IN TEACHER PROFESSIONALISM EFFECTS

While Figure 4.19 and Figure 4.20 clearly illustrate the positive association between increasing professional knowledge and peer networks and increasing teacher satisfaction, the ideal policy approach – investing in comprehensive teacher support practices that address multiple teacher professionalism scales simultaneously – may not be practical in countries that suffer from constrained resources. To help resource constrained systems target their support practices, this section explores the relative benefits of increased support in professional knowledge with the benefits of increased support in peer networks by calculating effect differentials[6] (see Box 4.5).

Box 4.5 Calculating effect differentials

Each differential is calculated by subtracting the country coefficient for the low concentration category from the country coefficient for the high concentration category ($\beta_{high} - \beta_{low}$). Associations that were not significantly different from zero were set at zero. Negative differentials suggest that the effect of the teacher professionalism domain on teacher satisfaction with their current work environment is greater for teachers in low concentration schools, while a positive differential suggests the association is greater for teachers in high concentration schools.

By mapping the difference in the effects found on Figure 4.19 (see above, i.e. the knowledge base gap differential) onto the knowledge base support gap, one can identify which countries with large gaps would benefit most from investing in practices that support teacher professional knowledge. Figure 4.21 presents a scatterplot with the axes centred at their respective means. In the bottom-right quadrant there are five systems with a knowledge base support gap but positive knowledge effect differentials. This suggests that closing the knowledge base support gap by targeting appropriate investments to teachers in high-needs schools, in Brazil; Estonia; Flanders, Belgium; Portugal; and Serbia, may have a great impact on teacher satisfaction and subsequently teacher attrition. In the top-right quadrant, England, United Kingdom is providing more equitable support for teachers in high-needs schools and benefiting from high effect differentials, indicating that when a system aggressively supports teachers in high-needs schools, it can have a substantial influence on teacher satisfaction.

Figure 4.22 maps each system's peer networks support gap onto the peer networks effect differential. The bottom-right quadrant in this graph is significantly more crowded than that in Figure 4.21, suggesting that a large number of systems have a lot to gain by improving peer networks in high-needs schools. Countries/economies with above average peer networks support gaps and above average peer networks effect differentials include Alberta, Canada; Brazil; Bulgaria; England, United Kingdom; France; Mexico; Portugal; Serbia; Shanghai, China; and Singapore. The upper-right quadrant includes systems that provide greater peer networks support for teachers in high-needs schools and benefit from the additional positive effect associated with such support in high-needs schools. This includes Georgia, where teachers in high socio-economically disadvantaged schools are provided with substantially more peer networks support, which is related with a larger return on teacher satisfaction. Japan appears to be an outlier; teachers in high-needs schools in Japan, on average, have peer networks scores well below their peers in low-needs schools and the influence those practices have on their satisfaction is not as great.

■ Figure 4.21 ■
Knowledge support gap, by knowledge effect differential

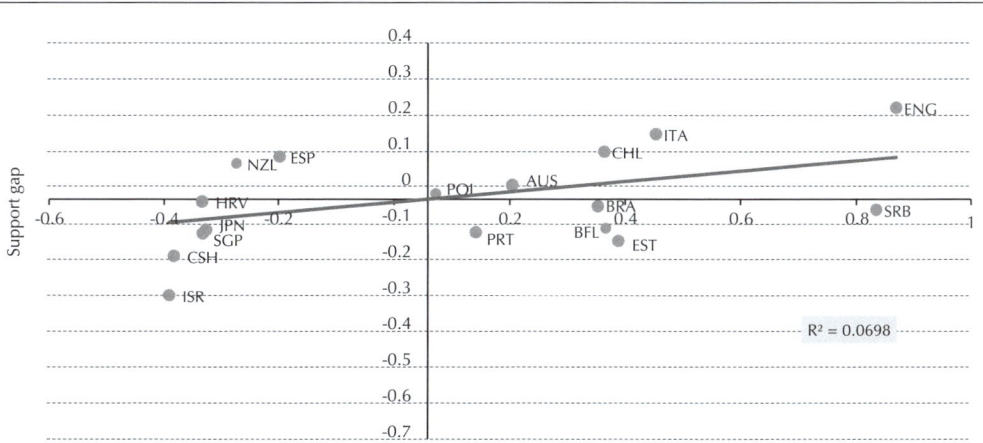

Note: Country and economy data points at the mean knowledge effect differential have been removed to increase image clarity.
Source: OECD (2013), *Teaching and Learning International Survey (TALIS): 2013 complete database*, http://stats.oecd.org/index.aspx?datasetcode=talis_2013%20.

■ Figure 4.22 ■
Peer networks support gap, by peer networks differential

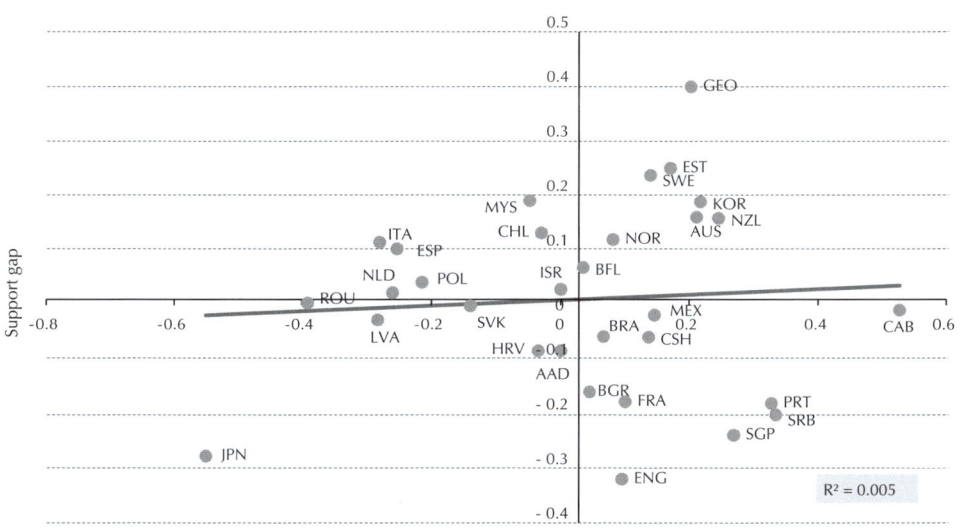

Source: OECD (2013), *Teaching and Learning International Survey (TALIS): 2013 complete database*, http://stats.oecd.org/index.aspx?datasetcode=talis_2013%20.

Although investments in support for teacher peer networks and teacher professional knowledge are positively associated with teacher satisfaction, there may be times where resource restraints mean a more targeted approach must be identified. This is especially true in countries with a high percentage of teachers working in high-needs schools, where per-teacher investment leads to a large total sum. To provide guidance to countries looking for targeted areas to provide teacher support, Figure 4.23 plots knowledge base and peer networks effect differentials onto the percentage of teachers who work in high socio-economically disadvantaged schools. Seven countries emerge with over 40% of teachers working in high socio-economically disadvantaged schools: Brazil, Chile, France, Israel, Malaysia, Mexico and Portugal. The four with large differences between the knowledge base effect differential and peer networks effect differential are included in Figure 4.23. In these four countries, three (Israel, Mexico and Portugal) benefit more from investments in teacher peer networks in high-needs schools than investments in teacher professional knowledge. Alternatively, the figure suggests that if Malaysia had to target their teacher support resources, it would be wise to focus resources on practices that increase professional knowledge first, as they have a relatively greater effect on teacher satisfaction in high-needs schools.

■ Figure 4.23 ■
Effect differentials, by percentage of teachers in high socio-economically disadvantaged schools

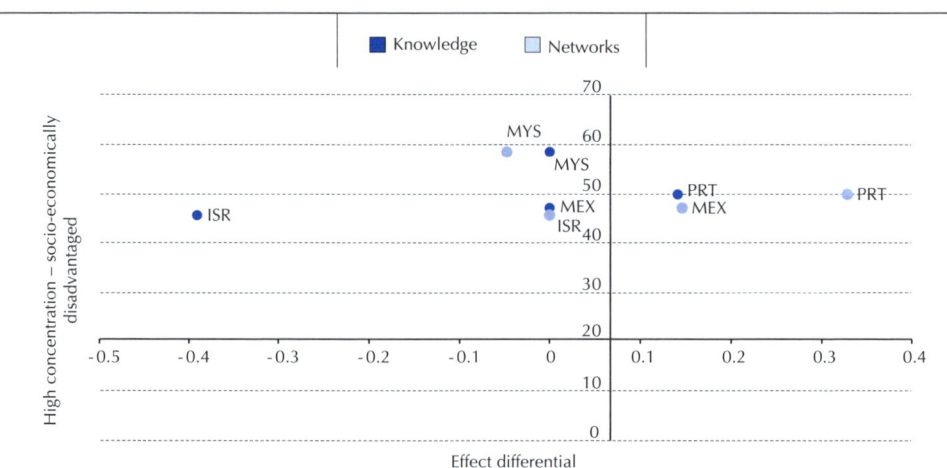

Source: OECD (2013), *Teaching and Learning International Survey (TALIS): 2013 complete database*, http://stats.oecd.org/index.aspx?datasetcode=talis_2013%20.

DISCUSSION

This chapter identified teacher professionalism support gaps and explored how supportive teacher professionalism practices that contribute to a professional knowledge base, provide teachers with autonomy and encourage high peer networks are related to teachers' satisfaction. Results suggest that teacher professionalism gaps are most apparent when comparing teachers in high and low socio-economically disadvantaged schools. Regardless of high-needs student group (socio-economically disadvantaged, special needs, or second language), the greatest amount of within-system diversity in teacher support is found in the autonomy domain.

Four equity patterns were identified to examine within-system patterns of teacher support by the school context in which they work. More equitable patterns are found in countries that have average scores significantly higher for teachers in high-needs schools in at least one teacher professionalism domain. Equal patterns are found in countries where there is no statistically significant difference between high and low categories in all teacher professionalism domains. Less equitable patterns are found in systems that have average scores significantly higher for teachers in relatively low-needs schools in at least one teacher professionalism domain. Replacement patterns are present when a system has at least one significant support gap and one significant advantage across teacher professionalism domains. By looking across all high-needs groups, five exemplary, most equitable systems become clear: England, United Kingdom; Korea; Latvia; Spain; and Sweden. Future research should further explore how these countries support teachers in high-needs schools and how this support affects teacher and student performance and well-being.

Additional findings suggest that teacher professionalism support gaps are not associated with system average PISA score. However, the system average score can hide large within-country achievement differences. When the measure of differences in teacher support (teacher professionalism support gap) was compared with the more appropriate measure of within-system differences in student achievement (PISA standard deviation), an interesting relationship was revealed. Specifically, a marginal correlation was found with increases in equity (i.e. more support for teachers in high-needs schools) associated with decreases in the country average PISA standard deviation. The relationship between teacher professionalism support gap and average PISA standard deviation was best highlighted when the support gap was limited to the autonomy scale.

The ways in which teachers' professionalism is supported can influence their satisfaction with their current work environment. The results here indicate that teacher professionalism practices are almost always positively associated with increased teacher satisfaction, especially when the support comes in the form of increased professional knowledge or increased peer networks. Important for equity concerns, this positive association is largely amplified in high-needs schools, suggesting that one of the best investments schools can make in increasing teacher satisfaction is providing practices that support teacher professionalism. Finally, although part of this analysis compares teacher professionalism domains to one another, it is best to approach teacher professionalism as a complex set of interdependent practices that are best implemented in unison to provide holistic support for teachers in high-needs schools.

Notes

1. See Box 4.3 for more information on omission of the second-language and special-needs categories from this analysis.

2. Within-system findings on the autonomy domain should be interpreted cautiously as the autonomy measures were included only in the principal questionnaire, therefore all autonomy gaps represent between-school differences within a system.

3. The within-system support gaps are more difficult to interpret for special needs due to the lack of schools in many countries with a special-needs population above 30%. In these instances the medium group was used in place of the high group to calculate the support gap; however, doing so leads to a different interpretation and likely smaller gaps and advantages as the school compositions under comparison are not as drastically different.

4. The average teacher professionalism support gap equals the sum of the support gap in the three teacher professionalism domains (knowledge, autonomy, and peer networks) divided by three.

5. The non-significant relationship between autonomy and teacher satisfaction can be partially attributed to the lack of individual level data in the autonomy domain.

6. The autonomy domain is not included in this analysis as it is generally not significantly related to teachers' satisfaction with their current work environment. This is potentially due to the lack of individual level data discussed in note 2.

> **A note regarding Israel**
> The statistical data for Israel are supplied by and under the responsibility of the relevant Israeli authorities. The use of such data by the OECD is without prejudice to the status of the Golan Heights, East Jerusalem and Israeli settlements in the West Bank under the terms of international law.

References

Alberta Education (2014), *Teaching and Learning International Survey (TALIS) 2013: Alberta Report*, Alberta Education, Edmonton, Canada, http://education.alberta.ca/media/15225545/2014talisreport.pdf.

Darling-Hammond, L. et al. (2009), "Professional learning in the learning profession: A status report on teacher development in the United States and abroad", National Staff Development Council, http://learningforward.org/docs/pdf/nsdcstudy2009.pdf.

Guarino, C.M., L. Santibañez and **G.A. Daley** (2006), "Teacher recruitment and retention: A review of the recent empirical literature", *Review of Educational Research*, Vol. 76/2, pp. 173-208.

Imazeki, J. and **L. Goe** (2009), "The distribution of highly qualified, experienced teachers: Challenges and opportunities", *TQ Research and Quality Brief, August 2009*, National Comprehensive Center for Teacher Quality, www.gtlcenter.org/sites/default/files/docs/August2009Brief.pdf.

Jacob, A., E. Vidyarthi and **K. Carroll** (2012), "The irreplaceables: Understanding the real retention crisis in America's urban schools", TNTP, http://tntp.org/assets/documents/TNTP_Irreplaceables_2012.pdf.

Johnson, S.M. et al. (2004), "The support gap: New teachers' early experiences in high-income and low-income schools", *Education Policy Analysis Archives*, Vol. 12/61, 29 October 2004, pp. 1-25, http://dx.doi.org/10.14507/epaa.v12n61.2004.

Kertesi, G. and **G. Kézdia** (2011), "The Roma/non-Roma test score gap in Hungary", *The American Economic Review*, Vol. 101/3, pp. 519-525.

Mulkeen, A. (2006), "Teachers for rural schools: A challenge for Africa", Association for the Development for Education in Africa.

OECD (2014a), "PISA 2012 results in focus: What 15-year-olds know and what they can do with what they know", PISA, OECD Publishing, www.oecd.org/pisa/keyfindings/pisa-2012-results-overview.pdf.

OECD (2014b), *TALIS 2013 Results: An International Perspective on Teaching and Learning*, TALIS, OECD Publishing, Paris, http://dx.doi.org/10.1787/9789264196261-en.

OECD (2005), *Teachers Matter: Attracting, Developing and Retaining Effective Teachers*, Education and Training Policy, OECD Publishing, Paris, http://dx.doi.org/10.1787/9789264018044-en.

Smith, T.M. and **R.M. Ingersoll** (2004), "What are the effects of induction and mentoring on beginning teacher turnover?", *American Educational Research Journal*, Vol. 41/3, pp. 681-714.

5

Policy recommendations to support teacher professionalism

> This chapter summarises policy implications arising from the findings of this report. It highlights the role of pre-service and in-service professional development, opportunities for deepening peer networks and the value of focusing efforts for teacher professionalism on higher levels of schooling. Recognising substantial variations across education systems, the chapter discusses the need for more research into country-specific effects of teacher professionalism.

POLICY RECOMMENDATIONS TO SUPPORT TEACHER PROFESSIONALISM

POLICY RECOMMENDATIONS

This report defines teacher professionalism as the knowledge, skills and practices that teachers' must have to be effective educators. It examines support for teacher professionalism along three domains: 1) a knowledge base, which includes necessary knowledge for teaching; 2) autonomy, which is defined as teachers' decision making over aspects related to their work; and 3) peer networks, which provide opportunities for information exchange and support needed to maintain high standards of teaching. The report identifies best practices for supporting teacher professionalism, including pre-service education, in-service professional development, opportunities for decision making and programmes to develop peer networks. It then measures the extent of teacher professionalism in an education system by calculating the average number of best practices that teachers benefit from across Teaching and Learning International Survey (TALIS) countries and economies.

It finds that, across surveyed countries and economies, there is a strong and positive relationship between teachers' knowledge base and their participation in networks of peers and important policy-relevant outcomes, including teachers' perceived status, satisfaction with their profession and environment and their perceived self-efficacy. In light of these findings, the following policy recommendations are suggested:

1) Provide concrete forms of support for teachers to continue learning and developing their knowledge base.

Supporting teachers' knowledge base is positively associated with teachers' self-efficacy, and their satisfaction with both their current work environment and the teaching profession. That said, this report has found that teachers benefit from support for in-service professional development. In particular, the findings indicate that teachers need additional monetary and non-monetary supports for pursuing professional development, including salary supplements or non-monetary supports such as transportation to and from professional development programmes, or time devoted specifically to professional development. Policy makers can invest in additional supports for teachers' professional development by further investigating what types of monetary and non-monetary supports are needed by teachers in their own countries. One recommended policy might be to incentivise professional development through financial aid or salary supplements for teachers' who pursue advanced professional development opportunities. Policy makers may also want to encourage professional development that occurs over an extended period of time, such as a semester-long course or programme, rather than one-off day-long trainings. These programmes present added barriers, such as costs, and a need for private transportation, in contrast to day-long trainings that can be held in schools. Extended-period professional development is likely to need the most support.

Additionally, teachers may need more opportunities to apply their learning to classroom practice – specifically, opportunities to conduct research and experiment with how to make the theoretical knowledge gained in professional development applicable to their own teaching. One recommendation includes creating additional opportunities for teachers to get engaged in individual or collaborative research in their own schools and classrooms. Policy makers can facilitate the adoption of these best practices at the school level by funding programmes that provide concrete supports for teachers' participation in professional development and facilitate individual or collaborative research.

2) Implement policies that support teachers' networks of peer feedback and learning, specifically induction programmes and teacher professional networks.

Peer networks of collaboration and learning are strongly linked to teachers' self-efficacy and job satisfaction. The more opportunities teachers have within their schools to participate in formal programmes, including induction, mentoring and peer networks, the more effective and satisfied they are. This report shows that while many teachers benefit from certain forms of peer feedback – such as feedback after direct observations of their teaching – only about half participate in formal induction programmes and even fewer in networks of teachers for the purpose of professional development. Policy makers can encourage teachers' professionalism by supporting initiatives that bring together teachers. One option is to disseminate models for effective formal induction programmes for new teachers – either within a particular school or for new teachers across schools within similar localities.

3) Supporting teachers' professional knowledge base and peer networks is especially important for teachers' satisfaction in high-needs schools.

Teachers with access to practices that support their professional knowledge base and encourage peer networks are more satisfied with their current employment. In approximately two of every three systems that participated in the 2013 TALIS, the positive association between these professional support practices and teacher satisfaction is greater for teachers in high-needs schools. This suggests that investments in teacher professional knowledge and peer networks may be able to reduce the high teacher attrition rates common in high-needs schools (Imazeki and Goe, 2009). Reduction in attrition rates adds stability to both the schools and the lives of students. Additionally, more satisfied novice teachers eventually become more experienced teacher leaders. As Akiba, LeTendre and Scribner (2007) found, more-experienced teachers – those with at least three years of experience – have a positive, significant impact on their students' achievement relative to less-experienced teachers, the latter being more common in high-turnover, high-needs schools.

4) Improving equity in access to teacher professionalism support can reduce within-country differences in student achievement.

Differences between the support provided for teachers in high-needs schools and those in low-needs schools are associated with the country's mean PISA standard deviation. This suggests that reducing variance in teacher professionalism support can be an important policy point in reducing achievement gaps. Teacher professionalism practices, such as induction programmes (Feiman-Nemser, 2003), mentoring programmes (Borman and Dowling, 2008), increased autonomy (Watkins, 2005) and greater peer-to-peer collaboration (Darling-Hammond, 2006), are associated with greater teacher retention, improved pedagogic skills and ultimately student outcomes.

Focusing attention on high-needs schools where investments in teacher professionalism support have a greater impact (Peske and Haycock, 2006) can help reduce the disparities in teaching quality commonly found between high-needs and low-needs schools, thus decreasing differences in student achievement. Results here suggest that increasing the decision-making authority of teachers in high-needs schools is an important step, as system autonomy gaps account for approximately 20% of the variance in system mean PISA standard deviations. However, this increase in teacher autonomy in high-needs schools should be coupled with investments in professional knowledge and peer networks to ensure that teachers have the skills necessary to address the complex realities that are found in high-needs schools.

POLICY RECOMMENDATIONS TO SUPPORT TEACHER PROFESSIONALISM

5) Focus teacher professionalism efforts on the levels where teachers need the most support.

The study finds that teachers in lower and upper secondary schools, in countries participating in these TALIS optional surveys, have lower levels of teacher professionalism overall than do teachers in primary schools. Moreover, the study finds that teacher professionalism has a larger impact on teachers' job satisfaction and their perceptions of self-efficacy at the secondary level than the primary level. This finding suggests the need to target teacher professionalism on higher levels of schooling, where it can make the largest impact.

Teachers in secondary schools have lower levels of support for their pre-service knowledge base and lower levels of support for professional development, meaning that teachers at the upper secondary level likely need more supports for professional development. In particular, the descriptive analyses in Chapter 2 find that upper secondary teachers in many countries enter the teaching profession with less exposure to the principles of pedagogy and less experience with practice teaching than do teachers at the primary and lower secondary level. High-quality teaching requires not only content knowledge, but also an understanding of how to translate content knowledge into student learning, meaning that teachers, and particularly beginning teachers, need programmes that introduce them to pedagogy and provide opportunities for concrete practice.

6) Conduct research into the system-specific relationships between teacher professionalism and outcomes.

This report has found large variations in the nature and extent of teacher professionalism across the participating education systems. Additionally, it has found that, even while teacher professionalism is positively associated with outcomes of interest in all the surveyed education systems, the magnitude of relationships varies quite a bit cross-nationally. Chapter 3 also indicates that autonomy may be linked to outcomes in certain contexts, but not others. Although a detailed investigation of these differences was outside the scope of this report, there is a clear need for national and local policy makers to understand better how teacher professionalism in their education system is linked to teacher outcomes. Further studies should investigate which system-specific factors mediate the relationships between teacher professionalism and outcomes – there are a number of possible mediators, such as policies governing teacher pay or recruitment, or school-based management.

CONCLUSION

It is clear that supporting teacher professionalism has an important and positive relationship with teachers' perceptions of status and self-efficacy and on their satisfaction with their jobs and profession. This report has also found that supporting teachers' professionalism is perhaps most important in contexts of high disadvantage, particularly socio-economic disadvantage. Given these findings, policy makers must commit to enhancing teacher professionalism through concrete and targeted policies. In some cases, these policies will need to be specific to the needs of the education system. In other cases, this report has found that there are a number of ways in which most education systems can further support teachers – including by requiring formal teacher education programmes that expose teachers to pedagogy and provide opportunities to practice teaching in order to enter the profession, as well as supporting induction and mentoring programmes.

POLICY RECOMMENDATIONS TO SUPPORT TEACHER PROFESSIONALISM

Other policy recommendations include supporting teachers in conducing classroom-based individual or collaborative research and encouraging their participation in networks of other teachers for information exchange. These policy interventions may be particularly beneficial in schools with high proportions of students who suffer from socio-economic disadvantage and in secondary schools. This report has shown that teacher professionalism matters and is an important investment for education systems. More research is still needed to understand how teacher policies to support professionalism interact with other policies to support teachers, for instance, policies for hiring practice or pay performance.

References

Akiba, M., G.K. LeTendre and J.P. Scribner (2007), "Teacher quality, opportunity gap, and national achievement in 46 countries", *Educational Researcher*, Vol. 36/7, pp. 369-387.

Borman, G.D. and N.M. Dowling (2008), "Teacher attrition and retention: A meta-analytic and narrative review of the research", *Review of Educational Research*, Vol. 78/3, pp. 367-409.

Darling-Hammond, L. (2006), "Securing the right to learn: Policy and practice for powerful teaching and learning", *Educational Researcher*, Vol. 35/7, pp. 13-24.

Feiman-Nemser, S. (2003), "What new teachers need to learn", *Educational Leadership*, Vol. 60/8, pp. 25-29.

Imazeki, J. and L. Goe (2009), "The distribution of highly qualified, experienced teachers: Challenges and opportunities", *TQ Research and Quality Brief*, August 2009, National Comprehensive Center for Teacher Quality, www.gtlcenter.org/sites/default/files/docs/August2009Brief.pdf.

Peske, H.G. and K. Haycock (2006), "Teaching inequality: How poor and minority students are shortchanged on teacher quality," a report and recommendations by the Education Trust, http://edtrust.org/wp-content/uploads/2013/10/TQReportJune2006.pdf.

Watkins, P. (2005), "The principal's role in attracting, retaining, and developing new teachers: Three strategies for collaboration and support", *The Clearing House*, Vol. 79/2, pp. 83-87.

Annex A
TECHNICAL ANNEX

ANNEX A
TECHNICAL ANNEX

Approach to index construction

This technical annex outlines how the indices of professionalism are constructed, and contains additional information on their distribution. The approach to scale construction in this study differs from that used by the Teaching and Learning International Survey (TALIS) for complex scales, such as their scales for job satisfaction and teacher efficacy, which weigh factors differently based on their contribution to an underlying latent variable. In this report, additive scales are created based on implementation of best practices, rather than complex scales based on latent variables. Following recommendations of the *TALIS 2013 Technical Report* (OECD, 2014b), similar scales are created using confirmatory factor analysis and test for overall fit and scalar invariance. In most cases, the scales exhibit a relatively good fit overall cross-nationally, but are not scalar invariant across all countries. We also find that additive component scales are very highly correlated to factor scales (~0.90+), while also having the added advantages of comparability. As such, we made the decision to work with the additive composite indices because they are more intuitive, comparable and have better distributions for subsequent analyses.

Index construction methodology

Following the theoretical literature, we outlined the best practices and policies that are shown to support teacher professionalism. Within each of the three domains (i.e. knowledge, autonomy and peer networks), we identified the TALIS questions that align to best practices and recoded them as binary variables. We conduct the index construction by ISCED level to decrease the possibility that variations in professionalism practices differ by school level. Additive composite indices were then created based on the literature, scaled to zero to five for comparability.

Following the *TALIS 2013 Technical Report* (OECD 2014b), we also tested how additive indices align to scales created by using structural equation modelling that treats each domain as a latent concept, rather than a total of observed practices. To carry out the structural equation models, we drew a random subset of 100 observations (teachers in the case of knowledge and peer networks and principals in the case of autonomy) from each country. This weighs each country equally in the construction of the scale. We then used structural equation modelling to predict latent factor scales for each domain, and tested the scale's goodness of fit overall and across all countries. As discussed in the literature review, we find that the two approaches are highly correlated and opt for the additive index approach.

Knowledge domain

Drawing on the literature, we focus on ten variables related to the types of knowledge teachers need to have to be successful, outlined in Chapter 1. We recode the knowledge variables to binary variables when appropriate such that a 1 represents higher requirements for professional knowledge and more support for professional learning. Although the literature suggests that a graduate-level degree is important to a teacher's knowledge base, we found that the overwhelming majority of respondents in TALIS reported that a Bachelor's degree is their highest degree (~90%), which left little variation in the index. Instead, we prioritise the variable for participation in a teacher education programme, along with other supports for professionalism.

Removing the question on highest level of education, the knowledge domain includes the following ten variables:

Table A.1 **Knowledge domain variables**

Sub-domain	Variables	Recoding
Pre-service education requirements	11. Did you complete a teacher education programme?	0 – No 1 – Yes
	12a) Content of the subject I teach included [in formal education or training].	0 – No / some subjects 1 – Yes, all subjects
	12b) Pedagogy of the subject I teach included [in formal education or training].	0 – No / some subjects 1 – Yes, all subjects
	12c) Classroom practice in the subject I teach included [in formal education or training].	0 – No / some subjects 1 – Yes, all subjects
Support for in-service professional learning (for teachers who participated in professional development in the last 12 months)	23) For the professional development in which you participated in the last 12 months, how much did you personally have to pay for?	0 – Some or all 1 – None
	24a) For the professional development in which you participated in the last 12 months, did you receive scheduled time for activities that took place during regular working hours at the school?	0 – No 1 – Yes
	24b) For the professional development in which you participated in the last 12 months, did you receive a salary supplement for activities outside regular working hours?	0 – No 1 – Yes
	24c) For the professional development in which you participated in the last 12 months, did you receive non-monetary support for activities outside working hours?	0 – No 1 – Yes
	25d) Considering the professionnal development activities you took part in during the last 12 months, to what extent have they included an extended time-period (several occasions spread out over several weeks or months)	0 – None 1 – Some, most or all
Support for practitioner research	21h) In the past 12 months, did you participate in individual or collaborative research on a professional topic of interest.	0 – No 1 – Yes

Confirmatory factor analysis

To conduct the confirmatory factor analysis, in line with the methodology adopted by TALIS 2013, we first draw a random sample of 100 observations of teachers from each country, which weighs each country equally in the analysis. The Cronbach's alpha for all ten of the knowledge domain variables is lower than the acceptable threshold and the inter-item correlation is very low in all ISCED levels, which suggests that factor analysis may not be the best approach.

Table A.2 **Cronbach's alpha of knowledge domain items, by ISCED level**

ISCED level	Cronbach's alpha	Inter-item correlation
ISCED 1	0.494	0.0158
ISCED 2	0.490	0.016
ISCED 3	0.450	0.014

We then conduct a confirmatory factor analysis using structural equation commands to test the model fit of a scale developed from knowledge items. We examine three goodness of fit statistics – root mean squared error of approximation (RMSEA), comparative fit index (CFI) and standardised root mean squared residual (SRMR) – from the structural equation model, suggesting that a knowledge scale is a relatively good fit for a scale on the overall data.

Table A.3 **SEM goodness of fit indicators of knowledge scales**

Indicator	ISCED 1	ISCED 2	ISCED 3
RMSEA	0.050	0.065	0.069
CFI	0.932	0.904	0.872
SRMR	0.049	0.050	0.053

ANNEX A: TECHNICAL ANNEX

Additional analysis indicates that the factor loadings for the scale strongly emphasise formal education components (content, pedagogy and practice) over school-specific supports for ongoing professional development.

Additive index

We then create an additive index that weights all items equally and is scaled from zero to five. The additive scale has the advantage of being normally distributed and continuous.

Correlations between knowledge base scales

The scale is positively correlated with the other two scales; however, the correlation between the latent scales and additive indices is less than we would like – roughly 0.70. The relatively low correlation between the additive component and the latent variable approach comes from the differential weighting of factors in the construction of the scales. To disaggregate the pre-service and in-service professional development factors, we create two separate knowledge factors, one focusing on pre-service knowledge requirements and a second on in-school support for professional learning. The goodness of fit indicators suggest that this is generally a better fit for the data.

Table A.4 Goodness of fit indicators for a two-factor latent knowledge variable

Indicator	ISCED 1	ISCED 2	ISCED 3
RMSEA	0.029	0.043	0.055
CFI	0.978	0.959	0.921
SRMR	0.041	0.032	0.043

We then equally weigh each scale in the construction of a composite knowledge-base scale. This approach is more highly correlated with the additive composite scale, suggesting that a latent factor approach and additive composite index approach produce more similar indicators of professionalism when both pre-service and in-service professional learning are considered equally important to overall teacher professionalism. Because the theoretical literature on the topic consistently emphasises both pre- and in-service learning, we adopt the additive, composite approach that weighs both equally.

Table A.5 Correlations between knowledge domain scales and indices

	PCF	SEM – 1 latent	SEM – 2 latent
SEM – 1 latent variable	0.994		
SEM – 2 latent variables	0.943	0.937	
Additive composite	0.759	0.730	0.787

Autonomy domain

The variables on teachers' involvement in decision making are asked in only the principal questionnaire; to conduct the scale construction and analysis, we select a subsample of 100 principals from each country, as the questions in the autonomy scale are drawn from principal responses.

TECHNICAL ANNEX: ANNEX A

Table A.6 Autonomy domain variables

Domain	Question	Re-code
Autonomous decision making	Principal 18i) Do teachers have significant responsibility for choosing which learning materials are used?	0 – No 1 – Yes
	Principal 18j) Do teachers have significant responsibility for determining course content including (national/regional) curricula?	0 – No 1 – Yes
	Principal 18k) Do teachers have significant responsibility for deciding which courses are offered?	0 – No 1 – Yes
	Principal 18f) Do teachers have significant responsibility for establishing student disciplinary policies and procedures?	0 – No 1 – Yes
	Principal 18g) Do teachers have significant responsibility for establishing student assessment policies?	0 – No 1 – Yes

The Cronbach's alpha for these five items is quite high in all ISCED levels, roughly 0.75, which is above the conventional cut-off of 0.70.

Table A.7 Cronbach's alpha and inter-item correlation for autonomy

ISCED Level	Cronbach's alpha	Inter-item correlation
ISCED 1	0.79	0.09
ISCED 2	0.768	0.092
ISCED 3	0.797	0.102

Confirmatory factor analysis

Given the single factor score, we also conduct confirmatory factor analysis using structural equation modelling. The standardised coefficients are all very close to one another, ranging from roughly 0.50-0.70 – which suggests that, while some may be slightly more significant to autonomy, they may all also be equally weighted.

Table A.8 Goodness of fit indicators for autonomy scale, by ISCED level

Indicator	ISCED 1	ISCED 2	ISCED 3
RMSEA	0.127	0.167	0.151
CFI	0.946	0.887	0.923
SRMR	0.044	0.051	0.044

Additive composite index

Because the structural equation model suggests that all five components of the scale are likely to be equally weighted, there is support for constructing an additive index that takes each component or best practice as part of an additive, composite index.

Correlations between autonomy scales and additive index

Table A.9 Correlations between autonomy domain scales and indices

	PCF	SEM
SEM	0.980	
Component	0.999	0.976

The correlations are very high among all three approaches to measuring autonomy, which suggests that whether we use either a latent factor approach or a composite additive approach, the two are capturing the same phenomenon. We proceed with the creation of the additive scale due to its distributional benefits and ease of interpretation.

ANNEX A: TECHNICAL ANNEX

Peer networks

Based on the literature, the scale of peer networks draws on five practices: 1) induction; 2) mentoring; 3) peer feedback from direct observations; 4) existence of a personal professional development plan; and 5) participation in a professional learning community. The variables from TALIS are outlined below in Table A.10.

Table A.10 Variables in peer networks domain

Sub-domain	Question	Recoding
Induction	19a) I took part in an induction programme. (0/1)	0 – Did not take part in induction
		1 - Took part in induction
Mentoring[1]	20a) I presently have an assigned mentor to support me. (0/1)	0 – Responded no to all mentoring questions
	20b) I serve as an assigned mentor for one or more teachers. (0/1)	
	21i) During the last 12 months, did you participate in mentoring and/or peer observation and coaching as part of a formal school arrangement? (0/1)	1 – Responded yes to at least one mentoring question
	31h) A mentor is appointed to help the teacher improve his/her teaching.	0 – Disagree or strongly disagree 1 – Agree or strongly agree
Peer feedback[2]	28a) In this school, the school principal, members of the school management team, assigned teachers or other teachers provide feedback based on direct observations of your teaching.	0 – No 1 – Yes
Development plan	31d) How strongly do you agree or disagree with the following statements: a development or training plan is established for teachers to improve their work as a teacher.	0 – Disagree or strongly disagree 1 – Agree or strongly agree
Network of teachers	21g) In the last 12 months, did you participate in a network of teachers formed specifically for the professional development of teachers?	0 – No 1 – Yes

Notes:
1. The variable takes a value of 1 if there is an affirmative response to any of questions 20a, 20b or 21i, or a response of "agree" or "strongly agree" to question 31h. It is set to missing if responses to all three of 20a, 20b and 21i are missing, as we place emphasis on the teacher's experience with mentoring at their school.
2. This variable is set to missing if there are missing values for all of TT2g28A2 through TT2g28A5.

The Cronbach's alpha on the five factors is relatively low, ranging from 0.44 to .054 and the inter-item covariance is 0.03-0.04.

Table A.11 Cronbach's alpha for peer networks domain, by ISCED level

ISCED level	Cronbach's alpha	Inter-item correlation
ISCED 1	0.438	0.030
ISCED 2	0.498	0.038
ISCED 3	0.539	0.045

Conducting a principal components analysis, we find that the various elements do reflect one underlying concept of strong professional networks. Given the single underlying factor suggested by the principal components analysis, we conduct confirmatory factor analysis using structural equation modelling on the five items suggested by the literature, including induction. Additionally, standardised coefficients are also quite close to one another (ranging from roughly 0.3-0.4) – which suggests that, while some may be slightly more significant to high peer networks overall, the differences are not substantial.

Table A.12 Goodness of fit indicators for the peer networks scale

Indicator	ISCED 1	ISCED 2	ISCED 3
RMSEA	0.044	0.019	0.049
CFI	0.965	0.992	0.965
SRMR	0.025	0.011	0.024

TECHNICAL ANNEX: ANNEX A

As shown in Table A.12, the goodness of fit statistics for the peer networks scale are quite good for the index at each ISCED level.

Additive component analysis

Because the structural equation model suggests that all five components of the scale are not substantively different from one another, there is also strong rationale for creating a composite index that weighs all items equally. We proceed with the creation of the additive scale due to its distributional benefits and ease of interpretation, creating a scale that naturally ranges from zero to five.

Correlations between peer networks scales

Table A.13 Correlations between peer networks domain scales and indices

Peer networks	PCF	SEM
SEM	0.99	
Additive composite	0.94	0.95

The correlations between the three scales are all quite high for all three scales, which suggests that whether we use either a latent factor approach or the additive composite approach, the two are capturing the same phenomenon.

Descriptive analysis of additive indices

This section provides an overview of the additive composite indices of teacher professionalism domains used in the analysis. From the histogram plots, it is clear that each of the domains has quite a different distribution. The descriptives also suggest more emphasis generally on knowledge base, followed by high peer networks, with the least emphasis on teachers' decision-making autonomy.

■ Figure A.1 ■
Distribution of knowledge base scale

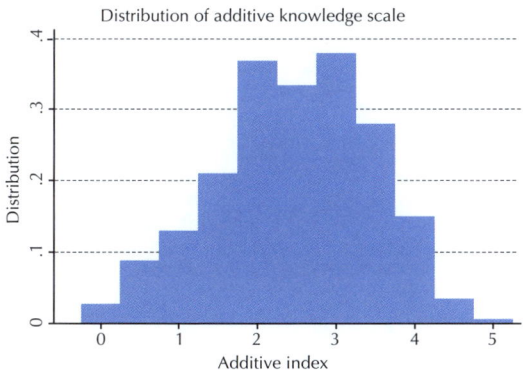

Source: OECD (2013), *Teaching and Learning International Survey (TALIS): 2013 complete database*, http://stats.oecd.org/index.aspx?datasetcode=talis_2013%20.

Table A.14 Distribution of knowledge base scale

ISCED level	Mean	Min	Max
ISCED 1	2.655	0	5
ISCED 2	2.657	0	5
ISCED 3	2.424	0	5

▪ Figure A.2 ▪
Distribution of autonomy scale

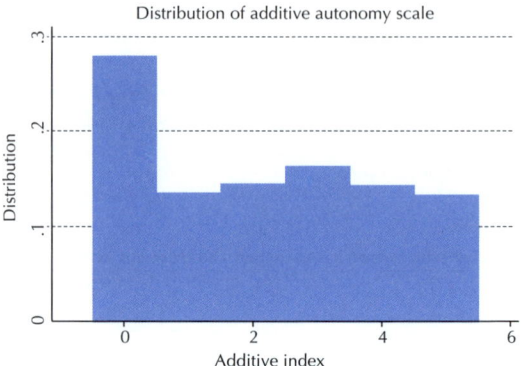

Source: OECD (2013), *Teaching and Learning International Survey (TALIS): 2013 complete database*, http://stats.oecd.org/index.aspx?datasetcode=talis_2013%20.

Table A.15   Distribution of autonomy domain scale

ISCED Level	Mean	Min	Max
ISCED 1	1.392	0	5
ISCED 2	1.978	0	5
ISCED 3	2.462	0	5

▪ Figure A.3 ▪
Distribution of peer networks scale

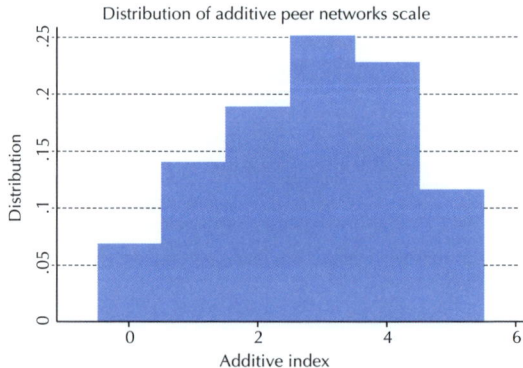

Source: OECD (2013), *Teaching and Learning International Survey (TALIS): 2013 complete database*, http://stats.oecd.org/index.aspx?datasetcode=talis_2013%20.

Table A.16   Distribution of peer networks domain scale

ISCED Level	Mean	Min	Max
ISCED 1	2.313	0	5
ISCED 2	2.772	0	5
ISCED 3	2.51	0	5

Treatment of missing values

Most of the variables in TALIS have some missing responses. Missing responses range from comprising 0% to up to 20% of all observations on some items. This is, in part, due to skip patterns in the TALIS questionnaire. Missing values need to be accounted for in scale construction wherever possible.

Observations with missing values are often not included in the construction of complex scales, which decreases the sample size and poses a risk of introducing selection bias, particularly if the missing pattern is not random. Missing values also pose a problem for additive scales, as a missing value mathematically does not contribute to the scale and, as a result, mathematically enters the scale equivalent to a response of zero, which is problematic for scale construction because we want to distinguish missing responses from negative responses.

To overcome the issue of missing data, we impute missing values with the school-mean for the questions where teachers are the respondents. This method is very effective at eliminating missing observations and has a minimal effect on overall distribution of responses to each question. The mean values hardly change, in the range of one-thousandth of a decimal point, while we are able to preserve many more observations. Understanding that mean imputation may underestimate variability in the values, which can lead to Type I error in interpretive analysis, we adjust the mean-imputed values by adding random variance equal to the amount of variability in the observed values prior to regression analysis.

With school-level variables, however, mean imputation was not possible, as schools were the primary sampling units. School-level variables were not imputed and missing values were list-wise deleted at the time of the analysis.

Regression analysis

Dependent variables

The four dependent variables were drawn from key items on TALIS. The unit of analysis for all dependent variables is the individual teacher.

Table A.17 **Teacher professionalism outcome variables**

Concept	Indicators
Status	I think that teaching is valued in society.
Satisfaction with work environment	I would recommend my school as a good place to work. I would like to change to another school if that were possible. I enjoy working at this school. All in all, I am satisfied with my job.
Satisfaction with profession	The advantages of being a teacher clearly outweigh the disadvantages. I regret that I decided to be a teacher. If I could decide again, I would still chose to work as a teacher. I wonder whether it would have been better to choose another profession.
Self-efficacy	To what extent do you believe that you can: Control disruptive behaviour in the classroom Make my expectations about student behaviour clear Get students to follow classroom rules Calm a student who is disruptive or noisy Craft good questions for my students Use a variety of assessment strategies Provide an alternative explanation or example when students are confused Implement alternative instructional strategies in my classroom Get students to believe they can do well in school work Help my students value learning Motivate students who show low interest in school work Help students think critically

For comparability, the dependent variables are all standardised, such that they have a mean of zero and a standard deviation.

Survey design and weights

The regression analyses in Chapter 3 use balanced repeated replicate survey weights, along with final teacher weights, using Stata 14 (StataCorp, 2015). The complex structure of the TALIS 2013 dataset necessitates specifying the survey characteristics of the dataset using the survey set command in Stata 14, which is done by using teacher weights, as well as the balanced repeated replicate weights (svy:). The primary sampling unit is the unique school identifier, with the brr option specified, using the 100 teacher replicate weights in TALIS (trwgt1-trwgt100). Fay's adjustment is set at 0.5. The svy prefix is used throughout the analysis, which ensures consistency in the application of final teacher weight and brr weights.

Regression models

The analyses of outcomes presented in Chapter 3 applies a two-level regression framework that accounts for the nested structure of the data, in which teachers are nested within schools, which are embedded within national education systems. For each of the dependent variables, the outcome is examined as a function of measures of teacher professionalism captured at the teacher level, with clustering at the school level. Across all model specifications, results showed that between-schools variation captures nearly all the variation between countries, making the clustering at the country level redundant.

The basic model predicts the outcome at the teacher level, as follows:

$$\text{Outcome}_{ij} = \beta_0 + \beta_1 P_{ij} + \beta_2 X_{ij} + \beta_3 W_j + e_{ij} + \varepsilon_j$$

Where, β_0 is the intercept for all teachers, P_{ij} is the relevant measure of teacher professionalism or its domain (measured at the teacher level for knowledge base and peer networks, but at the school level for autonomy), X_{ij} is a vector of teacher-level controls, and W_j is a vector of school-level controls. Some of the initial models also included a school mean on each of the professionalism measures, however, the final model places teacher professionalism at the teacher level to account for the individual-level variation. While in some model specifications school mean values for teacher professionalism were also tested as predictors of interest, results showed that including both teacher and school mean of teacher professionalism was not possible due to high multi-collinearity between these variables.

In addition to this basic model, the analysis also includes a number of control variables measured at the system level. This allows us to examine whether other system-level factors (i.e. male-female ratio, teacher pay, etc.) affect the relationship between teacher professionalism and outcomes. The set of models that tests these factors includes a vector of system-level covariates (Z_{jk}), including the male-to-female ratio, starting salaries and salary progression ladders, and contract type. These control variables are each included in the models individually, due to high correlations.

This extended model is structured as follows:

$$\text{Outcome}_{ij} = \beta_0 + \beta_1 P_{ij} + \beta_2 X_{ij} + \beta_3 W_j + \beta_4 Z_{jk} + e_{ij} + \varepsilon_j$$

The pooled multilevel model predicts each of the outcomes (status, job satisfaction, commitment and self-efficacy) as a function of individual and school variables, with system-level controls. As noted above, all analyses are done using the final teacher weight and brr weights.

Control variables

Our regression models control for important covariates. At the individual teacher level, controls include teacher gender and years of teaching experience. At the school level, controls include whether the school is public or private, the percentage of students who are socio-economically disadvantaged and an index of school climate, created by TALIS 2013, which captures how positive student-teacher relations are in the school.

Table A.18 Covariates in regression models

Level	Control variables	TALIS variable
Individual	Teacher gender	TT2G01
	Years teaching experience	TT2G05B
	Subject taught (coded as a series of four binary variables: 1) maths or science; 2) social sciences; 3) humanities or literature; 4) other)	TT2G15A-L
School	% of students in school from socio-economically disadvantaged homes	TC2G15C
	School climate – mutual respect (complex scale)	PSCMUTRS
	Public or private school	TC2G10
System	Relative salary compared to tertiary graduate in the labour force	OECD Education GPS (2014a)
	Test-based accountability system	Coded from Smith (forthcoming)

Table A.19 Regression models

Analysis type	Predictor variable	Regression model	Control variables
Overall	Teacher professionalism index	Pooled, two-level random intercepts model at the school level	Individual and school
Domain specific	Knowledge base scale	Pooled, two-level random intercepts model at the school level	Individual and school
	Autonomy scale	Pooled, two-level random intercepts model at the school level	Individual and school
	Peer networks scale	Pooled, two-level random intercepts model at the school level	Individual and school
Country-specific	Teacher professionalism index	Country-specific, two-level model with random intercepts at the school level	Individual and school
	Knowledge base scale	Country-specific, two-level model with random intercepts at the school level	Individual and school
	Autonomy scale	Country-specific, two-level model with random intercepts at the school level	Individual and school
	Peer networks scale	Country-specific, two-level model with random intercepts at the school level	
Alternate teacher professionalism checks	Teacher professionalism index	Pooled, three-level model with random intercepts for each school	Individual, school and additional teacher professionalism controls (salary and testing)

Robustness checks

A series of robustness checks were performed to ensure that the findings are robust to multiple model specifications and are not biased by the specifics of the sample, treatment of missing data or omitted variables.

To test whether the findings are biased by the cross-national sample, all cross-national models were also tested on random subsamples of 1 000 teachers drawn from each country. This ensured that all countries were equally represented in the cross-national study.

ANNEX A: TECHNICAL ANNEX

In addition to the TALIS data, we draw on system-level data to control for biases introduced by system-level factors. We draw on data from the 2014 Education GPS (OECD, 2014a), which is drawn from the OECD's annual *Education at a Glance* publication, and include indicators such as the male-female teacher ratio (an indicator of feminisation of the profession), various teacher salary measures, teacher-student ratios, teaching hours per year and the percentage of teachers by age bracket.

As shown in Table A.20, a series of system-level controls that may affect both teacher professionalism and outcomes of interest are also tested. Due to a high level of correlation between system-level variables, they are entered individually. The controls tested include feminisation of the profession, the salary ladder, economic development and the percent of teachers with a permanent contract. The results concerning the sign, significance and magnitude of the coefficients on teacher professionalism indices are robust to the inclusion of all the system-level controls tested.

Table A.20 **Additional controls**

Control variable	Source
Male-female teacher ratio	Education GPS (OECD, 2014a)
Salary ladder (ratio of salary at bottom to top of teacher pay scale)	Education GPS (OECD, 2014a)
Percent of teachers with permanent contract	Education GPS (OECD, 2014a)
GDP per capita	World Bank (2015)

Finally, to test whether the coding of missing values affects the findings, all models were run with controls for missing data and on smaller samples with no missing data.

References

OECD (2014a), *Education GPS*, http://gpseducation.oecd.org/

OECD (2014b), "TALIS 2013 Technical Report", OECD, Paris, http://www.oecd.org/edu/school/TALIS-technical-report-2013.pdf.

OECD (2013), *Teaching and Learning International Survey (TALIS): 2013 complete database*, http://stats.oecd.org/index.aspx?datasetcode=talis_2013%20.

Smith, W. (forthcoming), "Exploring educator based testing for accountability: national testing policies and student achievement", in T. Burns (ed.), *Modern Governance in Education: The Challenge of Complexity*, OECD Publishing, Paris.

StataCorp, (2015), "Stata Statistical Software: Release 14", StataCorp LP, College Station, TX.

World Bank (The) (2015), *World Development Indicators 2015*, http://data.worldbank.org/products/wdi.

Annex B

SYSTEM-SPECIFIC PROFILES OF TEACHER PROFESSIONALISM

A note regarding Israel
The statistical data for Israel are supplied by and under the responsibility of the relevant Israeli authorities. The use of such data by the OECD is without prejudice to the status of the Golan Heights, East Jerusalem and Israeli settlements in the West Bank under the terms of international law.

ANNEX B: SYSTEM-SPECIFIC PROFILES OF TEACHER PROFESSIONALISM

■ Figure B.1 ■
Profile of Abu Dhabi (United Arab Emirates)

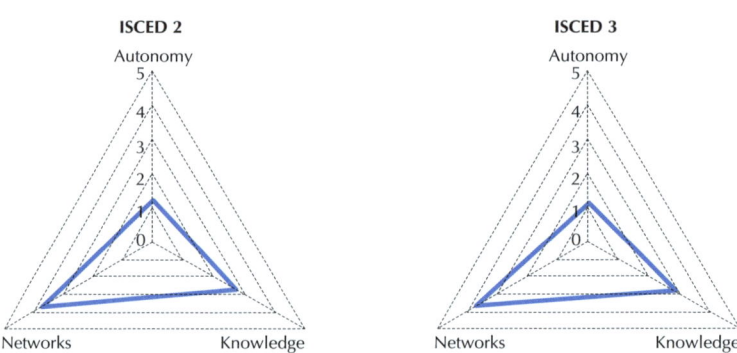

Table B.1 **Profile of Abu Dhabi (United Arab Emirates)**

Teacher professionalism best practice	ISCED 2	ISCED 3
Knowledge base scale	2.752	2.878
Autonomy scale	1.193	1.068
Peer networks scale	3.74	3.74
Knowledge base		
Participated in teacher education programme	83.30%	86.00%
Exposure to subject-specific content in teacher ed. programme	72.00%	77.10%
Exposure to pedagogy in teacher ed. programme	66.90%	73.70%
Exposure to practice in teacher ed. programme	70.70%	75.80%
Participates in individual or collaborative research	48.70%	50.20%
Receives financial support to pay for professional learning	64.20%	62.00%
Receives time release for professional learning	60.40%	66.60%
Receives salary supplement for professional learning	5.50%	6.30%
Receives non-monetary support for professional learning	14.50%	15.60%
Participates in extended-time professional learning activities	64.30%	62.40%
Autonomy		
Autonomy over content	23.20%	19.40%
Autonomy over course offerings	23.10%	19.50%
Autonomy over discipline practices	19.10%	20.10%
Autonomy over assessment	22.90%	19.10%
Autonomy over materials	31.60%	28.80%
Peer networks		
Participates in formal induction	70.90%	71.47%
Mentoring programme at school	88.33%	86.55%
Participates in network of teachers	44.40%	46.00%
Receives feedback from direct observations	93.78%	93.48%
Receives personalised professional development plan	77.40%	77.00%

SYSTEM-SPECIFIC PROFILES OF TEACHER PROFESSIONALISM: ANNEX B

▪ Figure B.2 ▪
Profile of Alberta (Canada)

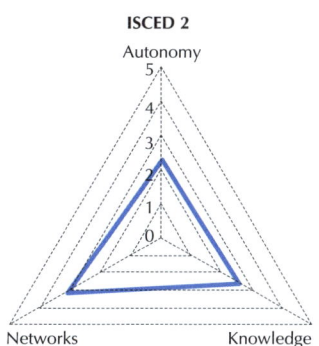

Table B.2   **Profile of Alberta (Canada)**

Teacher professionalism best practice	ISCED 2
Knowledge base scale	2.567
Autonomy scale	2.321
Peer networks scale	3.106
Knowledge base	
Participated in teacher education programme	98.27%
Exposure to subject-specific content in teacher ed. programme	44.23%
Exposure to pedagogy in teacher ed. programme	49.17%
Exposure to practice in teacher ed. programme	51.48%
Participates in individual or collaborative research	48.85%
Receives financial support to pay for professional learning	62.12%
Receives time release for professional learning	74.22%
Receives salary supplement for professional learning	8.09%
Receives non-monetary support for professional learning	16.88%
Participates in extended-time professional learning activities	60.44%
Autonomy	
Autonomy over content	30.52%
Autonomy over course offerings	49.10%
Autonomy over discipline practices	41.14%
Autonomy over assessment	43.34%
Autonomy over materials	69.71%
Peer networks	
Participates in formal induction	51.13%
Mentoring programme at school	62.64%
Participates in network of teachers	62.76%
Receives feedback from direct observations	82.29%
Receives personalised professional development plan	51.98%

ANNEX B: SYSTEM-SPECIFIC PROFILES OF TEACHER PROFESSIONALISM

▪ Figure B.3 ▪
Profile of Australia

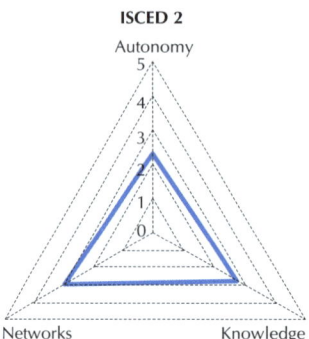
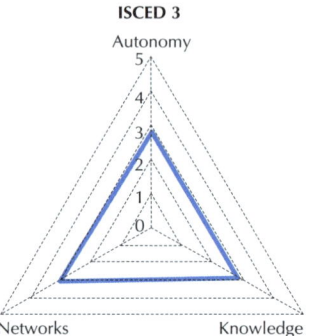

Table B.3 **Profile of Australia**

Teacher professionalism best practice	ISCED 2	ISCED 3
Knowledge base scale	2.772	2.852
Autonomy scale	2.241	2.780
Peer networks scale	2.967	3.046
Knowledge base		
Participated in teacher education programme	97.62%	97.11%
Exposure to subject-specific content in teacher ed. programme	62.19%	65.49%
Exposure to pedagogy in teacher ed. programme	63.98%	68.60%
Exposure to practice in teacher ed. programme	70.09%	72.57%
Participates in individual or collaborative research	37.23%	38.70%
Receives financial support to pay for professional learning	74.99%	73.37%
Receives time release for professional learning	79.37%	79.97%
Receives salary supplement for professional learning	3.95%	4.22%
Receives non-monetary support for professional learning	17.43%	20.48%
Participates in extended-time professional learning activities	47.62%	49.96%
Autonomy		
Autonomy over content	60.94%	60.75%
Autonomy over course offerings	27.08%	44.22%
Autonomy over discipline practices	33.15%	45.60%
Autonomy over assessment	35.33%	49.54%
Autonomy over materials	68.25%	78.57%
Peer networks		
Participates in formal induction	52.71%	53.25%
Mentoring programme at school	73.74%	76.22%
Participates in network of teachers	51.43%	57.15%
Receives feedback from direct observations	68.35%	67.15%
Receives personalised professional development plan	50.49%	50.85%

SYSTEM-SPECIFIC PROFILES OF TEACHER PROFESSIONALISM: ANNEX B

■ Figure B.4 ■
Profile of Brazil

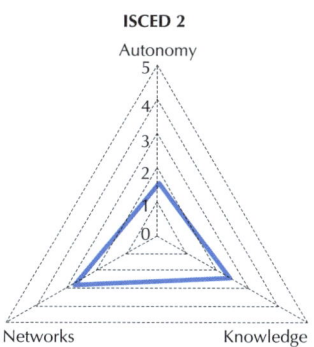

Table B.4 **Profile of Brazil**

Teacher professionalism best practice	ISCED 2
Knowledge base scale	2.374
Autonomy scale	1.564
Peer networks scale	2.773
Knowledge base	
Participated in teacher education programme	75.89%
Exposure to subject-specific content in teacher ed. programme	62.36%
Exposure to pedagogy in teacher ed. programme	50.80%
Exposure to practice in teacher ed. programme	61.25%
Participates in individual or collaborative research	46.70%
Receives financial support to pay for professional learning	58.15%
Receives time release for professional learning	43.38%
Receives salary supplement for professional learning	10.81%
Receives non-monetary support for professional learning	14.39%
Participates in extended-time professional learning activities	51.43%
Autonomy	
Autonomy over content	29.52%
Autonomy over course offerings	8.01%
Autonomy over discipline practices	31.49%
Autonomy over assessment	31.10%
Autonomy over materials	58.37%
Peer networks	
Participates in formal induction	32.22%
Mentoring programme at school	73.28%
Participates in network of teachers	25.81%
Receives feedback from direct observations	77.24%
Receives personalised professional development plan	69.10%

ANNEX B: SYSTEM-SPECIFIC PROFILES OF TEACHER PROFESSIONALISM

• Figure B.5 •
Profile of Bulgaria

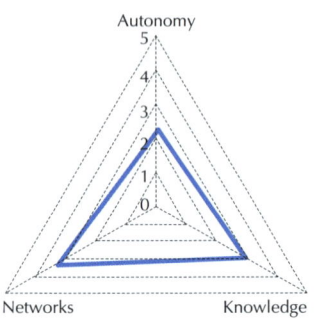

Table B.5 **Profile of Bulgaria**

Teacher professionalism best practice	ISCED 2
Knowledge base scale	2.904
Autonomy scale	2.266
Peer networks scale	3.315
Knowledge base	
Participated in teacher education programme	97.69%
Exposure to subject-specific content in teacher ed. programme	87.32%
Exposure to pedagogy in teacher ed. programme	86.81%
Exposure to practice in teacher ed. programme	84.45%
Participates in individual or collaborative research	22.60%
Receives financial support to pay for professional learning	84.63%
Receives time release for professional learning	50.57%
Receives salary supplement for professional learning	26.92%
Receives non-monetary support for professional learning	16.82%
Participates in extended-time professional learning activities	24.51%
Autonomy	
Autonomy over content	41.12%
Autonomy over course offerings	20.12%
Autonomy over discipline practices	37.05%
Autonomy over assessment	47.11%
Autonomy over materials	81.17%
Peer networks	
Participates in formal induction	68.82%
Mentoring programme at school	69.07%
Participates in network of teachers	21.55%
Receives feedback from direct observations	92.94%
Receives personalised professional development plan	79.11%

Figure B.6
Profile of Chile

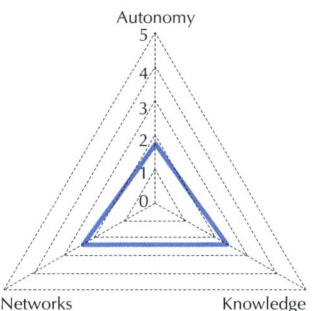

Table B.6 Profile of Chile

Teacher professionalism best practice	ISCED 2
Knowledge base scale	2.391
Autonomy scale	1.699
Peer networks scale	2.400
Knowledge base	
Participated in teacher education programme	85.75%
Exposure to subject-specific content in teacher ed. programme	60.90%
Exposure to pedagogy in teacher ed. programme	59.92%
Exposure to practice in teacher ed. programme	56.88%
Participates in individual or collaborative research	32.74%
Receives financial support to pay for professional learning	57.02%
Receives time release for professional learning	44.34%
Receives salary supplement for professional learning	12.71%
Receives non-monetary support for professional learning	18.01%
Participates in extended-time professional learning activities	53.94%
Autonomy	
Autonomy over content	31.25%
Autonomy over course offerings	17.09%
Autonomy over discipline practices	38.54%
Autonomy over assessment	32.75%
Autonomy over materials	50.62%
Peer networks	
Participates in formal induction	36.69%
Mentoring programme at school	52.97%
Participates in network of teachers	21.33%
Receives feedback from direct observations	70.88%
Receives personalised professional development plan	58.11%

ANNEX B: SYSTEM-SPECIFIC PROFILES OF TEACHER PROFESSIONALISM

▪ Figure B.7 ▪
Profile of Croatia

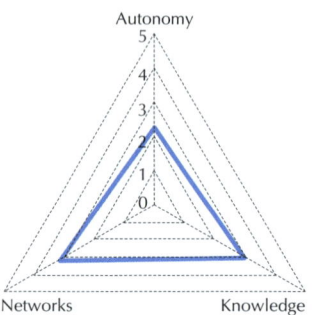

Table B.7   **Profile of Croatia**

Teacher professionalism best practice	ISCED 2
Knowledge base scale	3.025
Autonomy scale	2.288
Peer networks scale	3.176
Knowledge base	
Participated in teacher education programme	94.89%
Exposure to subject-specific content in teacher ed. programme	93.48%
Exposure to pedagogy in teacher ed. programme	88.34%
Exposure to practice in teacher ed. programme	85.91%
Participates in individual or collaborative research	34.95%
Receives financial support to pay for professional learning	73.60%
Receives time release for professional learning	73.05%
Receives salary supplement for professional learning	10.62%
Receives non-monetary support for professional learning	10.93%
Participates in extended-time professional learning activities	39.24%
Autonomy	
Autonomy over content	28.00%
Autonomy over course offerings	7.73%
Autonomy over discipline practices	60.63%
Autonomy over assessment	49.53%
Autonomy over materials	82.89%
Peer networks	
Participates in formal induction	68.04%
Mentoring programme at school	44.06%
Participates in network of teachers	62.62%
Receives feedback from direct observations	83.85%
Receives personalised professional development plan	59.01%

SYSTEM-SPECIFIC PROFILES OF TEACHER PROFESSIONALISM: ANNEX B

■ Figure B.8 ■
Profile of Cyprus[1]

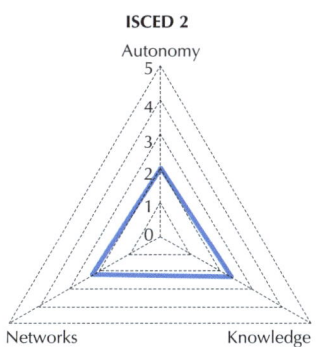

Table B.8   Profile of Cyprus[1]

Teacher professionalism best practice	ISCED 2
Knowledge base scale	2.487
Autonomy scale	1.906
Peer networks scale	2.613
Knowledge base	
Participated in teacher education programme	89.77%
Exposure to subject-specific content in teacher ed. programme	69.86%
Exposure to pedagogy in teacher ed. programme	61.76%
Exposure to practice in teacher ed. programme	56.18%
Participates in individual or collaborative research	24.54%
Receives financial support to pay for professional learning	81.58%
Receives time release for professional learning	58.02%
Receives salary supplement for professional learning	2.31%
Receives non-monetary support for professional learning	13.78%
Participates in extended-time professional learning activities	39.63%
Autonomy	
Autonomy over content	28.12%
Autonomy over course offerings	12.79%
Autonomy over discipline practices	43.30%
Autonomy over assessment	58.58%
Autonomy over materials	49.44%
Peer networks	
Participates in formal induction	50.90%
Mentoring programme at school	64.34%
Participates in network of teachers	24.70%
Receives feedback from direct observations	56.84%
Receives personalised professional development plan	64.49%

1. Note by Turkey: The information in this document with reference to "Cyprus" relates to the southern part of the Island. There is no single authority representing both Turkish and Greek Cypriot people on the Island. Turkey recognises the Turkish Republic of Northern Cyprus (TRNC). Until a lasting and equitable solution is found within the context of the United Nations, Turkey shall preserve its position concerning the "Cyprus issue".
Note by all the European Union Member States of the OECD and the European Union: The Republic of Cyprus is recognised by all members of the United Nations with the exception of Turkey. The information in this document relates to the area under the effective control of the Government of the Republic of Cyprus.

ANNEX B: SYSTEM-SPECIFIC PROFILES OF TEACHER PROFESSIONALISM

• Figure B.9 •
Profile of the Czech Republic

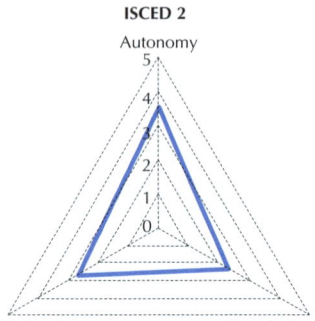

Table B.9   **Profile of the Czech Republic**

Teacher professionalism best practice	ISCED 2
Knowledge base scale	2.329
Autonomy scale	3.536
Peer networks scale	2.700
Knowledge base	
Participated in teacher education programme	76.68%
Exposure to subject-specific content in teacher ed. programme	57.18%
Exposure to pedagogy in teacher ed. programme	55.37%
Exposure to practice in teacher ed. programme	51.79%
Participates in individual or collaborative research	15.87%
Receives financial support to pay for professional learning	76.80%
Receives time release for professional learning	60.16%
Receives salary supplement for professional learning	14.21%
Receives non-monetary support for professional learning	14.91%
Participates in extended-time professional learning activities	42.84%
Autonomy	
Autonomy over content	75.23%
Autonomy over course offerings	51.97%
Autonomy over discipline practices	72.49%
Autonomy over assessment	66.96%
Autonomy over materials	86.98%
Peer networks	
Participates in formal induction	45.16%
Mentoring programme at school	56.67%
Participates in network of teachers	17.47%
Receives feedback from direct observations	91.53%
Receives personalised professional development plan	59.15%

SYSTEM-SPECIFIC PROFILES OF TEACHER PROFESSIONALISM: ANNEX B

• Figure B.10 •
Profile of Denmark

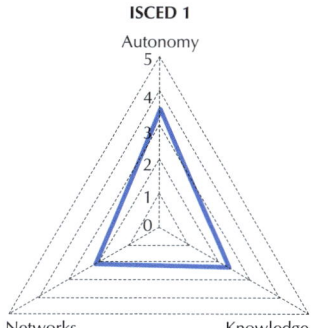
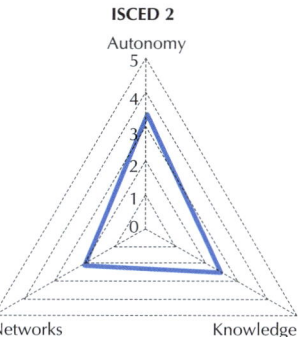
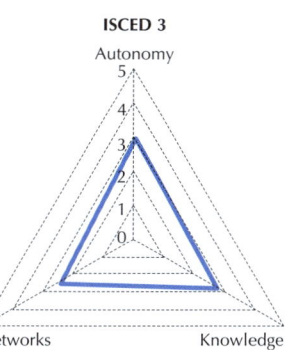

Table B.10 **Profile of Denmark**

Teacher professionalism best practice	ISCED 1	ISCED 2	ISCED 3
Knowledge base scale	2.334	2.458	2.728
Autonomy scale	3.457	3.359	2.963
Peer networks scale	2.149	2.057	2.464
Knowledge base			
Participated in teacher education programme	90.38%	93.54%	82.98%
Exposure to subject-specific content in teacher ed. programme	53.31%	60.02%	68.91%
Exposure to pedagogy in teacher ed. programme	52.69%	60.06%	66.99%
Exposure to practice in teacher ed. programme	43.99%	52.16%	66.61%
Participates in individual or collaborative research	18.52%	18.87%	28.54%
Receives financial support to pay for professional learning	84.92%	85.15%	85.44%
Receives time release for professional learning	64.22%	61.55%	76.73%
Receives salary supplement for professional learning	9.00%	11.97%	25.89%
Receives non-monetary support for professional learning	9.22%	10.45%	6.38%
Participates in extended-time professional learning activities	40.54%	38.78%	37.09%
Autonomy			
Autonomy over content	78.75%	76.87%	77.73%
Autonomy over course offerings	45.41%	47.29%	41.21%
Autonomy over discipline practices	62.39%	64.09%	42.77%
Autonomy over assessment	65.22%	52.31%	34.77%
Autonomy over materials	94.28%	95.29%	100.00%
Peer networks			
Participates in formal induction	28.43%	26.51%	44.93%
Mentoring programme at school	43.13%	45.07%	63.34%
Participates in network of teachers	41.47%	40.68%	40.90%
Receives feedback from direct observations	59.92%	52.98%	56.44%
Receives personalised professional development plan	41.93%	40.43%	40.81%

ANNEX B: SYSTEM-SPECIFIC PROFILES OF TEACHER PROFESSIONALISM

■ Figure B.11 ■
Profile of England (United Kingdom)

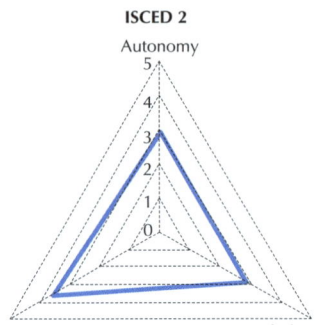

Table B.11 **Profile of England (United Kingdom)**

Teacher professionalism best practice	ISCED 2
Knowledge base scale	2.853
Autonomy scale	2.900
Peer networks scale	3.606
Knowledge base	
Participated in teacher education programme	91.90%
Exposure to subject-specific content in teacher ed. programme	71.92%
Exposure to pedagogy in teacher ed. programme	75.65%
Exposure to practice in teacher ed. programme	80.65%
Participates in individual or collaborative research	26.65%
Receives financial support to pay for professional learning	92.54%
Receives time release for professional learning	65.77%
Receives salary supplement for professional learning	4.02%
Receives non-monetary support for professional learning	9.02%
Participates in extended-time professional learning activities	52.57%
Autonomy	
Autonomy over content	79.27%
Autonomy over course offerings	59.70%
Autonomy over discipline practices	28.26%
Autonomy over assessment	36.11%
Autonomy over materials	88.58%
Peer networks	
Participates in formal induction	75.82%
Mentoring programme at school	87.23%
Participates in network of teachers	33.33%
Receives feedback from direct observations	98.60%
Receives personalised professional development plan	65.62%

SYSTEM-SPECIFIC PROFILES OF TEACHER PROFESSIONALISM: ANNEX B

■ Figure B.12 ■
Profile of Estonia

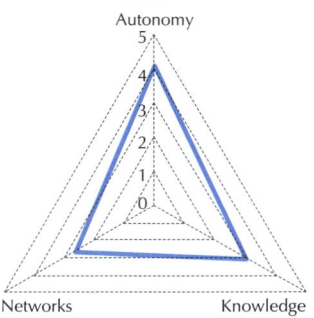

Table B.12   **Profile of Estonia**

Teacher professionalism best practice	ISCED 2
Knowledge base scale	3.053
Autonomy scale	4.094
Peer networks scale	2.637
Knowledge base	
Participated in teacher education programme	94.40%
Exposure to subject-specific content in teacher ed. programme	78.23%
Exposure to pedagogy in teacher ed. programme	78.23%
Exposure to practice in teacher ed. programme	69.00%
Participates in individual or collaborative research	34.01%
Receives financial support to pay for professional learning	69.13%
Receives time release for professional learning	81.87%
Receives salary supplement for professional learning	14.36%
Receives non-monetary support for professional learning	27.09%
Participates in extended-time professional learning activities	64.23%
Autonomy	
Autonomy over content	88.01%
Autonomy over course offerings	68.01%
Autonomy over discipline practices	78.38%
Autonomy over assessment	84.87%
Autonomy over materials	90.98%
Peer networks	
Participates in formal induction	19.45%
Mentoring programme at school	49.81%
Participates in network of teachers	51.28%
Receives feedback from direct observations	85.73%
Receives personalised professional development plan	57.46%

ANNEX B: SYSTEM-SPECIFIC PROFILES OF TEACHER PROFESSIONALISM

• Figure B.13 •
Profile of Finland

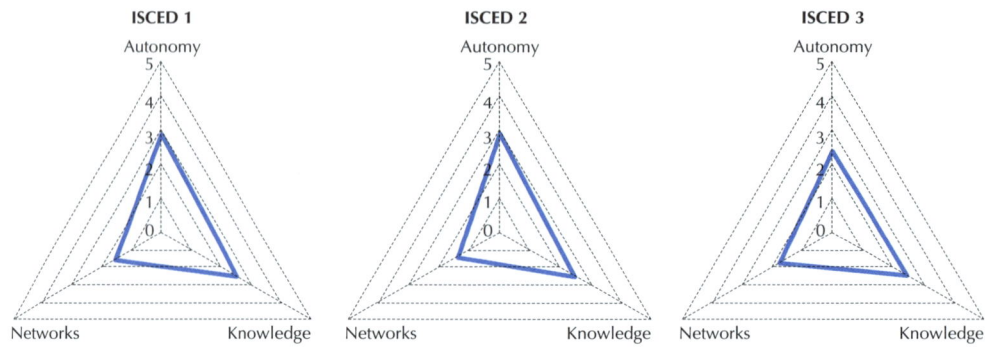

Table B.13 **Profile of Finland**

Teacher professionalism best practice	ISCED 1	ISCED 2	ISCED 3
Knowledge base scale	2.535	2.493	2.479
Autonomy scale	2.855	2.911	2.386
Peer networks scale	1.587	1.381	1.760
Knowledge base			
Participated in teacher education programme	91.98%	92.46%	90.81%
Exposure to subject-specific content in teacher ed. programme	78.69%	77.06%	64.09%
Exposure to pedagogy in teacher ed. programme	79.14%	75.12%	62.29%
Exposure to practice in teacher ed. programme	63.45%	69.16%	58.91%
Participates in individual or collaborative research	8.31%	7.59%	14.57%
Receives financial support to pay for professional learning	78.40%	72.17%	66.43%
Receives time release for professional learning	49.16%	50.82%	68.33%
Receives salary supplement for professional learning	5.20%	5.34%	9.10%
Receives non-monetary support for professional learning	13.25%	12.96%	14.33%
Participates in extended-time professional learning activities	39.36%	35.93%	46.86%
Autonomy			
Autonomy over content	54.77%	65.19%	72.57%
Autonomy over course offerings	43.39%	56.63%	34.63%
Autonomy over discipline practices	56.92%	42.43%	17.63%
Autonomy over assessment	48.10%	42.17%	29.45%
Autonomy over materials	85.38%	86.30%	84.58%
Peer networks			
Participates in formal induction	15.96%	16.33%	25.07%
Mentoring programme at school	23.67%	20.95%	23.20%
Participates in network of teachers	20.03%	20.48%	35.24%
Receives feedback from direct observations	55.88%	41.86%	47.79%
Receives personalised professional development plan	43.16%	38.44%	44.67%

Figure B.14
Profile of Flanders (Belgium)

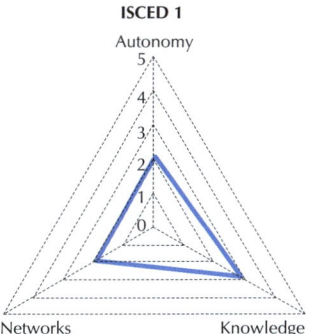
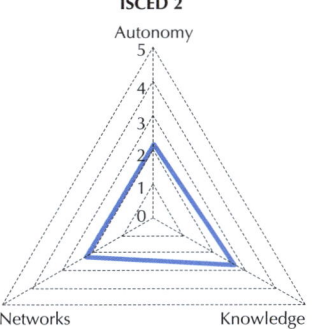

Table B.14 Profile of Flanders (Belgium)

Teacher professionalism best practice	ISCED 1	ISCED 2
Knowledge base scale	2.862	2.700
Autonomy scale	1.995	2.122
Peer networks scale	1.957	2.237
Knowledge base		
Participated in teacher education programme	99.31%	98.27%
Exposure to subject-specific content in teacher ed. programme	83.41%	76.51%
Exposure to pedagogy in teacher ed. programme	82.59%	80.44%
Exposure to practice in teacher ed. programme	81.14%	77.53%
Participates in individual or collaborative research	18.25%	18.81%
Receives financial support to pay for professional learning	88.78%	86.89%
Receives time release for professional learning	68.31%	61.81%
Receives salary supplement for professional learning	0.91%	0.67%
Receives non-monetary support for professional learning	2.35%	2.92%
Participates in extended-time professional learning activities	47.35%	36.14%
Autonomy		
Autonomy over content	27.07%	26.17%
Autonomy over course offerings	13.30%	18.22%
Autonomy over discipline practices	37.18%	28.40%
Autonomy over assessment	51.51%	47.30%
Autonomy over materials	73.37%	95.09%
Peer networks		
Participates in formal induction	18.82%	42.52%
Mentoring programme at school	46.48%	58.32%
Participates in network of teachers	22.12%	23.39%
Receives feedback from direct observations	77.18%	70.63%
Receives personalised professional development plan	31.12%	28.90%

ANNEX B: SYSTEM-SPECIFIC PROFILES OF TEACHER PROFESSIONALISM

Figure B.15
Profile of France

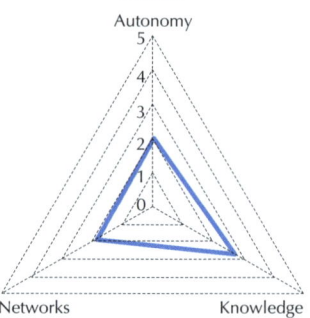

Table B.15 **Profile of France**

Teacher professionalism best practice	ISCED 2
Knowledge base scale	2.707
Autonomy scale	1.967
Peer networks scale	1.878
Knowledge base	
Participated in teacher education programme	90.08%
Exposure to subject-specific content in teacher ed. programme	85.00%
Exposure to pedagogy in teacher ed. programme	65.98%
Exposure to practice in teacher ed. programme	72.46%
Participates in individual or collaborative research	41.31%
Receives financial support to pay for professional learning	75.49%
Receives time release for professional learning	45.85%
Receives salary supplement for professional learning	4.74%
Receives non-monetary support for professional learning	16.59%
Participates in extended-time professional learning activities	43.90%
Autonomy	
Autonomy over content	18.92%
Autonomy over course offerings	16.23%
Autonomy over discipline practices	32.80%
Autonomy over assessment	50.97%
Autonomy over materials	79.10%
Peer networks	
Participates in formal induction	55.20%
Mentoring programme at school	45.73%
Participates in network of teachers	18.32%
Receives feedback from direct observations	26.21%
Receives personalised professional development plan	42.30%

Figure B.16
Profile of Georgia

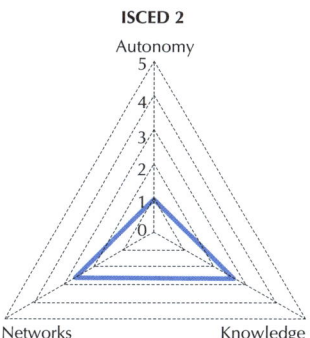

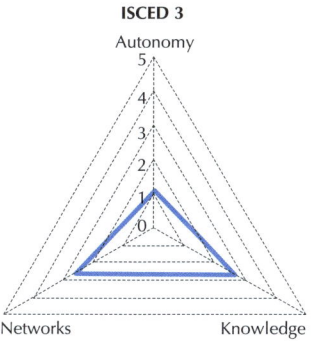

Table B.16 Profile of Georgia

Teacher professionalism best practice	ISCED 2	ISCED 3
Knowledge base scale	2.665	2.676
Autonomy scale	0.932	1.091
Peer networks scale	2.612	2.615
Knowledge base		
Participated in teacher education programme	90.87%	90.83%
Exposure to subject-specific content in teacher ed. programme	80.93%	81.24%
Exposure to pedagogy in teacher ed. programme	68.27%	70.27%
Exposure to practice in teacher ed. programme	67.63%	69.03%
Participates in individual or collaborative research	29.85%	28.91%
Receives financial support to pay for professional learning	86.50%	88.33%
Receives time release for professional learning	32.83%	30.26%
Receives salary supplement for professional learning	6.08%	5.77%
Receives non-monetary support for professional learning	9.21%	7.98%
Participates in extended-time professional learning activities	64.03%	65.81%
Autonomy		
Autonomy over content	11.29%	15.12%
Autonomy over course offerings	10.27%	12.53%
Autonomy over discipline practices	16.75%	13.24%
Autonomy over assessment	13.54%	15.24%
Autonomy over materials	41.36%	53.00%
Peer networks		
Participates in formal induction	13.44%	13.13%
Mentoring programme at school	61.55%	61.27%
Participates in network of teachers	29.01%	29.78%
Receives feedback from direct observations	62.45%	62.98%
Receives personalised professional development plan	94.73%	94.31%

ANNEX B: SYSTEM-SPECIFIC PROFILES OF TEACHER PROFESSIONALISM

■ Figure B.17 ■
Profile of Iceland

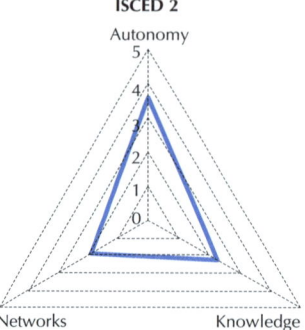
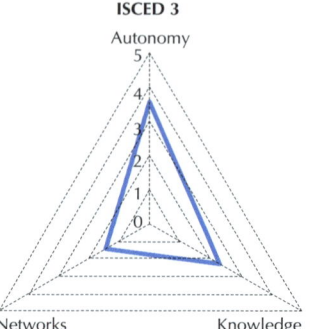

Table B.17 **Profile of Iceland**

Teacher professionalism best practice	ISCED 2	ISCED 3
Knowledge base scale	2.273	2.308
Autonomy scale	3.562	3.549
Peer networks scale	1.907	1.443
Knowledge base		
Participated in teacher education programme	92.44%	93.39%
Exposure to subject-specific content in teacher ed. programme	41.58%	53.28%
Exposure to pedagogy in teacher ed. programme	43.05%	47.78%
Exposure to practice in teacher ed. programme	42.15%	48.76%
Participates in individual or collaborative research	20.49%	28.09%
Receives financial support to pay for professional learning	61.47%	59.72%
Receives time release for professional learning	73.70%	54.15%
Receives salary supplement for professional learning	6.56%	13.91%
Receives non-monetary support for professional learning	14.77%	11.97%
Participates in extended-time professional learning activities	58.79%	50.59%
Autonomy		
Autonomy over content	61.08%	77.06%
Autonomy over course offerings	58.09%	64.08%
Autonomy over discipline practices	75.25%	55.90%
Autonomy over assessment	74.07%	63.34%
Autonomy over materials	94.24%	100.00%
Peer networks		
Participates in formal induction	29.43%	17.87%
Mentoring programme at school	39.23%	31.35%
Participates in network of teachers	56.06%	44.45%
Receives feedback from direct observations	30.57%	33.00%
Receives personalised professional development plan	35.51%	17.59%

SYSTEM-SPECIFIC PROFILES OF TEACHER PROFESSIONALISM: ANNEX B

• Figure B.18 •
Profile of Israel

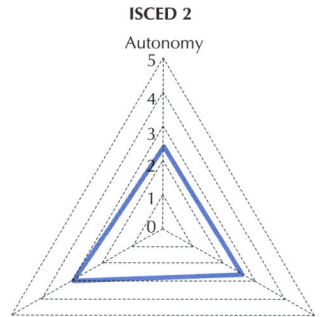

Table B.18   **Profile of Israel**

Teacher professionalism best practice	ISCED 2
Knowledge base scale	2.611
Autonomy scale	2.361
Peer networks scale	2.978
Knowledge base	
Participated in teacher education programme	93.63%
Exposure to subject-specific content in teacher ed. programme	77.09%
Exposure to pedagogy in teacher ed. programme	74.74%
Exposure to practice in teacher ed. programme	75.67%
Participates in individual or collaborative research	25.70%
Receives financial support to pay for professional learning	44.84%
Receives time release for professional learning	32.44%
Receives salary supplement for professional learning	12.70%
Receives non-monetary support for professional learning	12.38%
Participates in extended-time professional learning activities	74.85%
Autonomy	
Autonomy over content	52.75%
Autonomy over course offerings	30.32%
Autonomy over discipline practices	50.76%
Autonomy over assessment	44.13%
Autonomy over materials	61.34%
Peer networks	
Participates in formal induction	51.26%
Mentoring programme at school	71.30%
Participates in network of teachers	40.02%
Receives feedback from direct observations	72.22%
Receives personalised professional development plan	62.99%

ANNEX B: SYSTEM-SPECIFIC PROFILES OF TEACHER PROFESSIONALISM

■ Figure B.19 ■
Profile of Italy

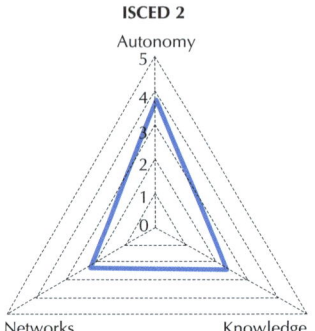
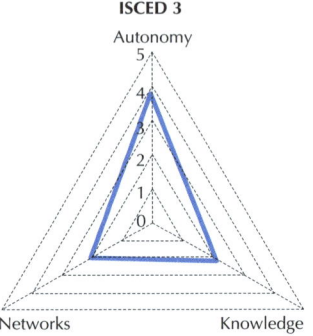

Table B.19 **Profile of Italy**

Teacher professionalism best practice	ISCED 2	ISCED 3
Knowledge base scale	2.326	2.179
Autonomy scale	3.726	3.709
Peer networks scale	2.229	1.995
Knowledge base		
Participated in teacher education programme	79.12%	71.44%
Exposure to subject-specific content in teacher ed. programme	69.39%	68.74%
Exposure to pedagogy in teacher ed. programme	62.61%	55.91%
Exposure to practice in teacher ed. programme	35.42%	27.45%
Participates in individual or collaborative research	45.56%	48.84%
Receives financial support to pay for professional learning	68.95%	59.02%
Receives time release for professional learning	26.34%	26.56%
Receives salary supplement for professional learning	5.55%	5.99%
Receives non-monetary support for professional learning	11.29%	13.43%
Participates in extended-time professional learning activities	60.94%	58.39%
Autonomy		
Autonomy over content	83.51%	84.36%
Autonomy over course offerings	87.70%	85.92%
Autonomy over discipline practices	43.06%	40.68%
Autonomy over assessment	72.81%	75.16%
Autonomy over materials	87.66%	86.58%
Peer networks		
Participates in formal induction	49.40%	46.51%
Mentoring programme at school	43.79%	37.55%
Participates in network of teachers	21.86%	18.95%
Receives feedback from direct observations	38.18%	35.18%
Receives personalised professional development plan	69.65%	61.33%

SYSTEM-SPECIFIC PROFILES OF TEACHER PROFESSIONALISM: ANNEX B

• Figure B.20 •
Profile of Japan

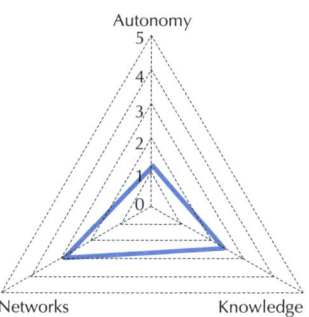

Table B.20 **Profile of Japan**

Teacher professionalism best practice	ISCED 2
Knowledge base scale	2.363
Autonomy scale	1.210
Peer networks scale	2.925
Knowledge base	
Participated in teacher education programme	87.85%
Exposure to subject-specific content in teacher ed. programme	71.18%
Exposure to pedagogy in teacher ed. programme	67.64%
Exposure to practice in teacher ed. programme	69.50%
Participates in individual or collaborative research	22.62%
Receives financial support to pay for professional learning	57.35%
Receives time release for professional learning	57.48%
Receives salary supplement for professional learning	6.51%
Receives non-monetary support for professional learning	11.03%
Participates in extended-time professional learning activities	21.47%
Autonomy	
Autonomy over content	18.65%
Autonomy over course offerings	15.55%
Autonomy over discipline practices	30.01%
Autonomy over assessment	30.81%
Autonomy over materials	25.94%
Peer networks	
Participates in formal induction	83.31%
Mentoring programme at school	58.08%
Participates in network of teachers	23.15%
Receives feedback from direct observations	82.57%
Receives personalised professional development plan	45.37%

ANNEX B: SYSTEM-SPECIFIC PROFILES OF TEACHER PROFESSIONALISM

■ Figure B.21 ■
Profile of Korea

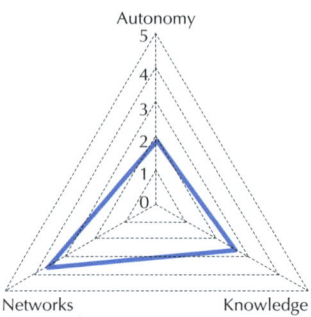

Table B.21   **Profile of Korea**

Teacher professionalism best practice	ISCED 2
Knowledge base scale	2.603
Autonomy scale	1.868
Peer networks scale	3.612
Knowledge base	
Participated in teacher education programme	96.14%
Exposure to subject-specific content in teacher ed. programme	90.36%
Exposure to pedagogy in teacher ed. programme	83.56%
Exposure to practice in teacher ed. programme	79.05%
Participates in individual or collaborative research	43.18%
Receives financial support to pay for professional learning	25.29%
Receives time release for professional learning	28.28%
Receives salary supplement for professional learning	23.01%
Receives non-monetary support for professional learning	10.57%
Participates in extended-time professional learning activities	41.21%
Autonomy	
Autonomy over content	38.26%
Autonomy over course offerings	54.62%
Autonomy over discipline practices	27.44%
Autonomy over assessment	17.24%
Autonomy over materials	50.33%
Peer networks	
Participates in formal induction	72.31%
Mentoring programme at school	77.06%
Participates in network of teachers	54.56%
Receives feedback from direct observations	87.90%
Receives personalised professional development plan	69.34%

SYSTEM-SPECIFIC PROFILES OF TEACHER PROFESSIONALISM: ANNEX B

• Figure B.22 •
Profile of Latvia

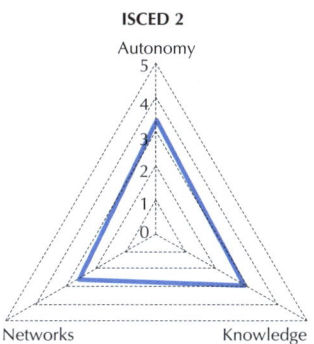

Table B.22   **Profile of Latvia**

Teacher professionalism best practice	ISCED 2
Knowledge base scale	2.937
Autonomy scale	3.288
Peer networks scale	2.597
Knowledge base	
Participated in teacher education programme	90.85%
Exposure to subject-specific content in teacher ed. programme	86.31%
Exposure to pedagogy in teacher ed. programme	85.13%
Exposure to practice in teacher ed. programme	80.34%
Participates in individual or collaborative research	28.61%
Receives financial support to pay for professional learning	71.10%
Receives time release for professional learning	63.73%
Receives salary supplement for professional learning	5.59%
Receives non-monetary support for professional learning	13.77%
Participates in extended-time professional learning activities	61.91%
Autonomy	
Autonomy over content	58.98%
Autonomy over course offerings	51.29%
Autonomy over discipline practices	67.10%
Autonomy over assessment	70.44%
Autonomy over materials	81.83%
Peer networks	
Participates in formal induction	35.87%
Mentoring programme at school	46.03%
Participates in network of teachers	36.59%
Receives feedback from direct observations	93.15%
Receives personalised professional development plan	48.03%

ANNEX B: SYSTEM-SPECIFIC PROFILES OF TEACHER PROFESSIONALISM

■ Figure B.23 ■
Profile of Malaysia

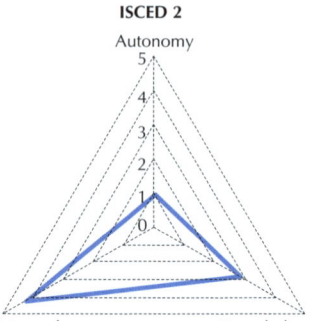

Table B.23 **Profile of Malaysia**

Teacher professionalism best practice	ISCED 2
Knowledge base scale	2.817
Autonomy scale	0.964
Peer networks scale	4.251
Knowledge base	
Participated in teacher education programme	92.12%
Exposure to subject-specific content in teacher ed. programme	76.96%
Exposure to pedagogy in teacher ed. programme	75.83%
Exposure to practice in teacher ed. programme	75.03%
Participates in individual or collaborative research	24.83%
Receives financial support to pay for professional learning	46.81%
Receives time release for professional learning	87.80%
Receives salary supplement for professional learning	14.02%
Receives non-monetary support for professional learning	19.09%
Participates in extended-time professional learning activities	50.88%
Autonomy	
Autonomy over content	5.58%
Autonomy over course offerings	17.64%
Autonomy over discipline practices	13.78%
Autonomy over assessment	7.28%
Autonomy over materials	52.16%
Peer networks	
Participates in formal induction	87.46%
Mentoring programme at school	90.66%
Participates in network of teachers	55.57%
Receives feedback from direct observations	95.54%
Receives personalised professional development plan	95.85%

Figure B.24
Profile of Mexico

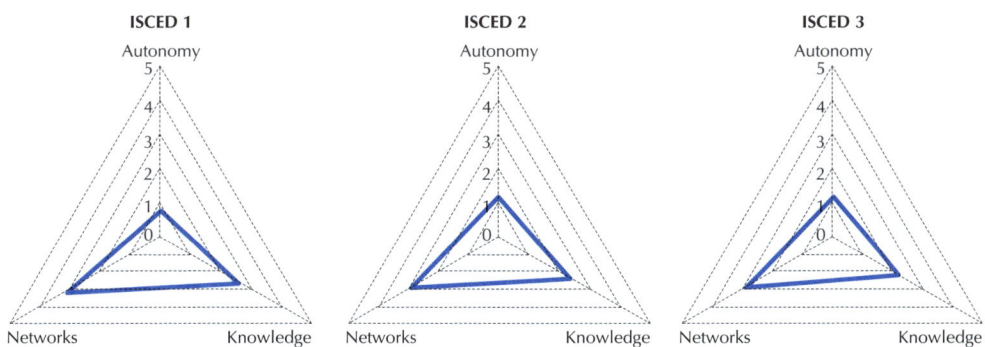

Table B.24 Profile of Mexico

Teacher professionalism best practice	ISCED 1	ISCED 2	ISCED 3
Knowledge base scale	2.581	2.400	2.190
Autonomy scale	0.815	1.180	1.186
Peer networks scale	3.110	2.925	2.899
Knowledge base			
Participated in teacher education programme	82.27%	61.50%	25.67%
Exposure to subject-specific content in teacher ed. programme	66.43%	67.32%	68.61%
Exposure to pedagogy in teacher ed. programme	63.68%	64.30%	61.03%
Exposure to practice in teacher ed. programme	65.15%	57.68%	53.48%
Participates in individual or collaborative research	50.95%	48.95%	48.13%
Receives financial support to pay for professional learning	67.26%	59.62%	59.10%
Receives time release for professional learning	44.28%	47.52%	44.66%
Receives salary supplement for professional learning	3.90%	3.64%	6.18%
Receives non-monetary support for professional learning	8.63%	11.69%	16.45%
Participates in extended-time professional learning activities	66.79%	57.98%	54.66%
Autonomy			
Autonomy over content	4.87%	8.27%	20.42%
Autonomy over course offerings	9.56%	10.79%	14.59%
Autonomy over discipline practices	17.49%	29.40%	14.02%
Autonomy over assessment	18.45%	19.43%	21.19%
Autonomy over materials	34.66%	52.50%	48.54%
Peer networks			
Participates in formal induction	59.41%	57.18%	64.16%
Mentoring programme at school	62.82%	57.44%	51.95%
Participates in network of teachers	38.05%	41.17%	36.30%
Receives feedback from direct observations	77.44%	73.00%	70.14%
Receives personalised professional development plan	74.05%	63.72%	67.40%

ANNEX B: SYSTEM-SPECIFIC PROFILES OF TEACHER PROFESSIONALISM

▪ Figure B.25 ▪
Profile of the Netherlands

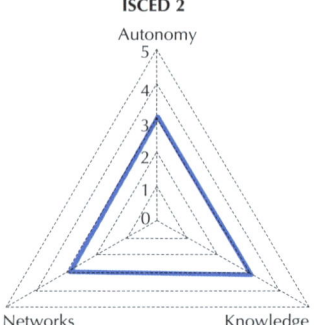

Table B.25 **Profile of the Netherlands**

Teacher professionalism best practice	ISCED 2
Knowledge base scale	3.085
Autonomy scale	3.038
Peer networks scale	2.908
Knowledge base	
Participated in teacher education programme	91.55%
Exposure to subject-specific content in teacher ed. programme	84.59%
Exposure to pedagogy in teacher ed. programme	86.55%
Exposure to practice in teacher ed. programme	82.43%
Participates in individual or collaborative research	38.32%
Receives financial support to pay for professional learning	77.05%
Receives time release for professional learning	69.89%
Receives salary supplement for professional learning	3.27%
Receives non-monetary support for professional learning	13.16%
Participates in extended-time professional learning activities	70.17%
Autonomy	
Autonomy over content	95.61%
Autonomy over course offerings	32.48%
Autonomy over discipline practices	25.72%
Autonomy over assessment	53.24%
Autonomy over materials	97.16%
Peer networks	
Participates in formal induction	45.62%
Mentoring programme at school	75.84%
Participates in network of teachers	30.36%
Receives feedback from direct observations	85.71%
Receives personalised professional development plan	53.28%

▪ Figure B.26 ▪
Profile of New Zealand

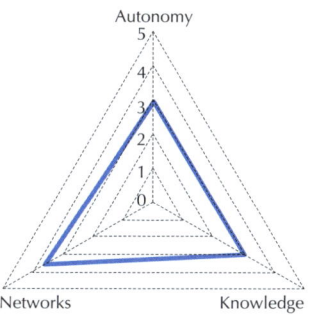

Table B.26 Profile of New Zealand

Teacher professionalism best practice	ISCED 2
Knowledge base scale	3.027
Autonomy scale	2.939
Peer networks scale	3.603
Knowledge base	
Participated in teacher education programme	99.14%
Exposure to subject-specific content in teacher ed. programme	72.64%
Exposure to pedagogy in teacher ed. programme	73.01%
Exposure to practice in teacher ed. programme	78.63%
Participates in individual or collaborative research	43.61%
Receives financial support to pay for professional learning	84.52%
Receives time release for professional learning	75.09%
Receives salary supplement for professional learning	4.68%
Receives non-monetary support for professional learning	15.63%
Participates in extended-time professional learning activities	58.52%
Autonomy	
Autonomy over content	80.66%
Autonomy over course offerings	57.91%
Autonomy over discipline practices	31.88%
Autonomy over assessment	38.17%
Autonomy over materials	85.48%
Peer networks	
Participates in formal induction	65.98%
Mentoring programme at school	85.04%
Participates in network of teachers	60.00%
Receives feedback from direct observations	93.67%
Receives personalised professional development plan	55.62%

ANNEX B: SYSTEM-SPECIFIC PROFILES OF TEACHER PROFESSIONALISM

■ Figure B.27 ■
Profile of Norway

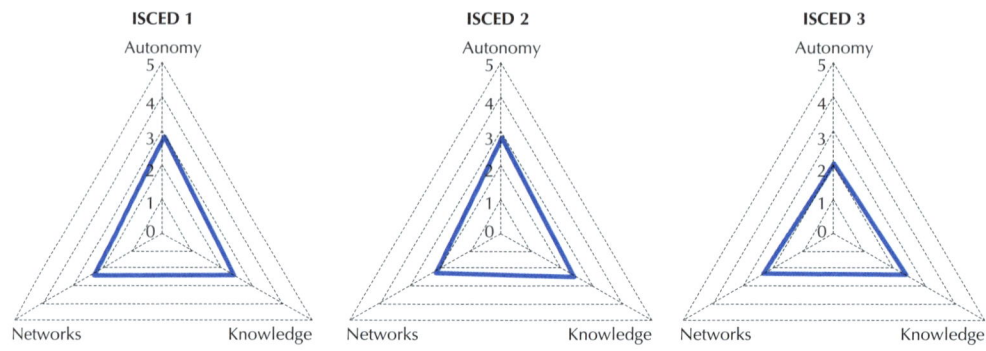

Table B.27   **Profile of Norway**

Teacher professionalism best practice	ISCED 1	ISCED 2	ISCED 3
Knowledge base scale	2.348	2.409	2.421
Autonomy scale	2.814	2.856	1.987
Peer networks scale	2.367	2.184	2.361
Knowledge base			
Participated in teacher education programme	84.51%	92.53%	88.09%
Exposure to subject-specific content in teacher ed. programme	42.35%	51.51%	58.49%
Exposure to pedagogy in teacher ed. programme	45.58%	50.64%	55.75%
Exposure to practice in teacher ed. programme	51.22%	50.78%	55.35%
Participates in individual or collaborative research	13.43%	15.07%	19.07%
Receives financial support to pay for professional learning	85.57%	81.19%	76.10%
Receives time release for professional learning	61.54%	59.71%	60.18%
Receives salary supplement for professional learning	6.89%	7.50%	7.70%
Receives non-monetary support for professional learning	21.46%	22.55%	22.13%
Participates in extended-time professional learning activities	58.87%	50.40%	41.44%
Autonomy			
Autonomy over content	77.32%	73.68%	56.64%
Autonomy over course offerings	11.06%	25.56%	17.36%
Autonomy over discipline practices	57.45%	59.60%	30.17%
Autonomy over assessment	57.72%	48.71%	18.43%
Autonomy over materials	80.56%	79.23%	76.30%
Peer networks			
Participates in formal induction	10.14%	10.36%	12.00%
Mentoring programme at school	46.55%	47.67%	52.12%
Participates in network of teachers	43.75%	37.79%	48.62%
Receives feedback from direct observations	76.72%	71.05%	69.31%
Receives personalised professional development plan	59.52%	51.57%	54.00%

SYSTEM-SPECIFIC PROFILES OF TEACHER PROFESSIONALISM: ANNEX B

• Figure B.28 •
Profile of Poland

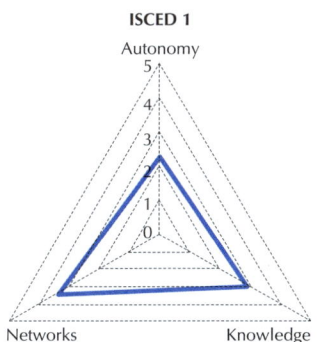
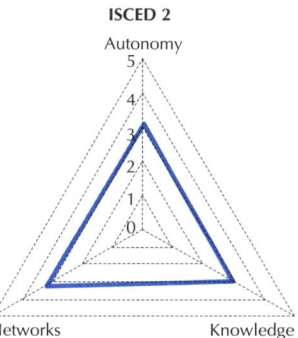
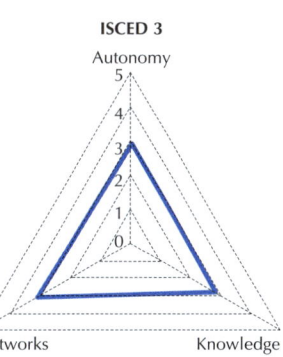

Table B.28 **Profile of Poland**

Teacher professionalism best practice	ISCED 1	ISCED 2	ISCED 3
Knowledge base scale	2.921	2.953	2.822
Autonomy scale	2.312	3.060	2.868
Peer networks scale	3.379	3.240	3.129
Knowledge base			
Participated in teacher education programme	99.48%	99.38%	97.65%
Exposure to subject-specific content in teacher ed. programme	93.49%	94.96%	88.85%
Exposure to pedagogy in teacher ed. programme	93.54%	94.74%	85.85%
Exposure to practice in teacher ed. programme	86.98%	88.10%	79.69%
Participates in individual or collaborative research	32.78%	37.80%	38.99%
Receives financial support to pay for professional learning	59.89%	60.72%	59.34%
Receives time release for professional learning	38.19%	39.12%	37.62%
Receives salary supplement for professional learning	5.46%	5.38%	5.14%
Receives non-monetary support for professional learning	10.03%	11.10%	9.24%
Participates in extended-time professional learning activities	64.45%	59.21%	61.97%
Autonomy			
Autonomy over content	55.53%	67.35%	66.48%
Autonomy over course offerings	14.45%	23.03%	38.67%
Autonomy over discipline practices	46.28%	61.94%	52.10%
Autonomy over assessment	53.05%	71.71%	57.82%
Autonomy over materials	62.23%	83.82%	72.08%
Peer networks			
Participates in formal induction	45.04%	37.85%	35.93%
Mentoring programme at school	67.73%	65.69%	64.19%
Participates in network of teachers	42.78%	40.58%	37.80%
Receives feedback from direct observations	97.21%	96.90%	94.92%
Receives personalised professional development plan	85.15%	83.03%	80.11%

ANNEX B: SYSTEM-SPECIFIC PROFILES OF TEACHER PROFESSIONALISM

■ Figure B.29 ■
Profile of Portugal

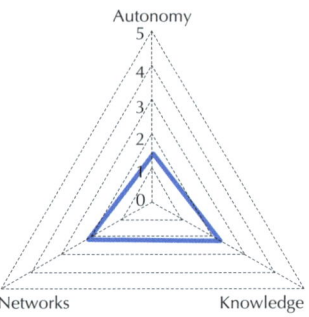

Table B.29   **Profile of Portugal**

Teacher professionalism best practice	ISCED 2
Knowledge base scale	2.224
Autonomy scale	1.386
Peer networks scale	2.149
Knowledge base	
Participated in teacher education programme	82.13%
Exposure to subject-specific content in teacher ed. programme	76.42%
Exposure to pedagogy in teacher ed. programme	74.24%
Exposure to practice in teacher ed. programme	70.94%
Participates in individual or collaborative research	36.51%
Receives financial support to pay for professional learning	42.89%
Receives time release for professional learning	15.00%
Receives salary supplement for professional learning	0.70%
Receives non-monetary support for professional learning	3.81%
Participates in extended-time professional learning activities	42.18%
Autonomy	
Autonomy over content	8.84%
Autonomy over course offerings	15.37%
Autonomy over discipline practices	26.06%
Autonomy over assessment	27.43%
Autonomy over materials	61.51%
Peer networks	
Participates in formal induction	35.51%
Mentoring programme at school	55.18%
Participates in network of teachers	19.12%
Receives feedback from direct observations	65.23%
Receives personalised professional development plan	39.82%

SYSTEM-SPECIFIC PROFILES OF TEACHER PROFESSIONALISM: ANNEX B

• Figure B.30 •
Profile of Romania

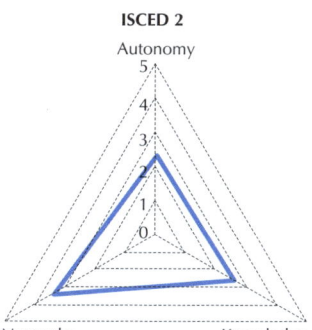

Table B.30   Profile of Romania

Teacher professionalism best practice	ISCED 2
Knowledge base scale	2.587
Autonomy scale	2.319
Peer networks scale	3.423
Knowledge base	
Participated in teacher education programme	97.16%
Exposure to subject-specific content in teacher ed. programme	84.16%
Exposure to pedagogy in teacher ed. programme	82.37%
Exposure to practice in teacher ed. programme	81.61%
Participates in individual or collaborative research	39.36%
Receives financial support to pay for professional learning	30.33%
Receives time release for professional learning	18.59%
Receives salary supplement for professional learning	1.44%
Receives non-monetary support for professional learning	7.57%
Participates in extended-time professional learning activities	74.87%
Autonomy	
Autonomy over content	31.75%
Autonomy over course offerings	42.95%
Autonomy over discipline practices	49.79%
Autonomy over assessment	35.22%
Autonomy over materials	72.66%
Peer networks	
Participates in formal induction	51.25%
Mentoring programme at school	79.31%
Participates in network of teachers	50.39%
Receives feedback from direct observations	92.38%
Receives personalised professional development plan	68.97%

ANNEX B: SYSTEM-SPECIFIC PROFILES OF TEACHER PROFESSIONALISM

• Figure B.31 •
Profile of the Russian Federation

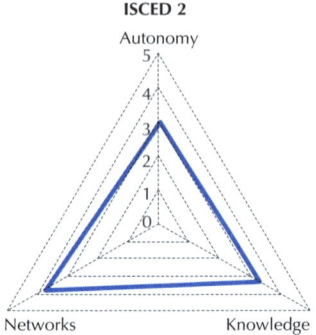

Table B.31   **Profile of the Russian Federation**

Teacher professionalism best practice	ISCED 2
Knowledge base scale	3.290
Autonomy scale	2.986
Peer networks scale	3.783
Knowledge base	
Participated in teacher education programme	94.58%
Exposure to subject-specific content in teacher ed. programme	85.66%
Exposure to pedagogy in teacher ed. programme	83.03%
Exposure to practice in teacher ed. programme	82.83%
Participates in individual or collaborative research	72.12%
Receives financial support to pay for professional learning	65.31%
Receives time release for professional learning	57.33%
Receives salary supplement for professional learning	34.39%
Receives non-monetary support for professional learning	24.07%
Participates in extended-time professional learning activities	58.76%
Autonomy	
Autonomy over content	57.58%
Autonomy over course offerings	70.06%
Autonomy over discipline practices	58.65%
Autonomy over assessment	47.84%
Autonomy over materials	64.71%
Peer networks	
Participates in formal induction	59.40%
Mentoring programme at school	77.90%
Participates in network of teachers	60.02%
Receives feedback from direct observations	90.20%
Receives personalised professional development plan	90.81%

SYSTEM-SPECIFIC PROFILES OF TEACHER PROFESSIONALISM: ANNEX B

▪ Figure B.32 ▪
Profile of Serbia

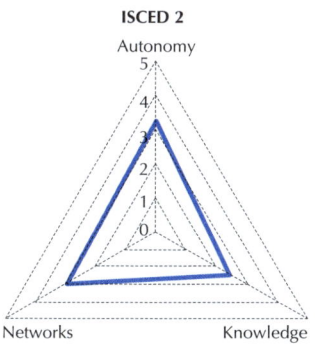

Table B.32   **Profile of Serbia**

Teacher professionalism best practice	ISCED 2
Knowledge base scale	2.452
Autonomy scale	3.199
Peer networks scale	2.970
Knowledge base	
Participated in teacher education programme	71.25%
Exposure to subject-specific content in teacher ed. programme	80.39%
Exposure to pedagogy in teacher ed. programme	74.91%
Exposure to practice in teacher ed. programme	65.00%
Participates in individual or collaborative research	31.91%
Receives financial support to pay for professional learning	53.26%
Receives time release for professional learning	46.99%
Receives salary supplement for professional learning	1.83%
Receives non-monetary support for professional learning	13.69%
Participates in extended-time professional learning activities	51.11%
Autonomy	
Autonomy over content	47.14%
Autonomy over course offerings	73.68%
Autonomy over discipline practices	55.45%
Autonomy over assessment	53.72%
Autonomy over materials	89.88%
Peer networks	
Participates in formal induction	59.05%
Mentoring programme at school	63.36%
Participates in network of teachers	33.03%
Receives feedback from direct observations	69.28%
Receives personalised professional development plan	72.31%

ANNEX B: SYSTEM-SPECIFIC PROFILES OF TEACHER PROFESSIONALISM

• Figure B.33 •
Profile of Shanghai (China)

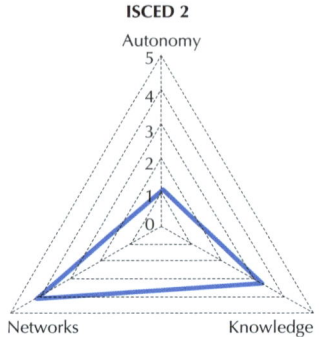

Table B.33 **Profile of Shanghai (China)**

Teacher professionalism best practice	ISCED 2
Knowledge base scale	3.277
Autonomy scale	1.091
Peer networks scale	4.161
Knowledge base	
Participated in teacher education programme	98.21%
Exposure to subject-specific content in teacher ed. programme	83.20%
Exposure to pedagogy in teacher ed. programme	78.44%
Exposure to practice in teacher ed. programme	77.29%
Participates in individual or collaborative research	54.36%
Receives financial support to pay for professional learning	80.42%
Receives time release for professional learning	87.67%
Receives salary supplement for professional learning	10.68%
Receives non-monetary support for professional learning	6.27%
Participates in extended-time professional learning activities	78.94%
Autonomy	
Autonomy over content	19.77%
Autonomy over course offerings	13.98%
Autonomy over discipline practices	23.58%
Autonomy over assessment	22.84%
Autonomy over materials	29.52%
Peer networks	
Participates in formal induction	89.76%
Mentoring programme at school	97.58%
Participates in network of teachers	55.17%
Receives feedback from direct observations	91.31%
Receives personalised professional development plan	82.22%

Figure B.34
Profile of Singapore

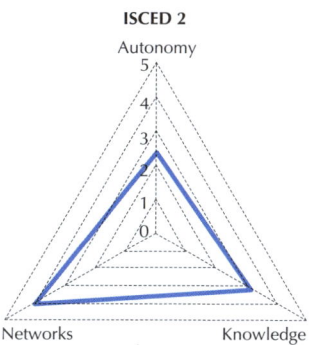
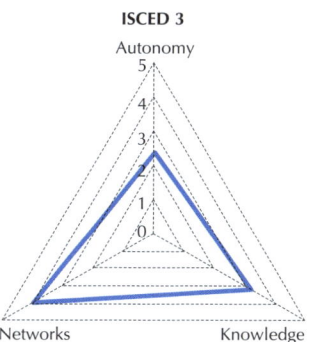

Table B.34 Profile of Singapore

Teacher professionalism best practice	ISCED 2	ISCED 3
Knowledge base scale	3.176	3.206
Autonomy scale	2.412	2.396
Peer networks scale	4.020	3.989
Knowledge base		
Participated in teacher education programme	99.10%	98.86%
Exposure to subject-specific content in teacher ed. programme	77.79%	78.61%
Exposure to pedagogy in teacher ed. programme	81.97%	84.53%
Exposure to practice in teacher ed. programme	82.56%	84.96%
Participates in individual or collaborative research	45.39%	45.14%
Receives financial support to pay for professional learning	89.72%	90.51%
Receives time release for professional learning	70.28%	70.93%
Receives salary supplement for professional learning	7.35%	6.60%
Receives non-monetary support for professional learning	16.61%	15.99%
Participates in extended-time professional learning activities	64.38%	64.99%
Autonomy		
Autonomy over content	57.66%	57.77%
Autonomy over course offerings	26.56%	25.29%
Autonomy over discipline practices	44.00%	42.99%
Autonomy over assessment	41.19%	40.96%
Autonomy over materials	72.09%	73.03%
Peer networks		
Participates in formal induction	80.03%	76.24%
Mentoring programme at school	93.57%	93.46%
Participates in network of teachers	52.71%	54.41%
Receives feedback from direct observations	96.16%	95.91%
Receives personalised professional development plan	79.57%	78.85%

ANNEX B: SYSTEM-SPECIFIC PROFILES OF TEACHER PROFESSIONALISM

▪ Figure B.35 ▪
Profile of the Slovak Republic

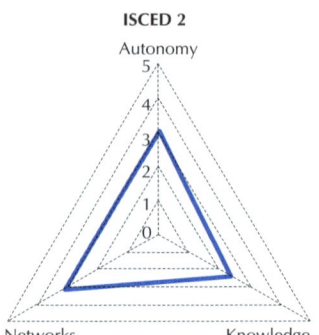

Table B.35   **Profile of the Slovak Republic**

Teacher professionalism best practice	ISCED 2
Knowledge base scale	2.362
Autonomy scale	3.036
Peer networks scale	3.126
Knowledge base	
Participated in teacher education programme	89.35%
Exposure to subject-specific content in teacher ed. programme	65.43%
Exposure to pedagogy in teacher ed. programme	63.18%
Exposure to practice in teacher ed. programme	54.22%
Participates in individual or collaborative research	11.20%
Receives financial support to pay for professional learning	54.88%
Receives time release for professional learning	54.00%
Receives salary supplement for professional learning	14.79%
Receives non-monetary support for professional learning	15.56%
Participates in extended-time professional learning activities	49.75%
Autonomy	
Autonomy over content	68.76%
Autonomy over course offerings	54.57%
Autonomy over discipline practices	51.74%
Autonomy over assessment	61.95%
Autonomy over materials	67.53%
Peer networks	
Participates in formal induction	60.44%
Mentoring programme at school	61.46%
Participates in network of teachers	34.29%
Receives feedback from direct observations	90.15%
Receives personalised professional development plan	66.31%

SYSTEM-SPECIFIC PROFILES OF TEACHER PROFESSIONALISM: ANNEX B

• Figure B.36 •
Profile of Spain

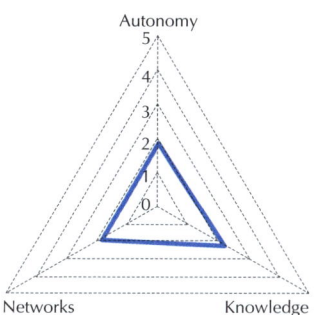

Table B.36   Profile of Spain

Teacher professionalism best practice	ISCED 2
Knowledge base scale	2.201
Autonomy scale	1.886
Peer networks scale	1.861
Knowledge base	
Participated in teacher education programme	97.46%
Exposure to subject-specific content in teacher ed. programme	64.57%
Exposure to pedagogy in teacher ed. programme	44.34%
Exposure to practice in teacher ed. programme	44.01%
Participates in individual or collaborative research	41.45%
Receives financial support to pay for professional learning	56.17%
Receives time release for professional learning	22.00%
Receives salary supplement for professional learning	2.33%
Receives non-monetary support for professional learning	6.34%
Participates in extended-time professional learning activities	61.55%
Autonomy	
Autonomy over content	27.24%
Autonomy over course offerings	12.00%
Autonomy over discipline practices	35.88%
Autonomy over assessment	26.60%
Autonomy over materials	87.48%
Peer networks	
Participates in formal induction	35.23%
Mentoring programme at school	35.28%
Participates in network of teachers	28.25%
Receives feedback from direct observations	36.97%
Receives personalised professional development plan	50.36%

ANNEX B: SYSTEM-SPECIFIC PROFILES OF TEACHER PROFESSIONALISM

■ Figure B.37 ■
Profile of Sweden

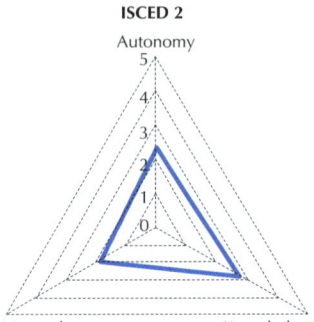

Table B.37 **Profile of Sweden**

Teacher professionalism best practice	ISCED 2
Knowledge base scale	2.747
Autonomy scale	2.371
Peer networks scale	1.889
Knowledge base	
Participated in teacher education programme	89.86%
Exposure to subject-specific content in teacher ed. programme	72.16%
Exposure to pedagogy in teacher ed. programme	67.75%
Exposure to practice in teacher ed. programme	68.57%
Participates in individual or collaborative research	9.69%
Receives financial support to pay for professional learning	85.91%
Receives time release for professional learning	63.64%
Receives salary supplement for professional learning	4.32%
Receives non-monetary support for professional learning	30.79%
Participates in extended-time professional learning activities	56.76%
Autonomy	
Autonomy over content	62.72%
Autonomy over course offerings	37.11%
Autonomy over discipline practices	15.43%
Autonomy over assessment	36.75%
Autonomy over materials	94.59%
Peer networks	
Participates in formal induction	10.79%
Mentoring programme at school	38.82%
Participates in network of teachers	41.61%
Receives feedback from direct observations	48.41%
Receives personalised professional development plan	49.27%

SYSTEM-SPECIFIC PROFILES OF TEACHER PROFESSIONALISM: ANNEX B

■ Figure B.38 ■
Profile of the United States

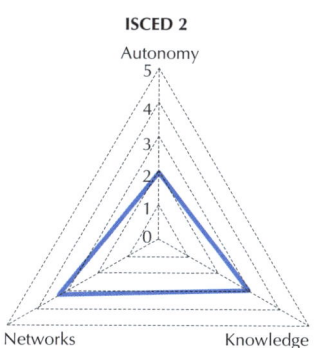

Table B.38 **Profile of the United States** [1]

Teacher professionalism best practice	ISCED 2
Knowledge base scale	3.004
Autonomy scale	1.929
Peer networks scale	3.280
Knowledge base	
Participated in teacher education programme	94.94%
Exposure to subject-specific content in teacher ed. programme	77.60%
Exposure to pedagogy in teacher ed. programme	74.09%
Exposure to practice in teacher ed. programme	74.77%
Participates in individual or collaborative research	41.13%
Receives financial support to pay for professional learning	73.91%
Receives time release for professional learning	65.39%
Receives salary supplement for professional learning	21.90%
Receives non-monetary support for professional learning	14.89%
Participates in extended-time professional learning activities	62.12%
Autonomy	
Autonomy over content	39.70%
Autonomy over course offerings	39.64%
Autonomy over discipline practices	26.85%
Autonomy over assessment	25.90%
Autonomy over materials	61.06%
Peer networks	
Participates in formal induction	59.35%
Mentoring programme at school	67.99%
Participates in network of teachers	47.39%
Receives feedback from direct observations	96.65%
Receives personalised professional development plan	56.60%

1. A country profile for the United States is presented to provide information about the levels of teachers' professionalism. However, the data should be interpreted carefully since the United States did not meet international participation rates.

Annex C

TEACHER PROFESSIONALISM SUPPORT GAPS BETWEEN HIGH AND LOW SECOND-LANGUAGE SCHOOLS

A note regarding Israel
The statistical data for Israel are supplied by and under the responsibility of the relevant Israeli authorities. The use of such data by the OECD is without prejudice to the status of the Golan Heights, East Jerusalem and Israeli settlements in the West Bank under the terms of international law.

ANNEX C

TEACHER PROFESSIONALISM SUPPORT GAPS BETWEEN HIGH AND LOW SECOND-LANGUAGE SCHOOLS

Table C.1 Gaps in teacher professionalism between high and low second-language schools

Country/economy	Knowledge	Autonomy	Networks
OVERALL MEAN	0.143	-0.089	0.143
Abu Dhabi (United Arab Emirates)	-0.095	1.25	-0.319
Alberta (Canada)	0.086	0.416	-0.261
Australia	0.233	-0.329	0.05
Brazil	-0.13	-1.01	0.38
Bulgaria	-0.161	0.508	0.27
Chile	-0.587	1.806	-0.21
Croatia	-0.034	-0.64	0.06
Cyprus[a, 1]	-0.157	1.258	0.62
Czech Republic	0.134	-2.427	0.76
Denmark	0.098	0.03	0.01
England (United Kingdom)	0.131	0.088	0.136
Estonia	0.134	-0.925	0.002
Finland	0.165	-1.107	1.014
Flanders (Belgium)	-0.021	0.157	0.075
France	0.054	0.041	0.127
Georgia	0.062	0.406	-0.04
Iceland	-0.027	-0.112	0.071
Israel	0.034	-0.026	-0.115
Italy	0.067	0.318	-0.313
Japan	0.102	NA	0.165
Korea[b]	NA	NA	NA
Latvia	0.389	1.148	0.332
Malaysia	-0.214	0.01	-0.145
Mexico	0.249	0.86	0.696
Netherlands	-0.03	-0.269	-0.13
New Zealand	0.012	-0.479	0.432
Norway	0.138	-0.952	0.301
Poland[a]	-0.252	NA	-0.446
Portugal	0.101	NA	-0.705
Romania	-0.028	-0.135	-0.129
Russian Federation	0.486	-1.139	0.298
Serbia	0.091	-1.228	0.333
Shanghai (China)	-0.406	NA	-0.321
Singapore	-0.028	0.028	-0.094
Slovak Republic	0.143	-0.089	0.143
Spain	-0.095	1.25	-0.319
Sweden	0.233	-0.329	0.05

Notes:

1. Note by Turkey: The information in this document with reference to "Cyprus" relates to the southern part of the Island. There is no single authority representing both Turkish and Greek Cypriot people on the Island. Turkey recognises the Turkish Republic of Northern Cyprus (TRNC). Until a lasting and equitable solution is found within the context of the United Nations, Turkey shall preserve its position concerning the "Cyprus issue".

Note by all the European Union Member States of the OECD and the European Union: The Republic of Cyprus is recognised by all members of the United Nations with the exception of Turkey. The information in this document relates to the area under the effective control of the Government of the Republic of Cyprus.

2. NA indicates adequate information is not present to calculate significant gap. [a] indicates gap was calculated using the middle category in place of high category. [b] indicates that 100% of schools in country fall in the low category. Significant differences are in dark grey or dark blue.

Annex D

TEACHER PROFESSIONALISM SUPPORT GAPS BETWEEN HIGH AND LOW SPECIAL-NEEDS SCHOOLS

A note regarding Israel
The statistical data for Israel are supplied by and under the responsibility of the relevant Israeli authorities. The use of such data by the OECD is without prejudice to the status of the Golan Heights, East Jerusalem and Israeli settlements in the West Bank under the terms of international law.

ANNEX D

TEACHER PROFESSIONALISM SUPPORT GAPS BETWEEN HIGH AND LOW SPECIAL-NEEDS SCHOOLS

Table D.1 Gaps in teacher professionalism between high and low special-needs schools

Country/economy	Knowledge	Autonomy	Networks
OVERALL MEAN	0.076	0.635	0.076
Abu Dhabi (United Arab Emirates) [a]	-0.046	0.254	-0.129
Alberta (Canada)	-0.001	1.347	-0.131
Australia	0.143	NA	0.25
Brazil	-0.143	-0.187	-0.23
Bulgaria [a]	-0.181	-0.561	-0.13
Chile	-0.05	0.798	0.11
Croatia [a]	0.042	-0.087	-0.06
Cyprus [a, 1]	0.081	-0.312	0.07
Czech Republic	0.186	-0.797	0.47
Denmark	-0.547	0.157	-0.4
England (United Kingdom)	0.061	1.538	0.116
Estonia	-0.149	0.043	-0.054
Finland	-0.418	NA	-0.082
Flanders (Belgium)	-0.107	0.426	-0.087
France	0.201	-0.604	0.38
Georgia [a]	-0.053	-0.523	0.617
Iceland	-0.085	-0.033	0.017
Israel	-0.1	0.143	-0.216
Italy	0.06	-0.202	-0.006
Japan [a]	-0.095	0.469	0.031
Korea	-0.283	1.12	-0.253
Latvia [a]	-0.082	0.794	-0.014
Malaysia	0.118	-0.382	-0.08
Mexico	0.114	-0.186	-0.013
Netherlands	-0.02	-0.893	-0.026
New Zealand	0.03	2.141	0.304
Norway	0.023	0.598	0.354
Poland	-0.028	0.213	-0.047
Portugal	0.1	NA	-0.687
Romania [a]	-0.265	1.54	-0.529
Russian Federation	-0.218	-0.8	-0.002
Serbia [a]	-0.026	0.141	-0.077
Shanghai (China) [a]	-0.011	-0.485	-0.299
Singapore [a]	0.119	0.26	0.128
Slovak Republic [a]	-0.063	-0.112	0.011
Spain	0.029	NA	-0.008
Sweden	-0.043	-0.099	0.148

Notes:

1. Note by Turkey: The information in this document with reference to "Cyprus" relates to the southern part of the Island. There is no single authority representing both Turkish and Greek Cypriot people on the Island. Turkey recognises the Turkish Republic of Northern Cyprus (TRNC). Until a lasting and equitable solution is found within the context of the United Nations, Turkey shall preserve its position concerning the "Cyprus issue".

Note by all the European Union Member States of the OECD and the European Union: The Republic of Cyprus is recognised by all members of the United Nations with the exception of Turkey. The information in this document relates to the area under the effective control of the Government of the Republic of Cyprus.

2. NA indicates adequate information is not present to calculate significant gap. [a] indicates gap was calculated using the middle category in place of high category. Significant differences are in dark grey or dark blue.

Annex E

TEACHER PROFESSIONALISM SUPPORT GAPS BETWEEN HIGH AND LOW SOCIO-ECONOMICALLY DISADVANTAGED SCHOOLS

A note regarding Israel
The statistical data for Israel are supplied by and under the responsibility of the relevant Israeli authorities. The use of such data by the OECD is without prejudice to the status of the Golan Heights, East Jerusalem and Israeli settlements in the West Bank under the terms of international law.

ANNEX E

TEACHER PROFESSIONALISM SUPPORT GAPS BETWEEN HIGH AND LOW SOCIO-ECONOMICALLY DISADVANTAGED SCHOOLS

Table E.1 Gaps in teacher professionalism between high and low socio-economically disadvantaged schools

Country/economy	Knowledge	Autonomy	Networks
OVERALL MEAN	-0.197	-0.539	-0.197
Abu Dhabi (United Arab Emirates)	-0.131	-0.809	-0.085
Alberta (Canada)	0.099	0.45	0.131
Australia	0.006	-0.65	0.16
Brazil	-0.069	0.365	-0.16
Bulgaria	-0.132	0.262	-0.01
Chile	-0.191	0.559	-0.06
Croatia	0.046	0.034	-0.04
Cyprus[a, 1]	0.221	-0.625	-0.32
Czech Republic	-0.149	-0.225	0.25
Denmark	-0.584	0.309	-0.178
England (United Kingdom)	0.197	0.116	0.399
Estonia	-0.3	-0.16	0.028
Finland	0.148	0.827	0.114
Flanders (Belgium)	-0.114	-0.205	0.068
France	0.286	-0.594	0.188
Georgia	-0.125	0.447	-0.028
Iceland	-0.037	0.588	0.473
Israel	0.007	-1.113	0.19
Italy	0.046	-0.417	0.022
Japan	0.066	-0.391	0.158
Korea	0.079	0.14	0.119
Latvia	-0.125	0.273	-0.181
Malaysia	-0.146	0.064	0.003
Mexico	-0.063	0.039	-0.202
Netherlands	-0.128	-0.102	-0.239
New Zealand	0.057	0.214	-0.002
Norway	0.188	-0.542	0.237
Poland	-0.053	-0.214	-0.059
Portugal	-0.118	-0.66	-0.277
Romania	-0.041	-0.119	-0.019
Russian Federation	-0.018	-0.124	0.038
Serbia	0.085	0.065	0.102
Shanghai (China)	-0.04	-0.496	-0.085
Singapore	0.22	-0.505	0.014
Slovak Republic	-0.11	0.036	0.044
Spain	0.018	-0.156	0.189
Sweden	-0.197	-0.539	-0.197

Notes:

1. Note by Turkey: The information in this document with reference to "Cyprus" relates to the southern part of the Island. There is no single authority representing both Turkish and Greek Cypriot people on the Island. Turkey recognises the Turkish Republic of Northern Cyprus (TRNC). Until a lasting and equitable solution is found within the context of the United Nations, Turkey shall preserve its position concerning the "Cyprus issue".

Note by all the European Union Member States of the OECD and the European Union: The Republic of Cyprus is recognised by all members of the United Nations with the exception of Turkey. The information in this document relates to the area under the effective control of the Government of the Republic of Cyprus.

2. Significant differences are in dark grey or dark blue.

Annex F

SYSTEM EQUITY PROFILES

A note regarding Israel
The statistical data for Israel are supplied by and under the responsibility of the relevant Israeli authorities. The use of such data by the OECD is without prejudice to the status of the Golan Heights, East Jerusalem and Israeli settlements in the West Bank under the terms of international law.

ANNEX F: SYSTEM EQUITY PROFILES

Figure F.1 **Equity profile of Abu Dhabi (United Arab Emirates)**

Equity gaps	Knowledge	Autonomy	Networks
Second language	-0.095	1.250	-0.319
Special needs	-0.046	0.254	-0.129
Economically disadvantaged	-0.131	-0.809	-0.085

Second language	# of Teachers	% of Teachers
Low concentration	1 172	61.20%
Medium concentration	18	0.94%
High concentration	725	37.86%

Special needs	# of Teachers	% of Teachers
Low concentration	1 798	93.89%
Medium concentration	117	6.11%

Economically disadvantaged	# of Teachers	% of Teachers
Low concentration	1 189	62.09%
Medium concentration	472	24.65%
High concentration	254	13.26%

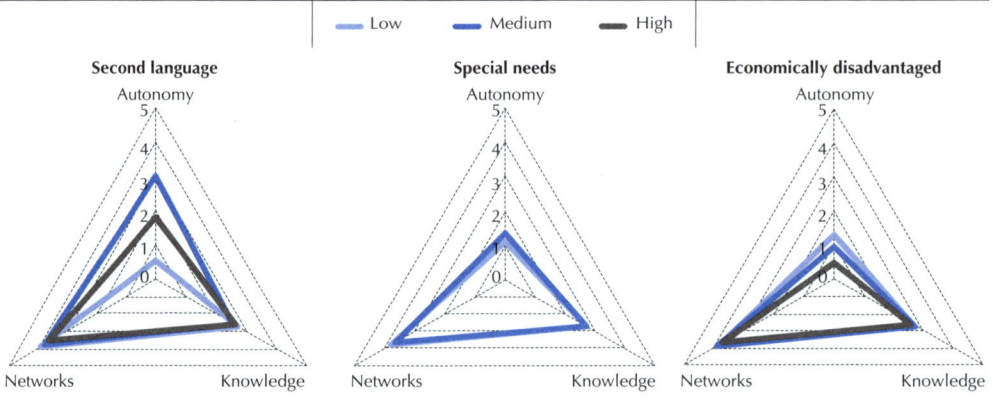

SYSTEM EQUITY PROFILES: ANNEX F

Figure F.2 Equity profile of Alberta (Canada)

Equity gaps	Knowledge	Autonomy	Networks
Second language	0.086	0.416	-0.261
Special needs	-0.001	1.347	-0.131
Economically disadvantaged	0.099	0.450	0.131
Most challenging*	0.040	0.507	-0.214

Note: * n = 202 (11.93% of teachers)

Second language	# of Teachers	% of Teachers
Low concentration	1 006	57.72%
Medium concentration	432	24.78%
High concentration	305	17.50%

Special needs	# of Teachers	% of Teachers
Low concentration	905	51.92%
Medium concentration	634	36.37%
High concentration	204	11.70%

Economically disadvantaged	# of Teachers	% of Teachers
Low concentration	829	48.00%
Medium concentration	540	31.27%
High concentration	358	20.73%

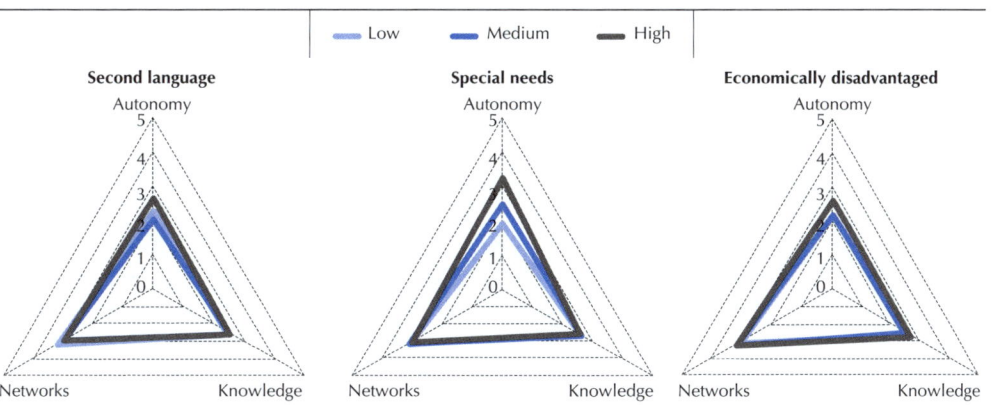

SUPPORTING TEACHER PROFESSIONALISM: INSIGHTS FROM TALIS 2013 © OECD 2016

ANNEX F: SYSTEM EQUITY PROFILES

Figure F.3 **Equity profile of Australia**

Equity gaps	Knowledge	Autonomy	Networks
Second language	0.233	-0.329	0.050
Special needs	0.143	NA	0.250
Economically disadvantaged	0.006	-0.650	0.160
Most challenging*	0.042	-0.961	0.220

Note: * n = 130 (7.05% of teachers)

Second language	# of Teachers	% of Teachers
Low concentration	1 244	67.50%
Medium concentration	329	17.85%
High concentration	270	14.65%

Special needs	# of Teachers	% of Teachers
Low concentration	1 415	76.78%
Medium concentration	409	22.19%
High concentration	19	1.03%

Economically disadvantaged	# of Teachers	% of Teachers
Low concentration	787	42.70%
Medium concentration	602	32.66%
High concentration	454	24.63%

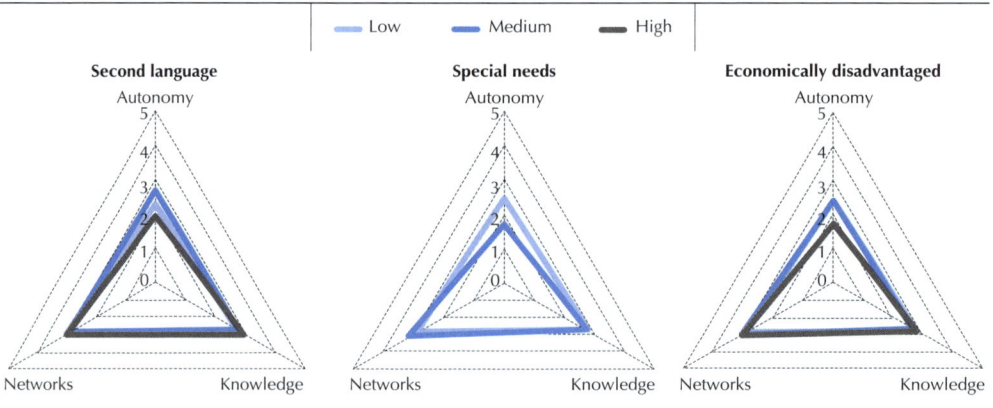

Figure F.4 Equity profile of Brazil

Equity gaps	Knowledge	Autonomy	Networks
Second language	-0.130	-1.010	0.380
Special needs	-0.143	-0.187	-0.230
Economically disadvantaged	-0.069	0.365	-0.160
Most challenging*	-0.048	3.423	-0.270

Note: * n = 15 (0.11% of teachers)

Second language	# of Teachers	% of Teachers
Low concentration	13 134	97.45%
Medium concentration	222	1.65%
High concentration	122	0.91%

Special needs	# of Teachers	% of Teachers
Low concentration	12 956	93.20%
Medium concentration	833	5.99%
High concentration	112	0.81%

Economically disadvantaged	# of Teachers	% of Teachers
Low concentration	3 830	27.68%
Medium concentration	3 618	26.15%
High concentration	6 388	46.17%

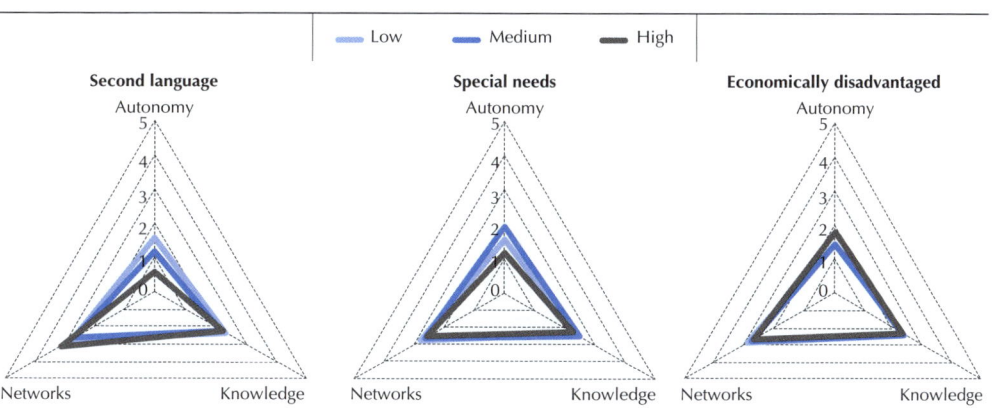

ANNEX F: SYSTEM EQUITY PROFILES

Figure F.5 Equity profile of Bulgaria

Equity gaps	Knowledge	Autonomy	Networks
Second language	-0.161	0.508	0.270
Special needs	-0.181	-0.561	-0.130
Economically disadvantaged	-0.132	0.262	-0.010
Most challenging*	-0.182	-0.561	-0.130

Note: * n = 23 (0.80% of teachers)

Second language	# of Teachers	% of Teachers
Low concentration	2 091	74.02%
Medium concentration	254	8.99%
High concentration	480	16.99%

Special needs	# of Teachers	% of Teachers
Low concentration	2 840	99.20%
Medium concentration	23	0.80%

Economically disadvantaged	# of Teachers	% of Teachers
Low concentration	1 404	49.04%
Medium concentration	924	32.27%
High concentration	535	18.69%

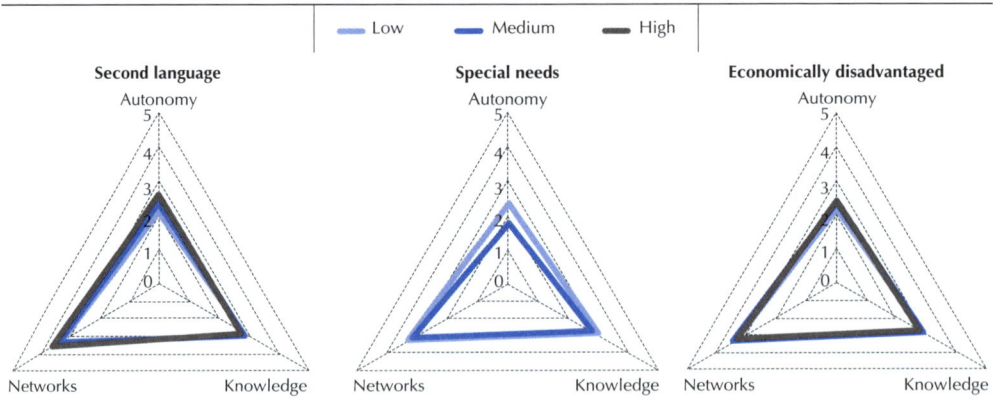

188 © OECD 2016 SUPPORTING TEACHER PROFESSIONALISM: INSIGHTS FROM TALIS 2013

SYSTEM EQUITY PROFILES: ANNEX F

Figure F.6 Equity profile of Chile

Equity gaps	Knowledge	Autonomy	Networks
Second language	-0.587	1.806	-0.210
Special needs	-0.050	0.798	0.110
Economically disadvantaged	-0.191	0.559	-0.060
Most challenging*	-0.527	1.852	-0.490

Note: * n = 34 (2.45% of teachers)

Second language	# of Teachers	% of Teachers
Low concentration	1 317	96.27%
Medium concentration	19	1.39%
High concentration	32	2.34%

Special needs	# of Teachers	% of Teachers
Low concentration	1 010	73.40%
Medium concentration	291	21.15%
High concentration	75	5.45%

Economically disadvantaged	# of Teachers	% of Teachers
Low concentration	404	29.15%
Medium concentration	245	17.68%
High concentration	737	53.17%

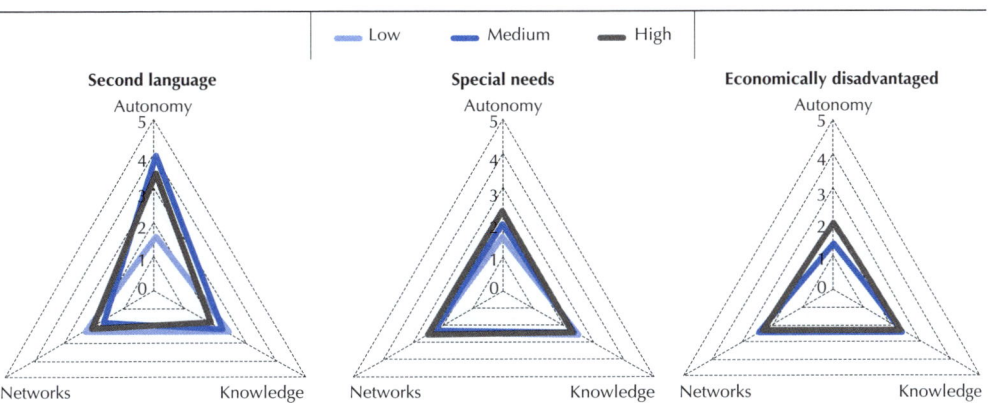

SUPPORTING TEACHER PROFESSIONALISM: INSIGHTS FROM TALIS 2013 © OECD 2016

ANNEX F: SYSTEM EQUITY PROFILES

Figure F.7 Equity profile of Croatia

Equity gaps	Knowledge	Autonomy	Networks
Second language	-0.034	-0.640	0.060
Special needs	0.042	-0.087	-0.060
Economically disadvantaged	0.046	0.034	-0.040
Most challenging*	0.382	NA	0.500

Note: * n = 111 (0.30% of teachers)

Second language	# of Teachers	% of Teachers
Low concentration	3 360	94.81%
Medium concentration	47	1.33%
High concentration	137	3.87%

Special needs	# of Teachers	% of Teachers
Low concentration	3 271	90.63%
Medium concentration	338	9.37%

Economically disadvantaged	# of Teachers	% of Teachers
Low concentration	1 879	52.35%
Medium concentration	1 423	39.65%
High concentration	287	8.00%

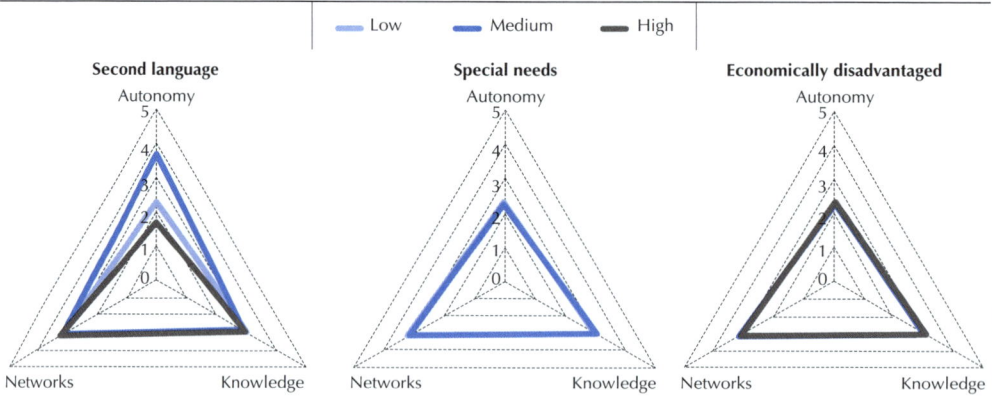

Figure F.8 Equity profile of Cyprus [1]

Equity gaps	Knowledge	Autonomy	Networks
Second language	-0.157	1.258	0.620
Special needs	0.081	-0.312	0.070
Economically disadvantaged	0.221	-0.625	-0.320
Most challenging*	0.347	0.066	-0.150

Note: * n = 20 (1.12% of teachers)

Second language	# of Teachers	% of Teachers
Low concentration	1 109	62.62%
Medium concentration	295	16.66%
High concentration	367	20.72%

Special needs	# of Teachers	% of Teachers
Low concentration	1 551	88.38%
Medium concentration	204	11.62%

Economically disadvantaged	# of Teachers	% of Teachers
Low concentration	868	48.46%
Medium concentration	771	43.05%
High concentration	152	8.49%

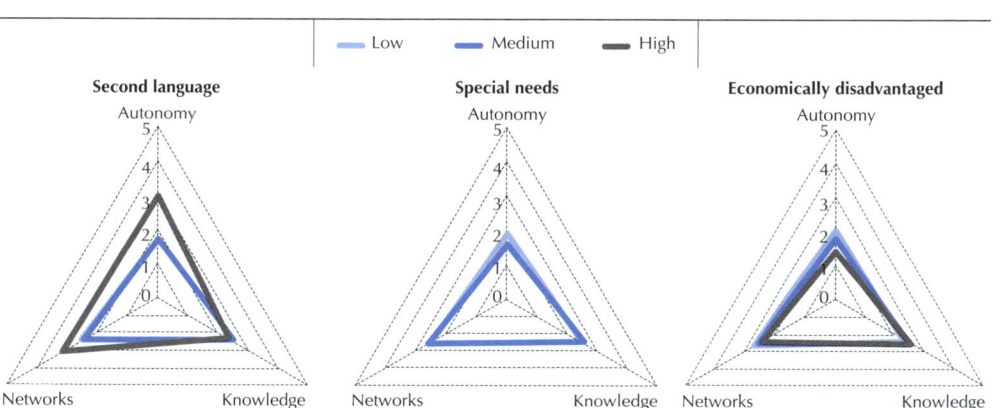

1. Note by Turkey: The information in this document with reference to "Cyprus" relates to the southern part of the Island. There is no single authority representing both Turkish and Greek Cypriot people on the Island. Turkey recognises the Turkish Republic of Northern Cyprus (TRNC). Until a lasting and equitable solution is found within the context of the United Nations, Turkey shall preserve its position concerning the "Cyprus issue".

Note by all the European Union Member States of the OECD and the European Union: The Republic of Cyprus is recognised by all members of the United Nations with the exception of Turkey. The information in this document relates to the area under the effective control of the Government of the Republic of Cyprus.

ANNEX F: SYSTEM EQUITY PROFILES

Figure F.9 **Equity profile of the Czech Republic**

Equity gaps	Knowledge	Autonomy	Networks
Second language	0.134	-2.427	0.760
Special needs	0.186	-0.797	0.470
Economically disadvantaged	-0.149	-0.225	0.250
Most challenging*	-0.119	0.066	0.460

Note: * n = 37 (1.15% of teachers)

Second language	# of Teachers	% of Teachers
Low concentration	3 122	96.99%
Medium concentration	76	2.36%
High concentration	21	0.65%

Special needs	# of Teachers	% of Teachers
Low concentration	2 599	80.74%
Medium concentration	524	16.28%
High concentration	96	2.98%

Economically disadvantaged	# of Teachers	% of Teachers
Low concentration	2 673	83.56%
Medium concentration	412	12.88%
High concentration	114	3.56%

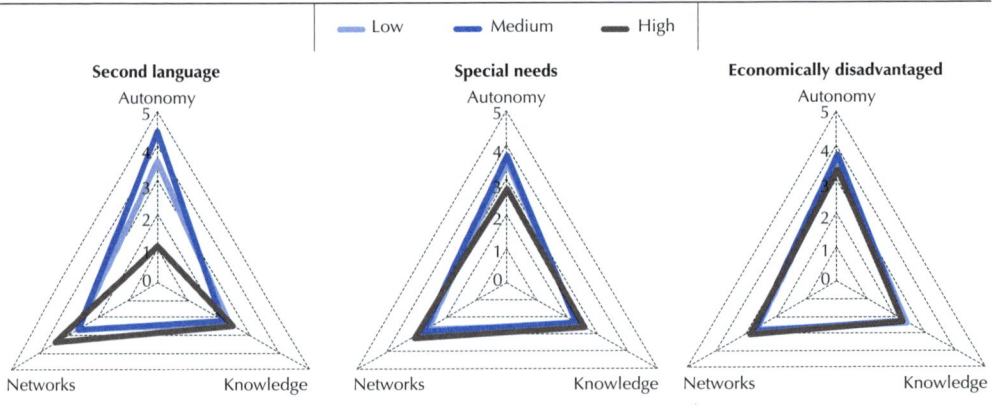

SYSTEM EQUITY PROFILES: ANNEX F

Figure F.10 Equity profile of Denmark

Equity gaps	Knowledge	Autonomy	Networks
Second language	0.098	0.030	0.010
Special needs	-0.547	0.157	-0.400
Economically disadvantaged	-0.584	0.309	-0.178
Most challenging*	-0.169	-0.362	0.026

Note: * n = 16 (1.13% of teachers)

Second language	# of Teachers	% of Teachers
Low concentration	1 080	76.60%
Medium concentration	233	16.52%
High concentration	97	6.88%

Special needs	# of Teachers	% of Teachers
Low concentration	995	70.57%
Medium concentration	377	26.74%
High concentration	38	2.70%

Economically disadvantaged	# of Teachers	% of Teachers
Low concentration	965	68.78%
Medium concentration	401	28.58%
High concentration	37	2.64%

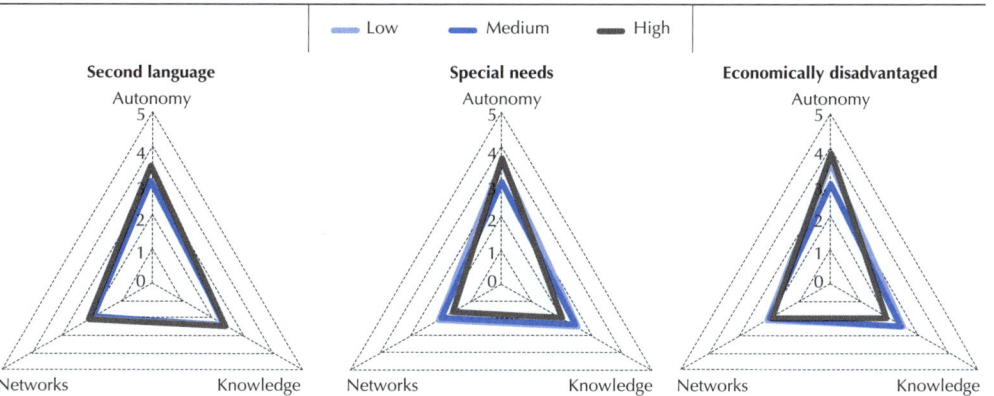

ANNEX F: SYSTEM EQUITY PROFILES

Figure F.11 Equity profile of England (United Kingdom)

Equity gaps	Knowledge	Autonomy	Networks
Second language	0.131	0.088	0.136
Special needs	0.061	1.538	0.116
Economically disadvantaged	0.197	0.116	0.399
Most challenging*	0.091	-0.318	0.192

Note: * n = 290 (11.99% of teachers)

Second language	# of Teachers	% of Teachers
Low concentration	1 798	74.33%
Medium concentration	344	14.22%
High concentration	277	11.45%

Special needs	# of Teachers	% of Teachers
Low concentration	717	29.64%
Medium concentration	1 432	59.20%
High concentration	270	11.16%

Economically disadvantaged	# of Teachers	% of Teachers
Low concentration	693	28.65%
Medium concentration	1 131	48.75%
High concentration	595	24.60%

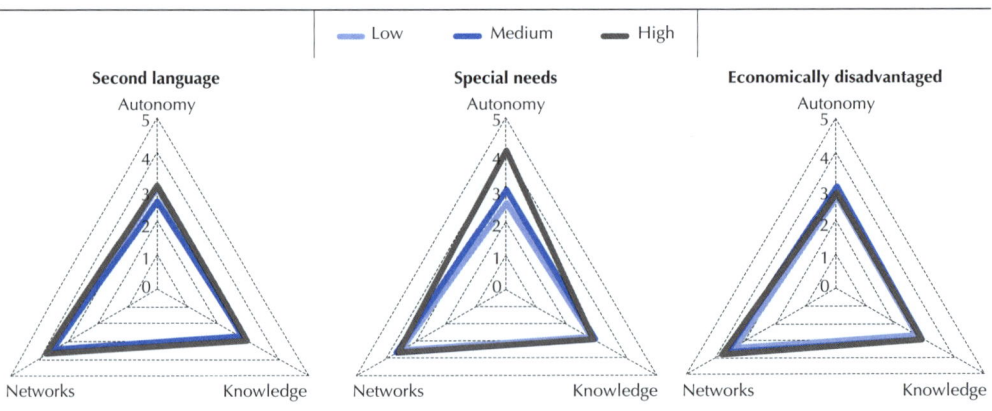

Figure F.12 Equity profile of Estonia

Equity gaps	Knowledge	Autonomy	Networks
Second language	0.134	-0.925	0.002
Special needs	-0.149	0.043	-0.054
Economically disadvantaged	-0.300	-0.160	0.028
Most challenging*	0.148	0.910	0.917

Note: * n = 20 (0.65% of teachers)

Second language	# of Teachers	% of Teachers
Low concentration	2 773	89.74%
Medium concentration	176	5.70%
High concentration	141	4.56%

Special needs	# of Teachers	% of Teachers
Low concentration	2 189	70.84%
Medium concentration	762	24.66%
High concentration	139	4.50%

Economically disadvantaged	# of Teachers	% of Teachers
Low concentration	1 435	46.44%
Medium concentration	1 305	42.23%
High concentration	350	11.33%

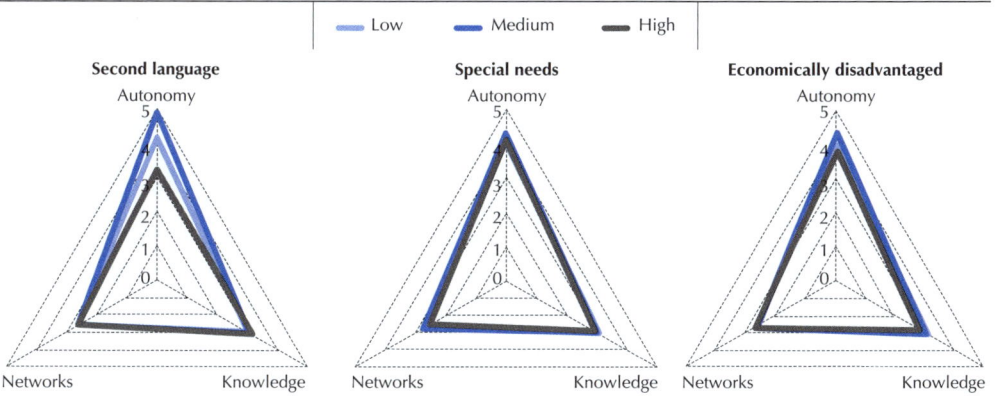

ANNEX F: SYSTEM EQUITY PROFILES

Figure F.13 Equity profile of Finland

Equity gaps	Knowledge	Autonomy	Networks
Second language	0.165	-1.107	1.014
Special needs	-0.418	NA	-0.082
Economically disadvantaged	0.148	0.827	0.114

Second language	# of Teachers	% of Teachers
Low concentration	2 439	89.05%
Medium concentration	216	7.89%
High concentration	84	3.07%

Special needs	# of Teachers	% of Teachers
Low concentration	1 988	72.58%
Medium concentration	740	27.02%
High concentration	11	0.40%

Economically disadvantaged	# of Teachers	% of Teachers
Low concentration	1 979	72.25%
Medium concentration	690	25.19%
High concentration	70	2.56%

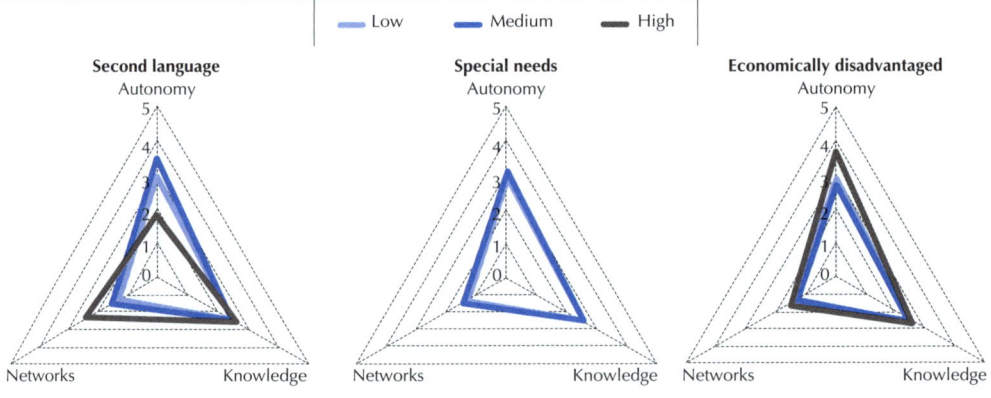

Figure F.14   Equity profile of Flanders (Belgium)

Equity gaps	Knowledge	Autonomy	Networks
Second language	-0.021	0.157	0.075
Special needs	-0.107	0.426	-0.087
Economically disadvantaged	-0.114	-0.205	0.068
Most challenging*	-0.133	-0.188	0.068

Note: * n = 404 (14.52% of teachers)

Second language	# of Teachers	% of Teachers
Low concentration	1 837	65.68%
Medium concentration	482	17.23%
High concentration	478	17.09%

Special needs	# of Teachers	% of Teachers
Low concentration	1 119	40.22%
Medium concentration	1 293	46.48%
High concentration	370	13.30%

Economically disadvantaged	# of Teachers	% of Teachers
Low concentration	1 120	40.04%
Medium concentration	1 111	39.72%
High concentration	566	20.24%

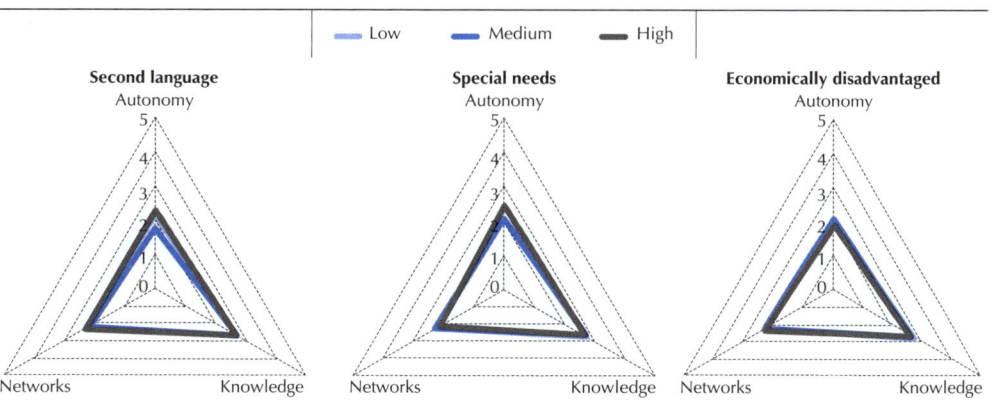

ANNEX F: SYSTEM EQUITY PROFILES

Figure F.15 **Equity profile of France**

Equity gaps	Knowledge	Autonomy	Networks
Second language	0.054	0.041	0.127
Special needs	0.201	-0.604	0.380
Economically disadvantaged	0.286	-0.594	0.188
Most challenging*	0.177	-0.176	0.117

Note: * n = 364 (13.88% of teachers)

Second language	# of Teachers	% of Teachers
Low concentration	2 126	50.56%
Medium concentration	289	10.95%
High concentration	224	8.49%

Special needs	# of Teachers	% of Teachers
Low concentration	1 510	57.61%
Medium concentration	890	33.96%
High concentration	221	8.43%

Economically disadvantaged	# of Teachers	% of Teachers
Low concentration	571	21.74%
Medium concentration	813	30.96%
High concentration	1 242	47.30%

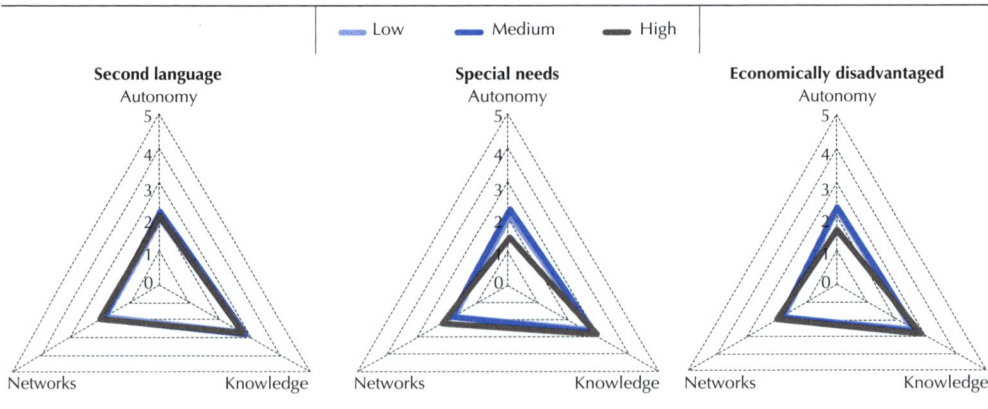

Figure F.16 Equity profile of Georgia

Equity gaps	Knowledge	Autonomy	Networks
Second language	0.062	0.406	-0.040
Special needs	-0.053	-0.523	0.617
Economically disadvantaged	-0.125	0.447	-0.028

Second language	# of Teachers	% of Teachers
Low concentration	2 288	92.37%
Medium concentration	80	3.23%
High concentration	109	4.40%

Special needs	# of Teachers	% of Teachers
Low concentration	2 449	97.49%
Medium concentration	63	2.51%

Economically disadvantaged	# of Teachers	% of Teachers
Low concentration	1 504	61.16%
Medium concentration	611	24.85%
High concentration	344	13.99%

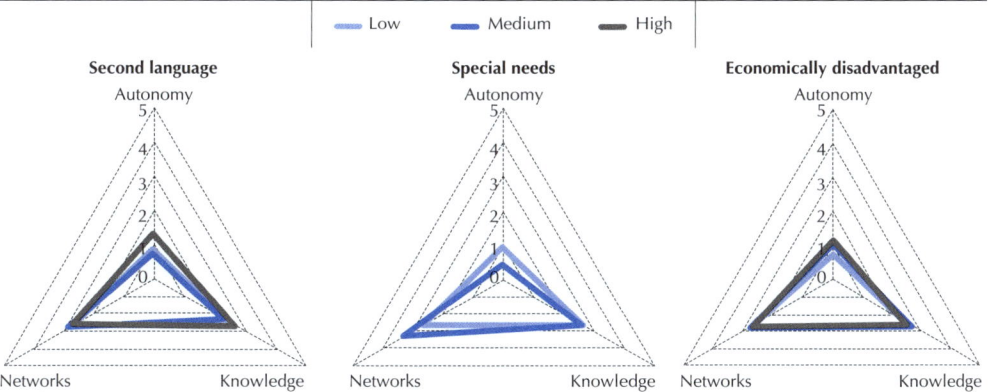

ANNEX F: SYSTEM EQUITY PROFILES

Figure F.17 Equity profile of Iceland

Equity gaps	Knowledge	Autonomy	Networks
Second language	-0.027	-0.112	0.071
Special needs	-0.085	-0.033	0.017
Economically disadvantaged	-0.037	0.588	0.473
Most challenging*	-0.216	NA	0.218

Note: * n = 12 (1.05% of teachers)

Second language	# of Teachers	% of Teachers
Low concentration	909	78.70%
Medium concentration	246	21.30%

Special needs	# of Teachers	% of Teachers
Low concentration	470	40.91%
Medium concentration	622	54.13%
High concentration	57	4.96%

Economically disadvantaged	# of Teachers	% of Teachers
Low concentration	878	77.15%
Medium concentration	229	20.12%
High concentration	31	2.72%

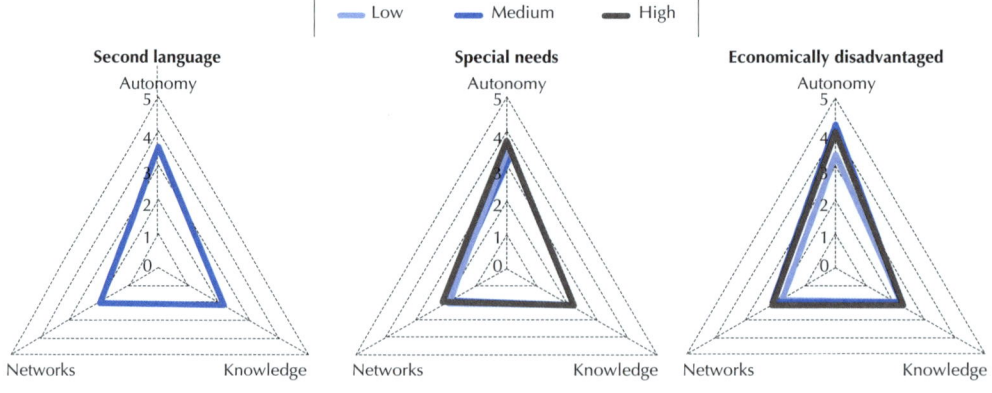

Figure F.18 Equity profile of Israel

Equity gaps	Knowledge	Autonomy	Networks
Second language	0.034	-0.026	-0.115
Special needs	-0.100	0.143	-0.216
Economically disadvantaged	0.007	-1.113	0.190
Most challenging*	-0.032	0.030	-0.199

Note: * n = 250 (8.03% of teachers)

Second language	# of Teachers	% of Teachers
Low concentration	2 485	79.85%
Medium concentration	365	11.73%
High concentration	262	8.42%

Special needs	# of Teachers	% of Teachers
Low concentration	1 825	59.20%
Medium concentration	1 032	33.47%
High concentration	226	7.33%

Economically disadvantaged	# of Teachers	% of Teachers
Low concentration	677	21.89%
Medium concentration	1 002	32.40%
High concentration	1 414	45.72%

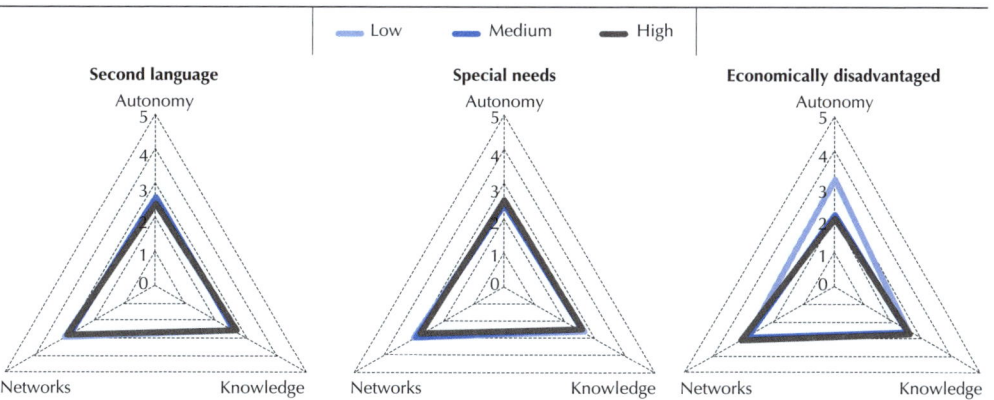

ANNEX F: SYSTEM EQUITY PROFILES

Figure F.19 Equity profile of Italy

Equity gaps	Knowledge	Autonomy	Networks
Second language	0.067	0.318	-0.313
Special needs	0.060	-0.202	-0.006
Economically disadvantaged	0.046	-0.417	0.022
Most challenging*	-0.090	-1.296	0.100

Note: * n = 76 (2.29% of teachers)

Second language	# of Teachers	% of Teachers
Low concentration	2 326	70.23%
Medium concentration	880	26.57%
High concentration	106	3.20%

Special needs	# of Teachers	% of Teachers
Low concentration	2 363	71.09%
Medium concentration	800	24.07%
High concentration	161	4.84%

Economically disadvantaged	# of Teachers	% of Teachers
Low concentration	1 827	54.96%
Medium concentration	1 203	36.19%
High concentration	294	8.84%

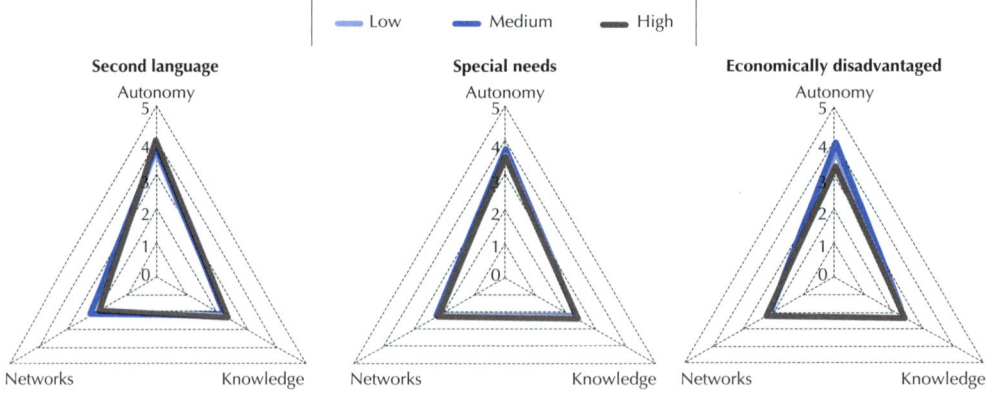

SYSTEM EQUITY PROFILES: ANNEX F

Figure F.20   Equity profile of Japan

Equity gaps	Knowledge	Autonomy	Networks
Second language	0.102	NA	0.165
Special needs	-0.095	0.469	0.031
Economically disadvantaged	0.066	-0.391	0.158

Second language	# of Teachers	% of Teachers
Low concentration	3 387	97.78%
Medium concentration	57	1.65%
High concentration	20	0.58%

Special needs	# of Teachers	% of Teachers
Low concentration	3 129	90.33%
Medium concentration	335	9.67%

Economically disadvantaged	# of Teachers	% of Teachers
Low concentration	1 833	52.92%
Medium concentration	1 431	41.31%
High concentration	200	5.77%

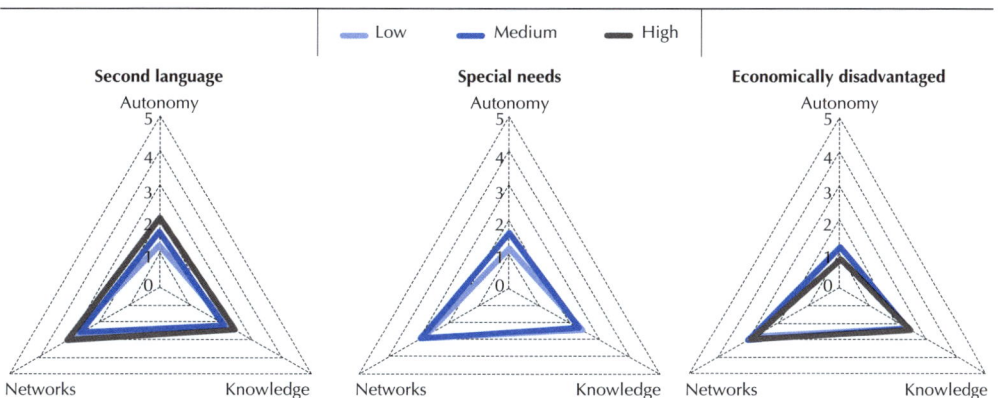

SUPPORTING TEACHER PROFESSIONALISM: INSIGHTS FROM TALIS 2013   © OECD 2016

ANNEX F: SYSTEM EQUITY PROFILES

Figure F.21 Equity profile of Korea

Equity gaps	Knowledge	Autonomy	Networks
Second language	NA	NA	NA
Special needs	-0.283	1.120	-0.253
Economically disadvantaged	0.079	0.140	0.119

Second language	# of Teachers	% of Teachers
Low concentration	2 721	100%

Special needs	# of Teachers	% of Teachers
Low concentration	2 520	92.61%
Medium concentration	187	6.87%
High concentration	14	0.51%

Economically disadvantaged	# of Teachers	% of Teachers
Low concentration	1 457	53.55%
Medium concentration	1 035	38.04%
High concentration	229	8.42%

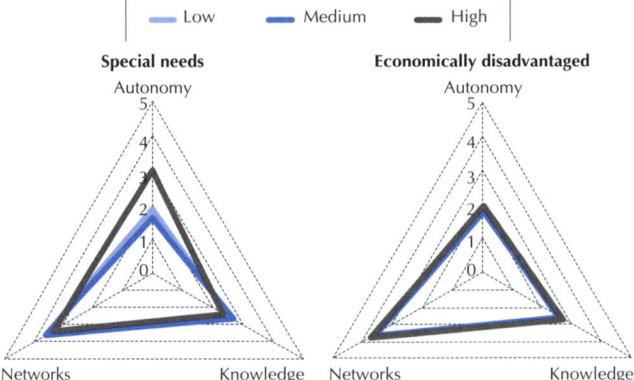

Figure F.22   Equity profile of Latvia

Equity gaps	Knowledge	Autonomy	Networks
Second language	0.389	1.148	0.332
Special needs	-0.082	0.794	-0.014
Economically disadvantaged	-0.125	0.273	-0.181
Most challenging*	0.245	1.735	0.084

Note: * n = 33 (1.62% of teachers)

Second language	# of Teachers	% of Teachers
Low concentration	1 624	79.92%
Medium concentration	263	14.42%
High concentration	115	5.66%

Special needs	# of Teachers	% of Teachers
Low concentration	1 839	91.08%
Medium concentration	180	8.92%

Economically disadvantaged	# of Teachers	% of Teachers
Low concentration	1 045	51.43%
Medium concentration	632	31.13%
High concentration	355	17.47%

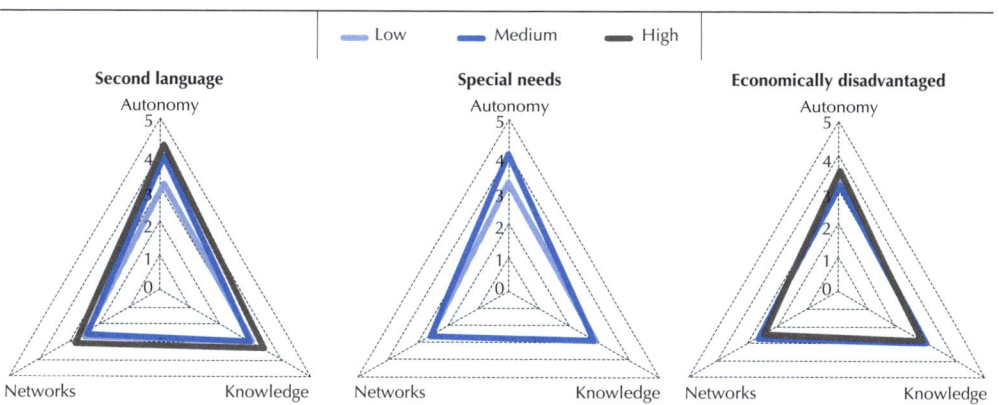

Figure F.23 Equity profile of Malaysia

Equity gaps	Knowledge	Autonomy	Networks
Second language	-0.214	0.010	-0.145
Special needs	0.118	-0.382	-0.080
Economically disadvantaged	-0.146	0.064	0.003
Most challenging*	0.125	-0.380	-0.073

Note: * n = 45 (1.56% of teachers)

Second language	# of Teachers	% of Teachers
Low concentration	1 291	44.66%
Medium concentration	446	15.43%
High concentration	1 154	39.92%

Special needs	# of Teachers	% of Teachers
Low concentration	2 773	95.92%
Medium concentration	73	2.53%
High concentration	45	1.56%

Economically disadvantaged	# of Teachers	% of Teachers
Low concentration	467	16.15%
Medium concentration	731	25.29%
High concentration	1 693	58.56%

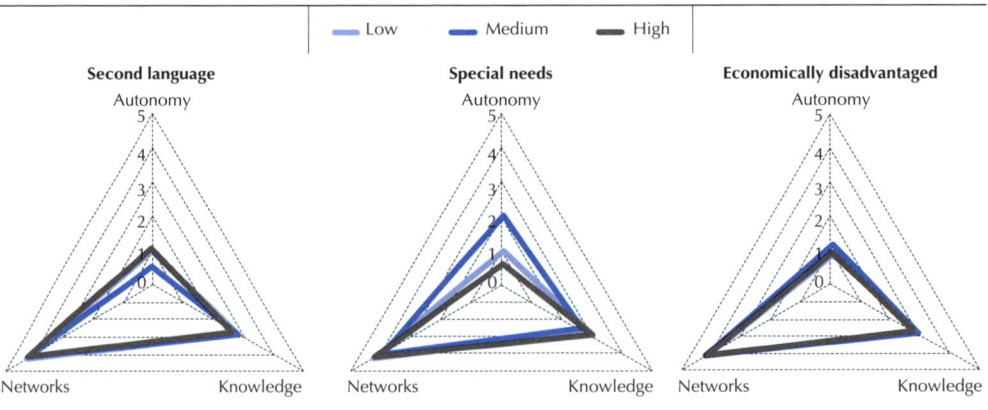

Figure F.24 Equity profile of Mexico

Equity gaps	Knowledge	Autonomy	Networks
Second language	0.249	0.860	0.696
Special needs	0.114	-0.186	-0.013
Economically disadvantaged	-0.063	0.039	-0.202

Second language	# of Teachers	% of Teachers
Low concentration	3 010	97.79%
Medium concentration	31	1.01%
High concentration	37	1.20%

Special needs	# of Teachers	% of Teachers
Low concentration	2 910	93.06%
Medium concentration	159	5.08%
High concentration	58	1.85%

Economically disadvantaged	# of Teachers	% of Teachers
Low concentration	861	27.53%
Medium concentration	790	25.26%
High concentration	1 476	47.20%

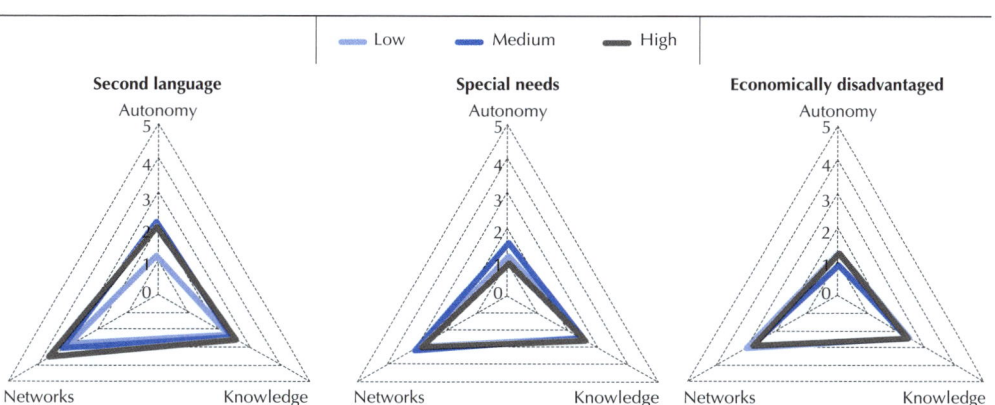

ANNEX F: SYSTEM EQUITY PROFILES

Figure F.25 Equity profile of the Netherlands

Equity gaps	Knowledge	Autonomy	Networks
Second language	-0.030	-0.269	-0.130
Special needs	-0.020	-0.893	-0.026
Economically disadvantaged	-0.128	-0.102	-0.239
Most challenging*	0.058	-0.342	-0.234

Note: * n = 78 (4.39 of teachers)

Second language	# of Teachers	% of Teachers
Low concentration	1 519	85.53%
Medium concentration	142	8.00%
High concentration	115	6.48%

Special needs	# of Teachers	% of Teachers
Low concentration	958	53.94%
Medium concentration	664	37.39%
High concentration	154	8.67%

Economically disadvantaged	# of Teachers	% of Teachers
Low concentration	1 088	61.26%
Medium concentration	550	30.97%
High concentration	138	7.77%

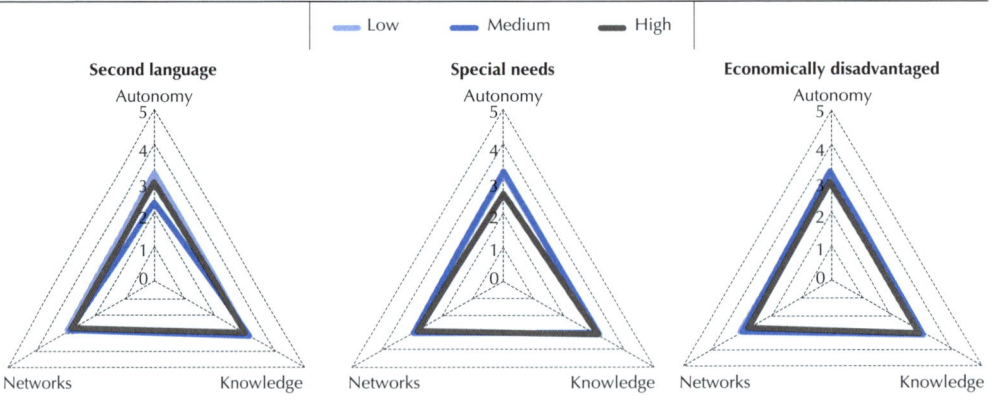

208 © OECD 2016 SUPPORTING TEACHER PROFESSIONALISM: INSIGHTS FROM TALIS 2013

SYSTEM EQUITY PROFILES: ANNEX F

Figure F.26 Equity profile of New Zealand

Equity gaps	Knowledge	Autonomy	Networks
Second language	0.012	-0.479	0.432
Special needs	0.030	2.141	0.304
Economically disadvantaged	0.057	0.214	-0.002
Most challenging*	0.246	-0.708	0.155

Note: * n = 94 (3.55% of teachers)

Second language	# of Teachers	% of Teachers
Low concentration	1 910	71.67%
Medium concentration	560	21.01%
High concentration	195	7.32%

Special needs	# of Teachers	% of Teachers
Low concentration	2 154	81.93%
Medium concentration	432	16.43%
High concentration	43	1.64%

Economically disadvantaged	# of Teachers	% of Teachers
Low concentration	1 219	46.05%
Medium concentration	907	34.27%
High concentration	521	19.68%

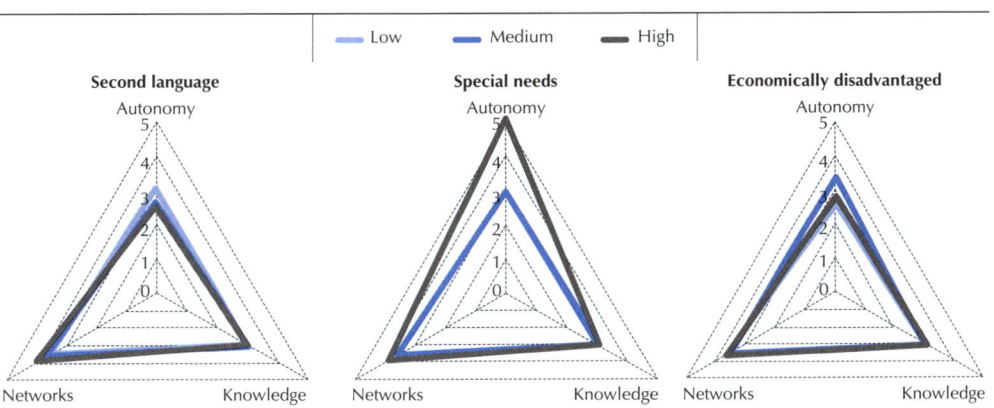

SUPPORTING TEACHER PROFESSIONALISM: INSIGHTS FROM TALIS 2013 © OECD 2016

ANNEX F: SYSTEM EQUITY PROFILES

Figure F.27 Equity profile of Norway

Equity gaps	Knowledge	Autonomy	Networks
Second language	0.138	-0.952	0.301
Special needs	0.023	0.598	0.354
Economically disadvantaged	0.188	-0.542	0.237
Most challenging*	0.075	-0.550	0.209

Note: * n = 68 (3.19% of teachers)

Second language	# of Teachers	% of Teachers
Low concentration	1 602	75.25%
Medium concentration	348	16.35%
High concentration	179	8.41%

Special needs	# of Teachers	% of Teachers
Low concentration	1 218	57.21%
Medium concentration	851	39.97%
High concentration	60	2.82%

Economically disadvantaged	# of Teachers	% of Teachers
Low concentration	1 512	71.02%
Medium concentration	493	23.16%
High concentration	124	5.82%

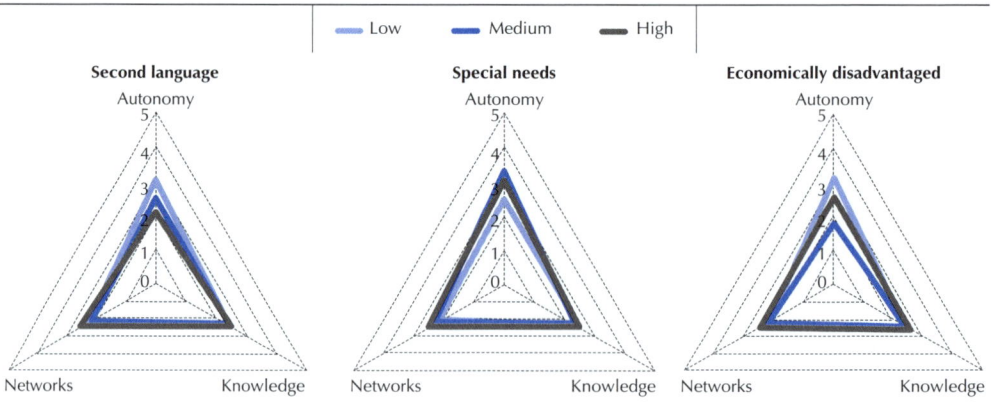

Figure F.28 Equity profile of Poland

Equity gaps	Knowledge	Autonomy	Networks
Second language	-0.252	NA	-0.446
Special needs	-0.028	0.213	-0.047
Economically disadvantaged	-0.053	-0.214	-0.059

Second language	# of Teachers	% of Teachers
Low concentration	3 657	99.35%
Medium concentration	24	0.65%

Special needs	# of Teachers	% of Teachers
Low concentration	1 423	38.99%
Medium concentration	1 856	50.85%
High concentration	371	10.16%

Economically disadvantaged	# of Teachers	% of Teachers
Low concentration	1 128	30.90%
Medium concentration	1 938	53.10%
High concentration	584	16.00%

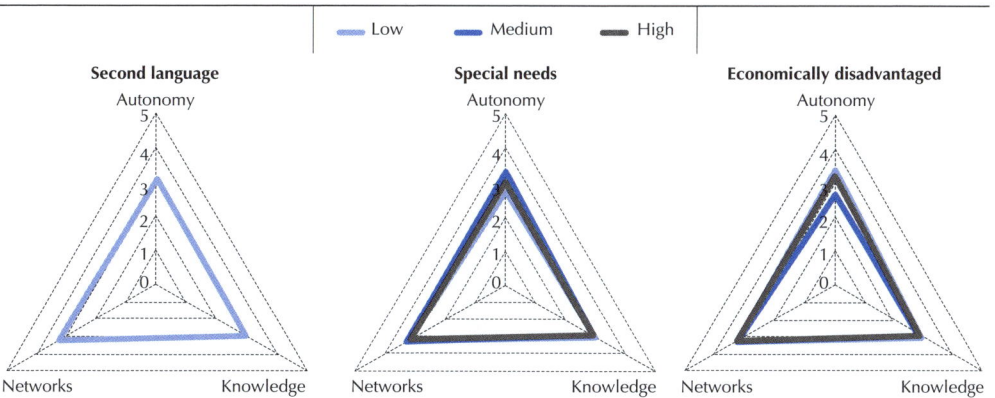

ANNEX F: SYSTEM EQUITY PROFILES

Figure F.29 **Equity profile of Portugal**

Equity gaps	Knowledge	Autonomy	Networks
Second language	0.101	NA	-0.705
Special needs	0.100	NA	-0.687
Economically disadvantaged	-0.118	-0.660	-0.277
Most challenging*	0.099	NA	-0.701

Note: * n = 21 (0.21% of teachers)

Second language	# of Teachers	% of Teachers
Low concentration	3 314	95.92%
Medium concentration	120	3.47%
High concentration	21	0.61%

Special needs	# of Teachers	% of Teachers
Low concentration	2 927	85.69%
Medium concentration	468	13.7%
High concentration	21	0.61%

Economically disadvantaged	# of Teachers	% of Teachers
Low concentration	358	10.50%
Medium concentration	1 349	39.56%
High concentration	1 703	49.94%

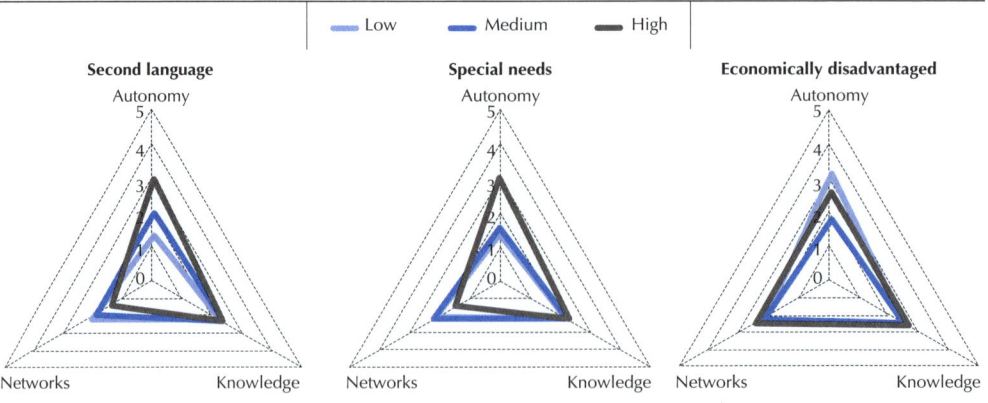

Figure F.30 Equity profile of Romania

Equity gaps	Knowledge	Autonomy	Networks
Second language	-0.028	-0.135	-0.129
Special needs	-0.265	1.540	-0.529
Economically disadvantaged	-0.041	-0.119	-0.019
Most challenging*	-0.179	0.691	-0.320

Note: * n = 12 (0.37% of teachers)

Second language	# of Teachers	% of Teachers
Low concentration	2 935	89.84%
Medium concentration	232	7.10%
High concentration	100	3.06%

Special needs	# of Teachers	% of Teachers
Low concentration	3 169	97.18%
Medium concentration	92	2.82%

Economically disadvantaged	# of Teachers	% of Teachers
Low concentration	1 461	44.72%
Medium concentration	950	29.08%
High concentration	856	26.20%

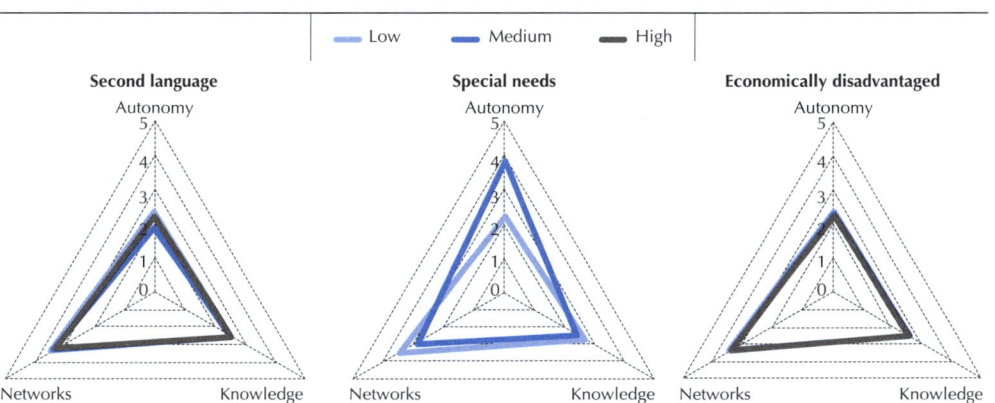

ANNEX F: SYSTEM EQUITY PROFILES

Figure F.31 Equity profile of the Russian Federation

Equity gaps	Knowledge	Autonomy	Networks
Second language	0.486	-1.139	0.298
Special needs	-0.218	-0.800	-0.002
Economically disadvantaged	-0.018	-0.124	0.038

Second language	# of Teachers	% of Teachers
Low concentration	3 430	88.91%
Medium concentration	261	6.77%
High concentration	167	4.33%

Special needs	# of Teachers	% of Teachers
Low concentration	3 682	95.09%
Medium concentration	138	3.56%
High concentration	52	1.34%

Economically disadvantaged	# of Teachers	% of Teachers
Low concentration	3 135	80.97%
Medium concentration	548	14.15%
High concentration	189	4.88%

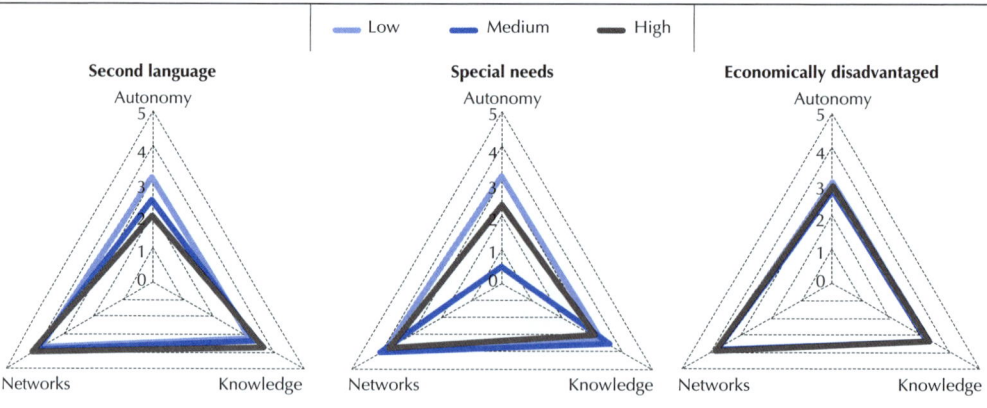

214 © OECD 2016 SUPPORTING TEACHER PROFESSIONALISM: INSIGHTS FROM TALIS 2013

SYSTEM EQUITY PROFILES: ANNEX F

Figure F.32   Equity profile of Serbia

Equity gaps	Knowledge	Autonomy	Networks
Second language	0.091	-1.228	0.333
Special needs	-0.026	0.141	-0.077
Economically disadvantaged	0.085	0.065	0.102
Most challenging*	0.041	-0.743	0.506

Note: * n = 38 (1.03% of teachers)

Second language	# of Teachers	% of Teachers
Low concentration	3 182	89.53%
Medium concentration	334	9.40%
High concentration	38	1.07%

Special needs	# of Teachers	% of Teachers
Low concentration	3 351	93.29%
Medium concentration	241	6.71%

Economically disadvantaged	# of Teachers	% of Teachers
Low concentration	1 758	48.79%
Medium concentration	1 597	44.32%
High concentration	248	6.88%

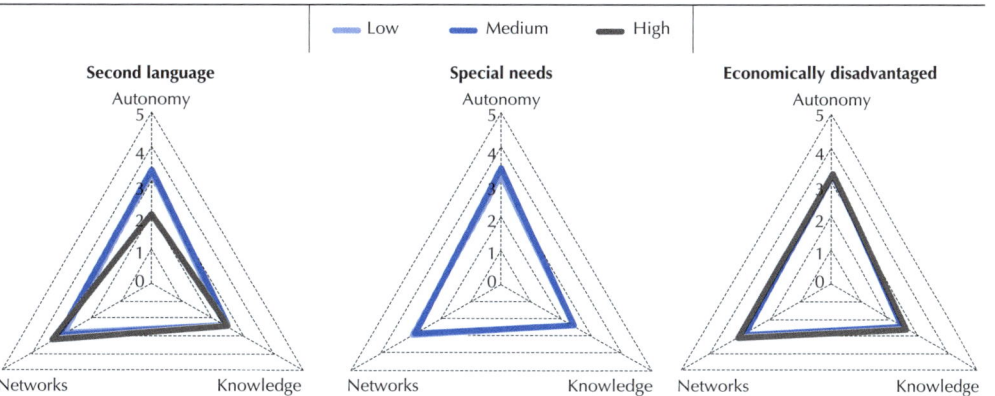

ANNEX F: SYSTEM EQUITY PROFILES

Figure F.33 Equity profile of Shanghai (China)

Equity gaps	Knowledge	Autonomy	Networks
Second language	-0.406	NA	-0.321
Special needs	-0.011	-0.485	-0.299
Economically disadvantaged	-0.040	-0.496	-0.085

Second language	# of Teachers	% of Teachers
Low concentration	3 778	98.87%
Medium concentration	23	0.60%
High concentration	20	0.52%

Special needs	# of Teachers	% of Teachers
Low concentration	3 782	98.98%
Medium concentration	39	1.02%

Economically disadvantaged	# of Teachers	% of Teachers
Low concentration	2 208	57.79%
Medium concentration	1 097	28.71%
High concentration	516	13.50%

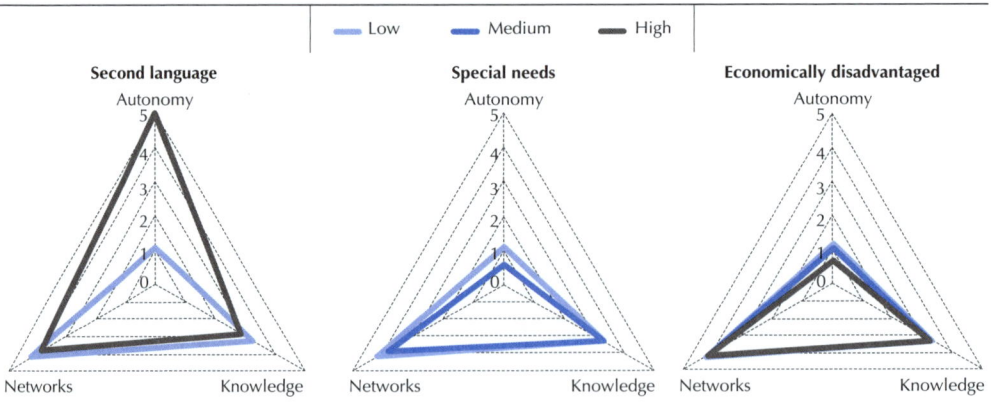

Figure F.34 Equity profile of Singapore

Equity gaps	Knowledge	Autonomy	Networks
Second language	-0.028	0.028	-0.094
Special needs	0.119	0.260	0.128
Economically disadvantaged	0.220	-0.505	0.014

Second language	# of Teachers	% of Teachers
Low concentration	314	11.24%
Medium concentration	679	24.30%
High concentration	1 801	64.46%

Special needs	# of Teachers	% of Teachers
Low concentration	2 753	98.53%
Medium concentration	41	1.47%

Economically disadvantaged	# of Teachers	% of Teachers
Low concentration	1 363	48.44%
Medium concentration	1 263	44.88%
High concentration	188	6.68%

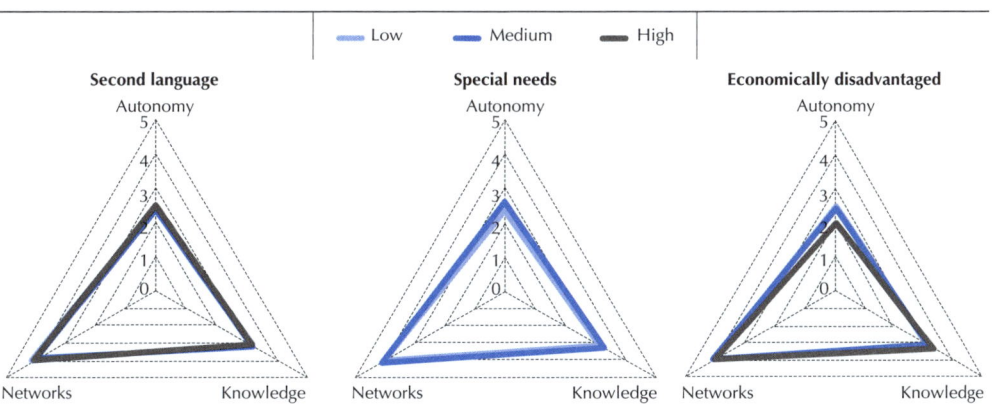

ANNEX F: SYSTEM EQUITY PROFILES

Figure F.35 Equity profile of the Slovak Republic

Equity gaps	Knowledge	Autonomy	Networks
Second language	-0.050	-0.508	0.001
Special needs	-0.063	-0.112	0.011
Economically disadvantaged	-0.110	0.036	0.044
Most challenging*	0.094	NA	0.473

Note: * n = 35 (1.06% of teachers)

Second language	# of Teachers	% of Teachers
Low concentration	3 003	91.03%
Medium concentration	165	5.00%
High concentration	131	3.97%

Special needs	# of Teachers	% of Teachers
Low concentration	2 922	88.25%
Medium concentration	389	11.75%

Economically disadvantaged	# of Teachers	% of Teachers
Low concentration	2 311	69.80%
Medium concentration	752	22.71%
High concentration	248	7.49%

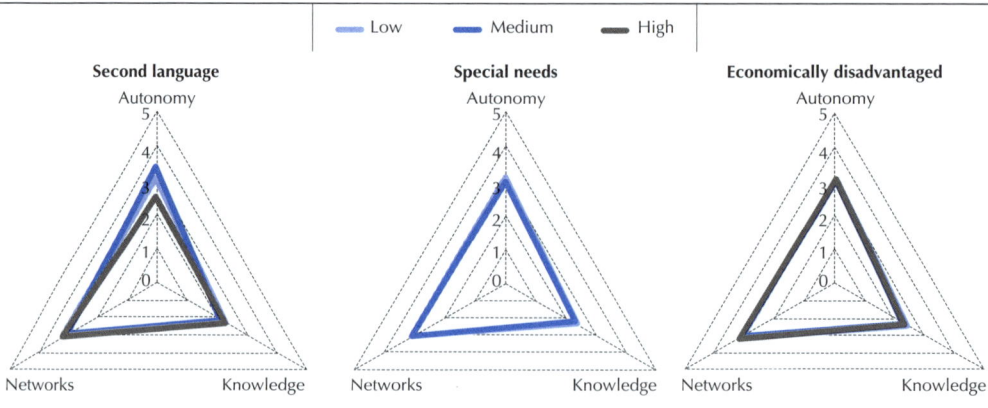

Figure F.36 Equity profile of Spain

Equity gaps	Knowledge	Autonomy	Networks
Second language	-0.032	0.817	-0.012
Special needs	0.029	NA	-0.008
Economically disadvantaged	0.018	-0.156	0.189
Most challenging*	0.141	-0.216	0.141

Note: * n = 87 (2.64% of teachers)

Second language	# of Teachers	% of Teachers
Low concentration	2 326	70.55%
Medium concentration	677	20.53%
High concentration	294	8.92%

Special needs	# of Teachers	% of Teachers
Low concentration	2 805	85.08%
Medium concentration	473	14.35%
High concentration	19	0.58%

Economically disadvantaged	# of Teachers	% of Teachers
Low concentration	2 000	60.66%
Medium concentration	831	25.20%
High concentration	466	14.13%

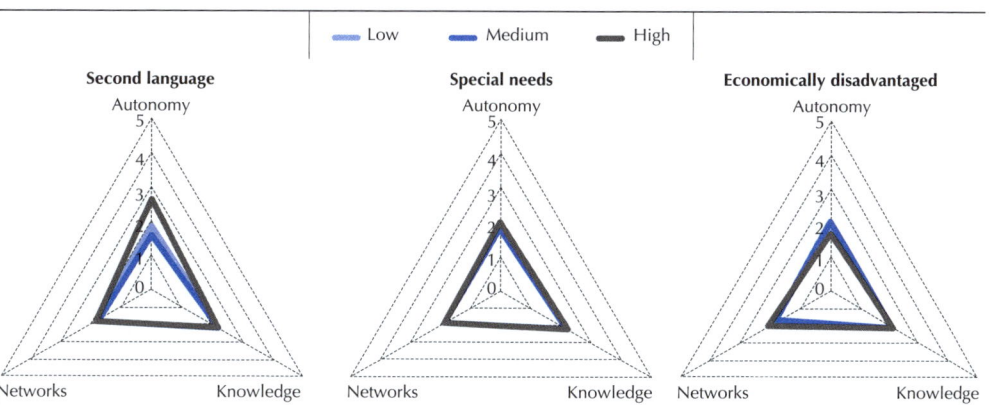

ANNEX F: SYSTEM EQUITY PROFILES

Figure F.37 **Equity profile of Sweden**

Equity gaps	Knowledge	Autonomy	Networks
Second language	-0.087	-0.127	0.312
Special needs	-0.043	-0.099	0.148
Economically disadvantaged	-0.068	-0.080	0.408
Most challenging*	-0.022	-0.333	0.432

Note: * n = 257 (8.31% of teachers)

Second language	# of Teachers	% of Teachers
Low concentration	1 731	55.93%
Medium concentration	851	27.50%
High concentration	513	16.58%

Special needs	# of Teachers	% of Teachers
Low concentration	1 150	36.91%
Medium concentration	1 727	55.42%
High concentration	239	7.67%

Economically disadvantaged	# of Teachers	% of Teachers
Low concentration	1 905	61.57%
Medium concentration	908	29.35%
High concentration	281	9.08%

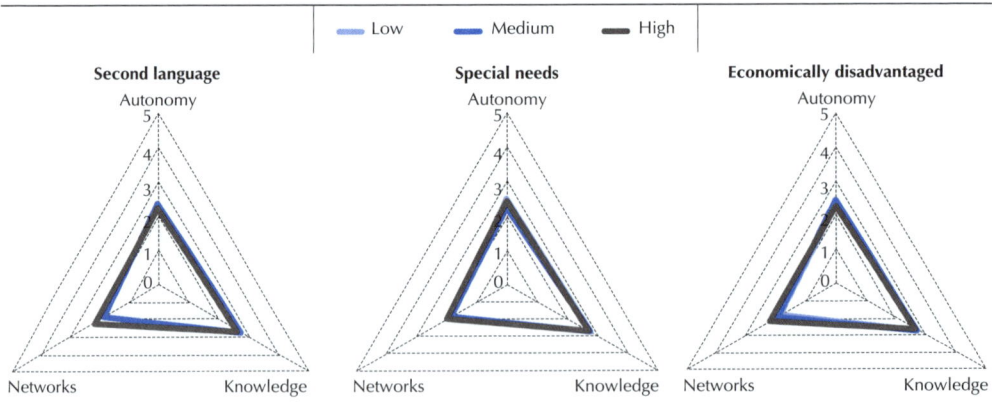

SYSTEM EQUITY PROFILES: ANNEX F

Figure F.38 Equity profile of the United States [1]

Equity gaps	Knowledge	Autonomy	Networks
Second language	0.056	-0.542	-0.109
Special needs	0.379	-1.302	0.147
Economically disadvantaged	0.230	-0.413	0.445
Most challenging*	0.120	-0.224	0.045

Note: * n = 250 (15.61% of teachers)

Second language	# of Teachers	% of Teachers
Low concentration	1 164	72.66%
Medium concentration	205	12.80%
High concentration	233	14.54%

Special needs	# of Teachers	% of Teachers
Low concentration	594	37.08%
Medium concentration	963	60.11%
High concentration	45	2.81%

Economically disadvantaged	# of Teachers	% of Teachers
Low concentration	175	10.92%
Medium concentration	337	21.04%
High concentration	1 090	68.04%

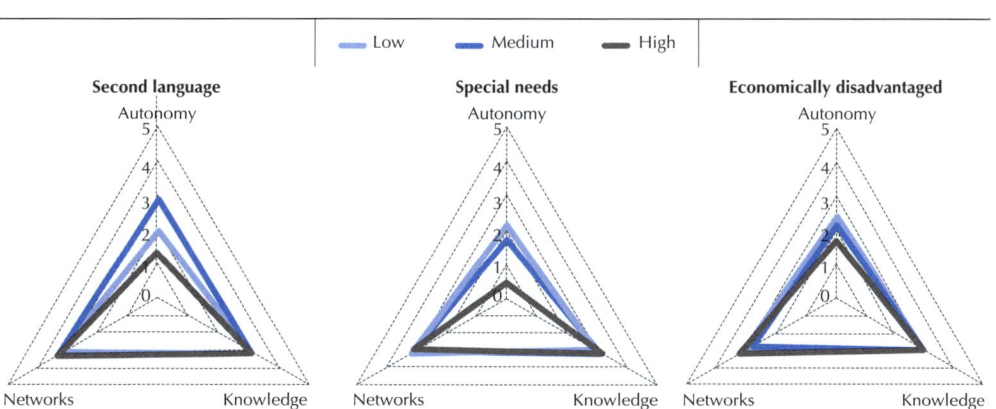

1. A country profile for the United States is presented to provide information about the school equity levels. However, the data should be interpreted carefully since the United States did not meet international participation rates.

ORGANISATION FOR ECONOMIC CO-OPERATION AND DEVELOPMENT

The OECD is a unique forum where governments work together to address the economic, social and environmental challenges of globalisation. The OECD is also at the forefront of efforts to understand and to help governments respond to new developments and concerns, such as corporate governance, the information economy and the challenges of an ageing population. The Organisation provides a setting where governments can compare policy experiences, seek answers to common problems, identify good practice and work to co-ordinate domestic and international policies.

The OECD member countries are: Australia, Austria, Belgium, Canada, Chile, the Czech Republic, Denmark, Estonia, Finland, France, Germany, Greece, Hungary, Iceland, Ireland, Israel, Italy, Japan, Korea, Luxembourg, Mexico, the Netherlands, New Zealand, Norway, Poland, Portugal, the Slovak Republic, Slovenia, Spain, Sweden, Switzerland, Turkey, the United Kingdom and the United States. The European Union takes part in the work of the OECD.

OECD Publishing disseminates widely the results of the Organisation's statistics gathering and research on economic, social and environmental issues, as well as the conventions, guidelines and standards agreed by its members.

OECD PUBLISHING, 2, rue André-Pascal, 75775 PARIS CEDEX 16
(872015021P1) ISBN 978-92-64-24859-5 – 2016